NETWORKED:

Carabella on the Run

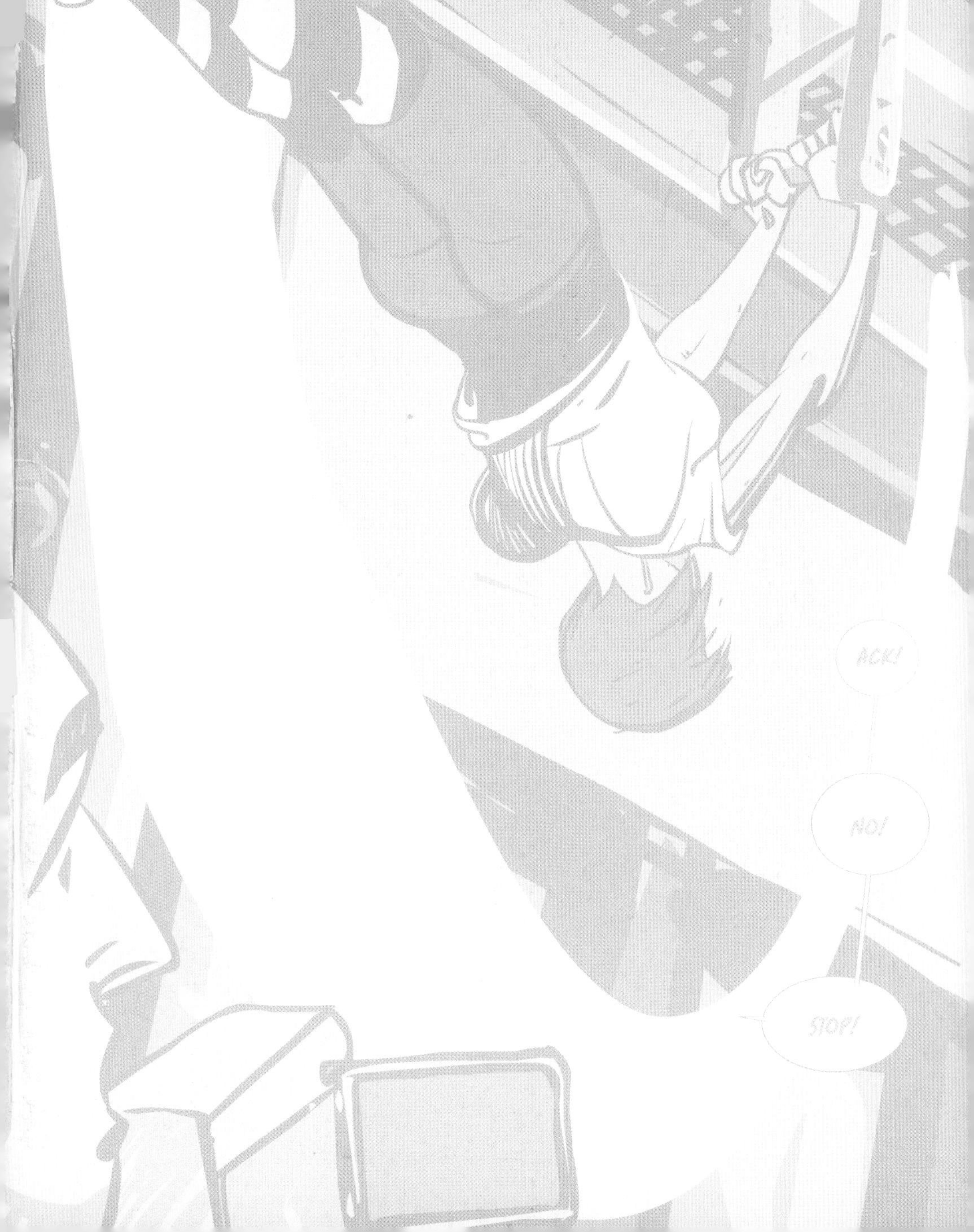
ACK!
NO!
STOP!

Networked: Carabella on the Run is a project of Privacy Activism and is funded by a generous grant from the Rose Foundation's Consumer Privacy Rights Fund.

Privacy Activism is a 501(c)(3) organization, based in California. Our goal is to enable people to make well-informed decisions about personal privacy and how privacy affects society as a whole. Because the field of privacy is so broad, we focus on areas of consumer privacy, including data mining of consumer information, identity theft, medical records privacy and online behavioral advertising and tracking. We focus on government surveillance issues only when there is a nexus between surveillance and consumer information, e.g. Real ID.

A key element of Privacy Activism's approach is to communicate information visually, in order to make the complexities of privacy law and policy more accessible to people with no specialized expertise in the issues. The creation of Carabella and her adventures has been our primary method of visually exploring the privacy landscape.

Two previous Carabella projects have been game oriented. "Carabella, the Quest for Tunes" educates players about digital privacy, copyright, and fair use. "Carabella Goes to College" looks at identity theft, consumer profiling, and spam. Our current Carabella project is a departure from our games and instead uses a graphic novel format. We intend to continue with the Carabella series to illustrate privacy concerns in the context of emerging technologies and how they impact personal privacy.

Privacy Activism's small staff works with volunteers and collaborates with like-minded organizations to maximize our contribution to educating the pubic about privacy and our impact on state and national policies.

www.privacyactivism.org

NETWORKED:
Carabella on the Run

GERARD JONES | MARK BADGER

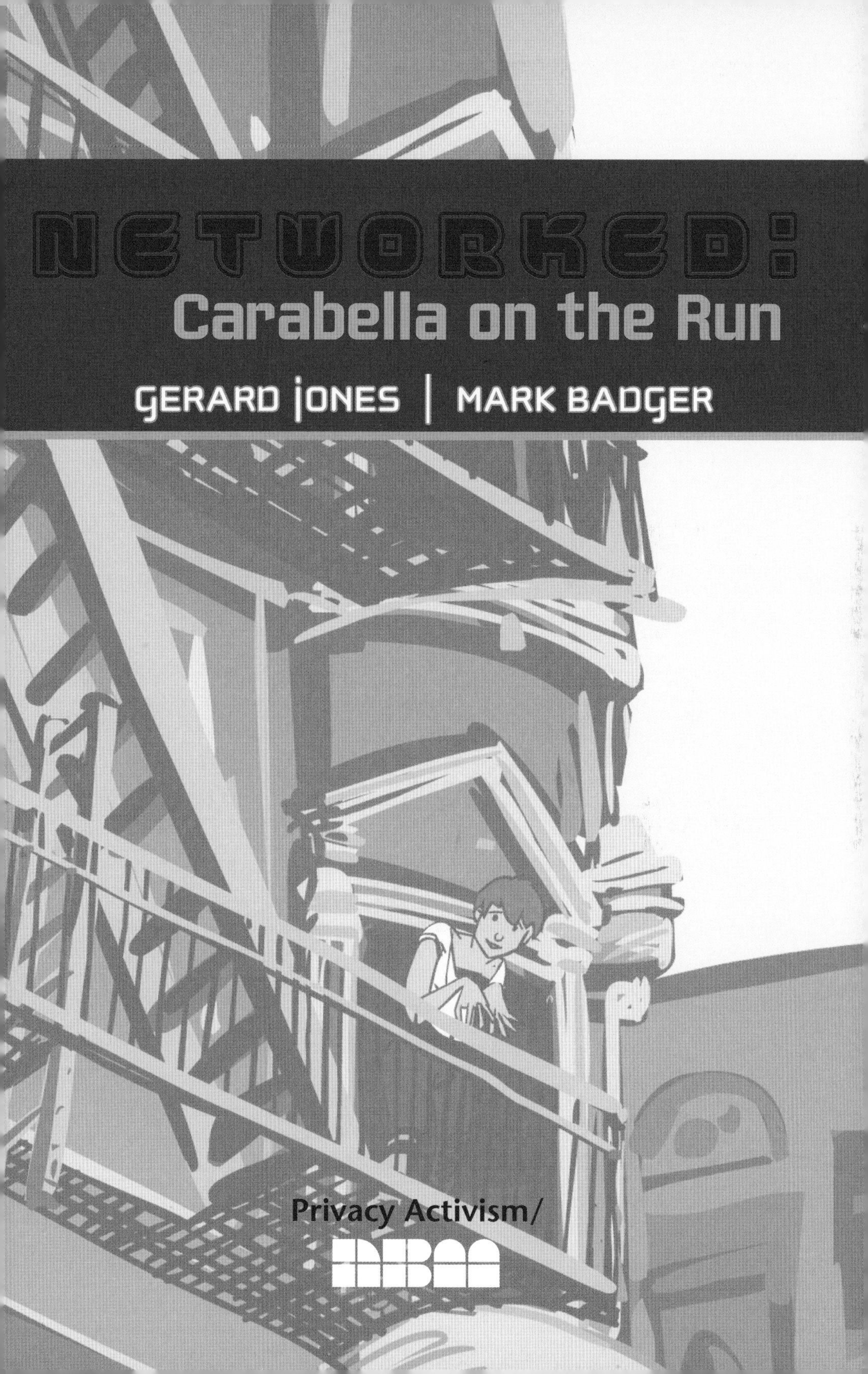

Privacy Activism/
NBM

writing and plot: Gerard Jones
drawing and plot: Mark Badger
cover design: Pete Friedrich

ISBN: 978-1-56163-586-3
© 2010 Privacy Activism
Library of Congress Control Number: 2010929157

We have over 200 titles,
write for our complete catalog:
NBM
40 Exchange Pl., Suite 1308
New York, NY 10005

See more at our website:
www.nbmpublishing.com

Printed in China

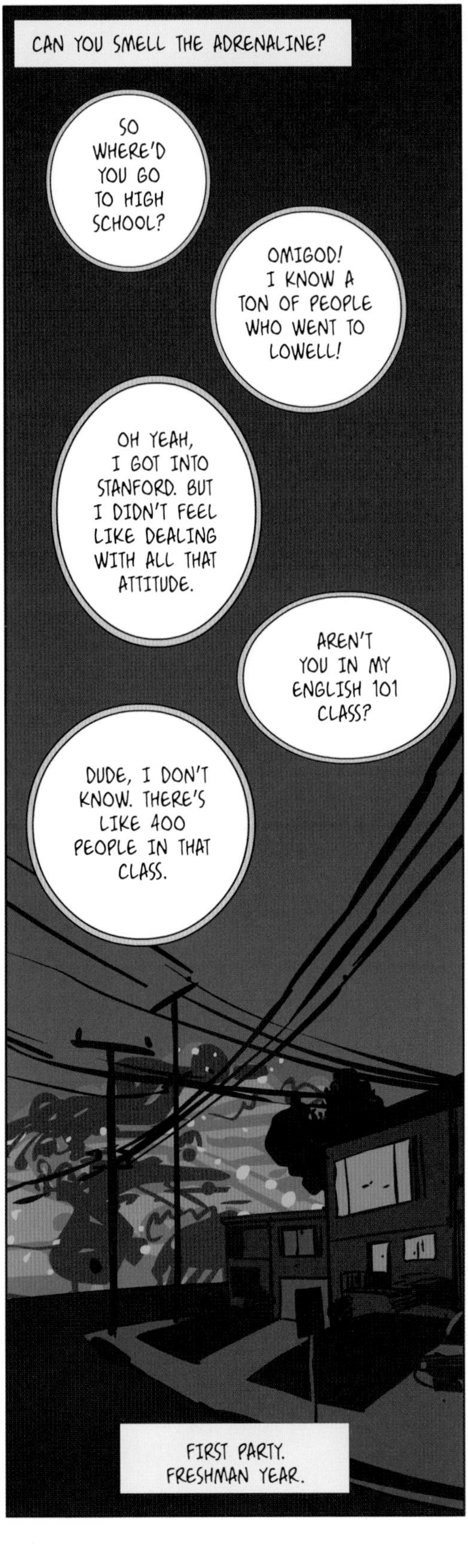
CAN YOU SMELL THE ADRENALINE?
SO WHERE'D YOU GO TO HIGH SCHOOL?
OMIGOD! I KNOW A TON OF PEOPLE WHO WENT TO LOWELL!
OH YEAH, I GOT INTO STANFORD. BUT I DIDN'T FEEL LIKE DEALING WITH ALL THAT ATTITUDE.
AREN'T YOU IN MY ENGLISH 101 CLASS?
DUDE, I DON'T KNOW. THERE'S LIKE 400 PEOPLE IN THAT CLASS.
FIRST PARTY. FRESHMAN YEAR.

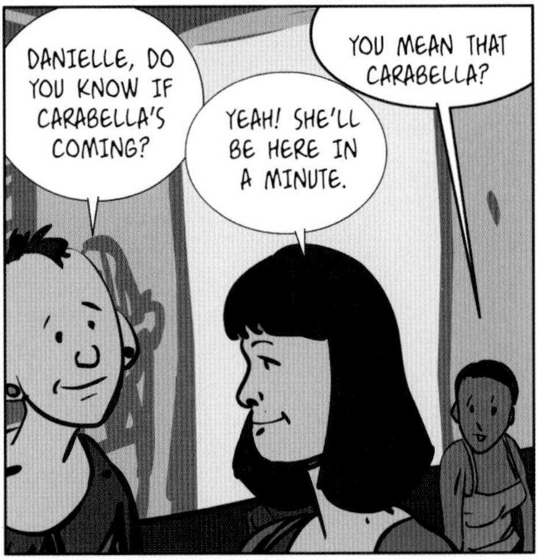
DANIELLE, DO YOU KNOW IF CARABELLA'S COMING?
YEAH! SHE'LL BE HERE IN A MINUTE.
YOU MEAN THAT CARABELLA?

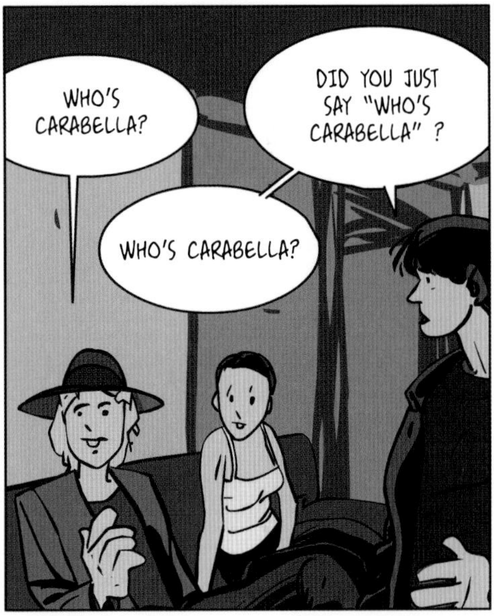
WHO'S CARABELLA?
DID YOU JUST SAY "WHO'S CARABELLA" ?
WHO'S CARABELLA?

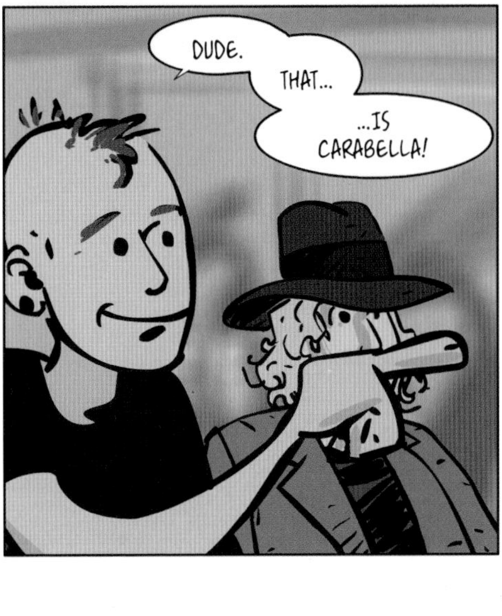
DUDE.
THAT...
...IS CARABELLA!

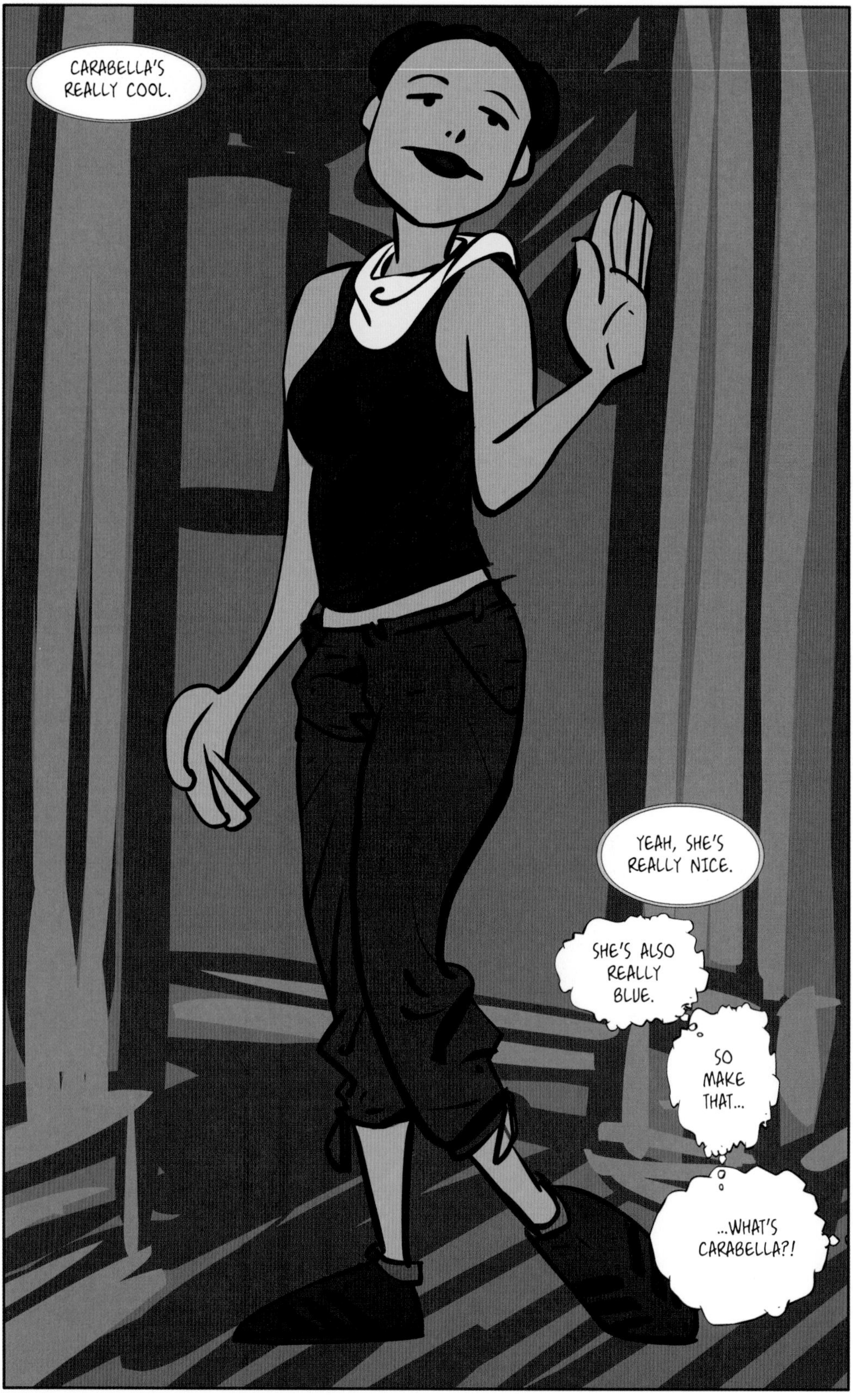
CARABELLA'S REALLY COOL.
YEAH, SHE'S REALLY NICE.
SHE'S ALSO REALLY BLUE.
SO MAKE THAT...
...WHAT'S CARABELLA?!

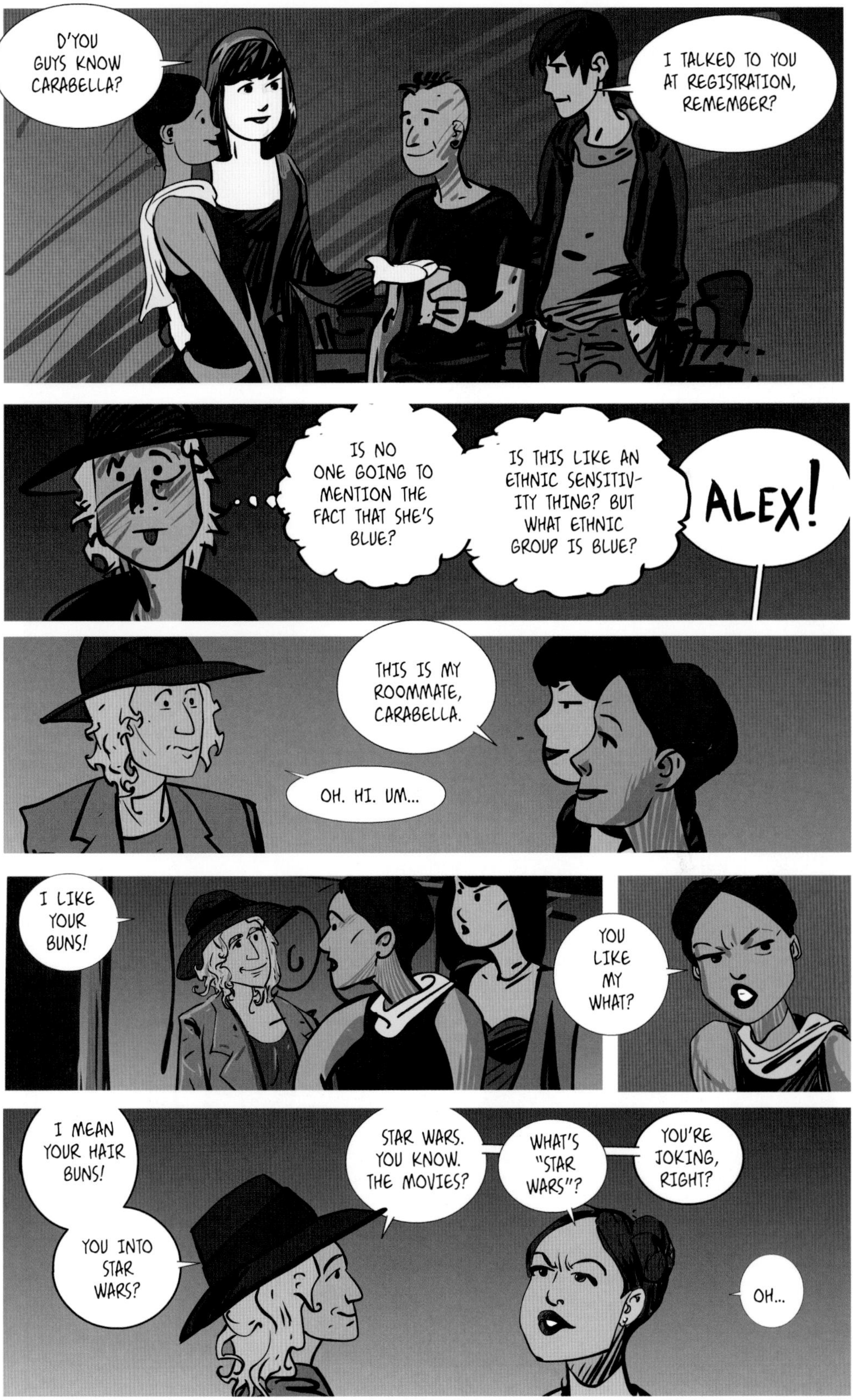
D'YOU GUYS KNOW CARABELLA?
I TALKED TO YOU AT REGISTRATION, REMEMBER?
IS NO ONE GOING TO MENTION THE FACT THAT SHE'S BLUE?
IS THIS LIKE AN ETHNIC SENSITIVITY THING? BUT WHAT ETHNIC GROUP IS BLUE?
ALEX!
THIS IS MY ROOMMATE, CARABELLA.
OH. HI. UM...
I LIKE YOUR BUNS!
YOU LIKE MY WHAT?
I MEAN YOUR HAIR BUNS!
YOU INTO STAR WARS?
STAR WARS. YOU KNOW. THE MOVIES?
WHAT'S "STAR WARS"?
YOU'RE JOKING, RIGHT?
OH...

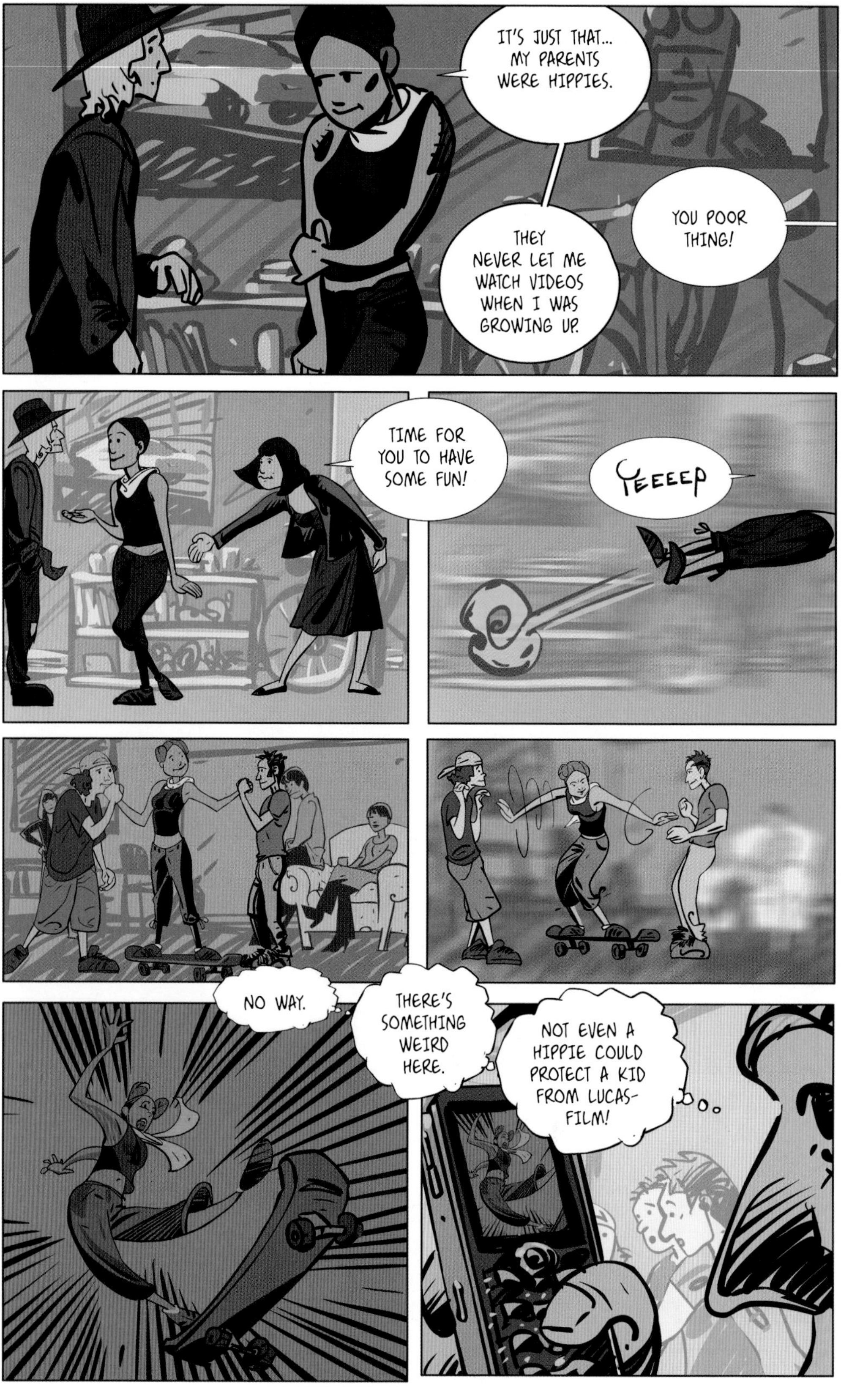
IT'S JUST THAT... MY PARENTS WERE HIPPIES.
THEY NEVER LET ME WATCH VIDEOS WHEN I WAS GROWING UP.
YOU POOR THING!
TIME FOR YOU TO HAVE SOME FUN!
YEEEEP
NO WAY.
THERE'S SOMETHING WEIRD HERE.
NOT EVEN A HIPPIE COULD PROTECT A KID FROM LUCAS-FILM!

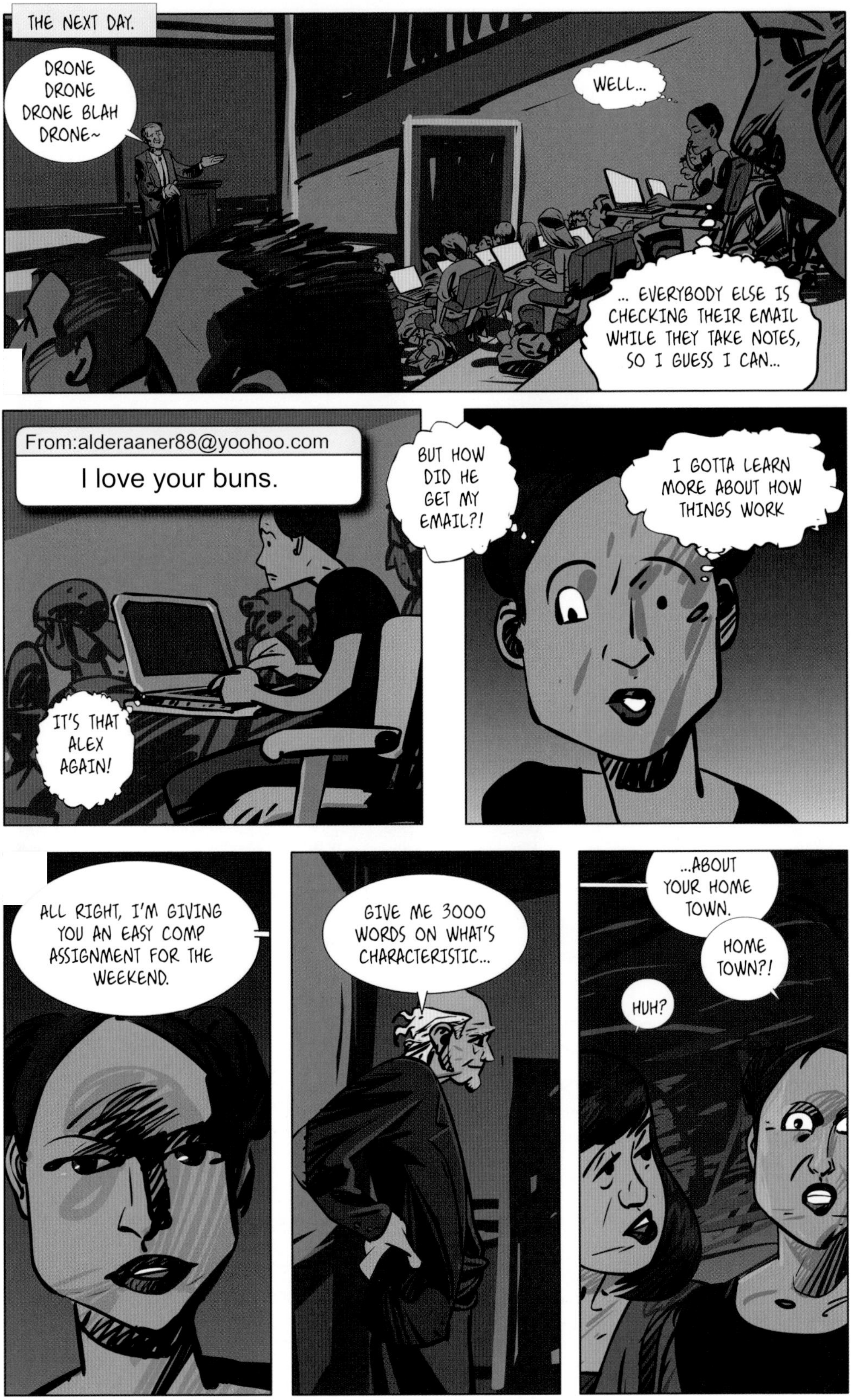
THE NEXT DAY.
DRONE DRONE DRONE BLAH DRONE~
WELL...
... EVERYBODY ELSE IS CHECKING THEIR EMAIL WHILE THEY TAKE NOTES, SO I GUESS I CAN...
From:alderaaner88@yoohoo.com
I love your buns.
IT'S THAT ALEX AGAIN!
BUT HOW DID HE GET MY EMAIL?!
I GOTTA LEARN MORE ABOUT HOW THINGS WORK
ALL RIGHT, I'M GIVING YOU AN EASY COMP ASSIGNMENT FOR THE WEEKEND.
GIVE ME 3000 WORDS ON WHAT'S CHARACTERISTIC...
...ABOUT YOUR HOME TOWN.
HOME TOWN?!
HUH?

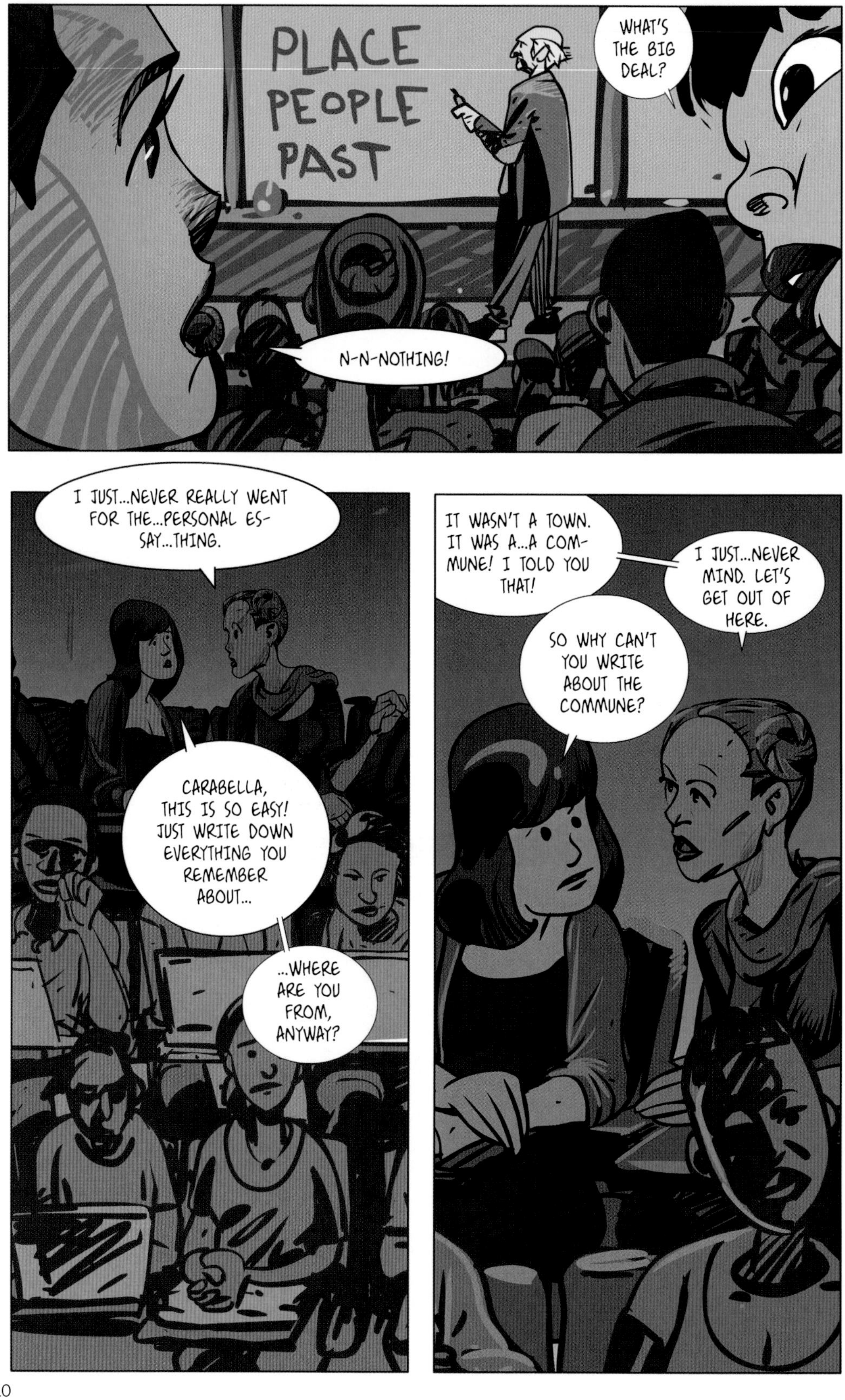
PLACE
PEOPLE
PAST
WHAT'S THE BIG DEAL?
N-N-NOTHING!
I JUST...NEVER REALLY WENT FOR THE...PERSONAL ES-SAY...THING.
CARABELLA, THIS IS SO EASY! JUST WRITE DOWN EVERYTHING YOU REMEMBER ABOUT...
...WHERE ARE YOU FROM, ANYWAY?
IT WASN'T A TOWN. IT WAS A...A COMMUNE! I TOLD YOU THAT!
I JUST...NEVER MIND. LET'S GET OUT OF HERE.
SO WHY CAN'T YOU WRITE ABOUT THE COMMUNE?

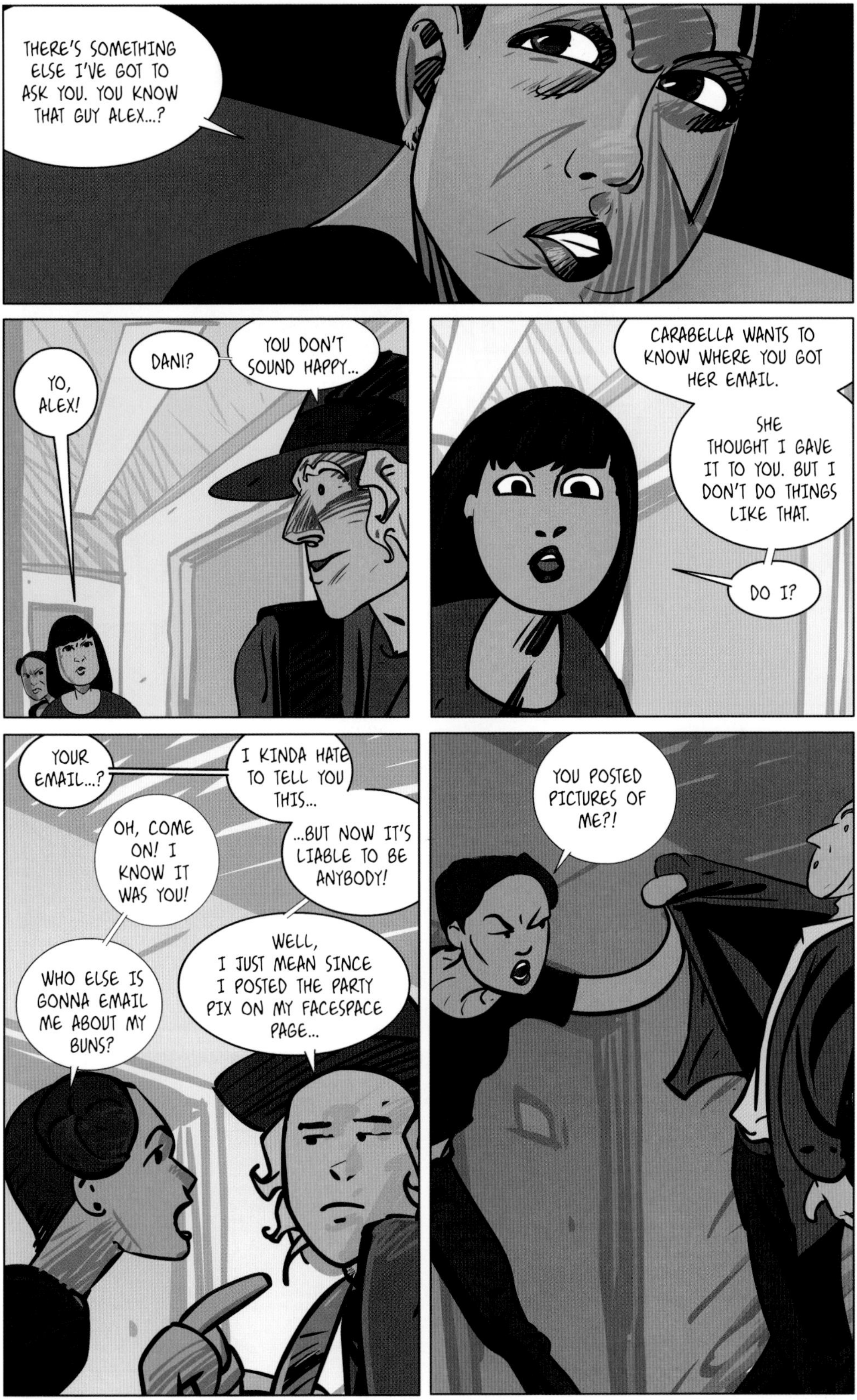

THERE'S SOMETHING ELSE I'VE GOT TO ASK YOU. YOU KNOW THAT GUY ALEX...?
YO, ALEX!
DANI?
YOU DON'T SOUND HAPPY...
CARABELLA WANTS TO KNOW WHERE YOU GOT HER EMAIL.
SHE THOUGHT I GAVE IT TO YOU. BUT I DON'T DO THINGS LIKE THAT.
DO I?
YOUR EMAIL...?
I KINDA HATE TO TELL YOU THIS...
OH, COME ON! I KNOW IT WAS YOU!
...BUT NOW IT'S LIABLE TO BE ANYBODY!
WHO ELSE IS GONNA EMAIL ME ABOUT MY BUNS?
WELL, I JUST MEAN SINCE I POSTED THE PARTY PIX ON MY FACESPACE PAGE...
YOU POSTED PICTURES OF ME?!

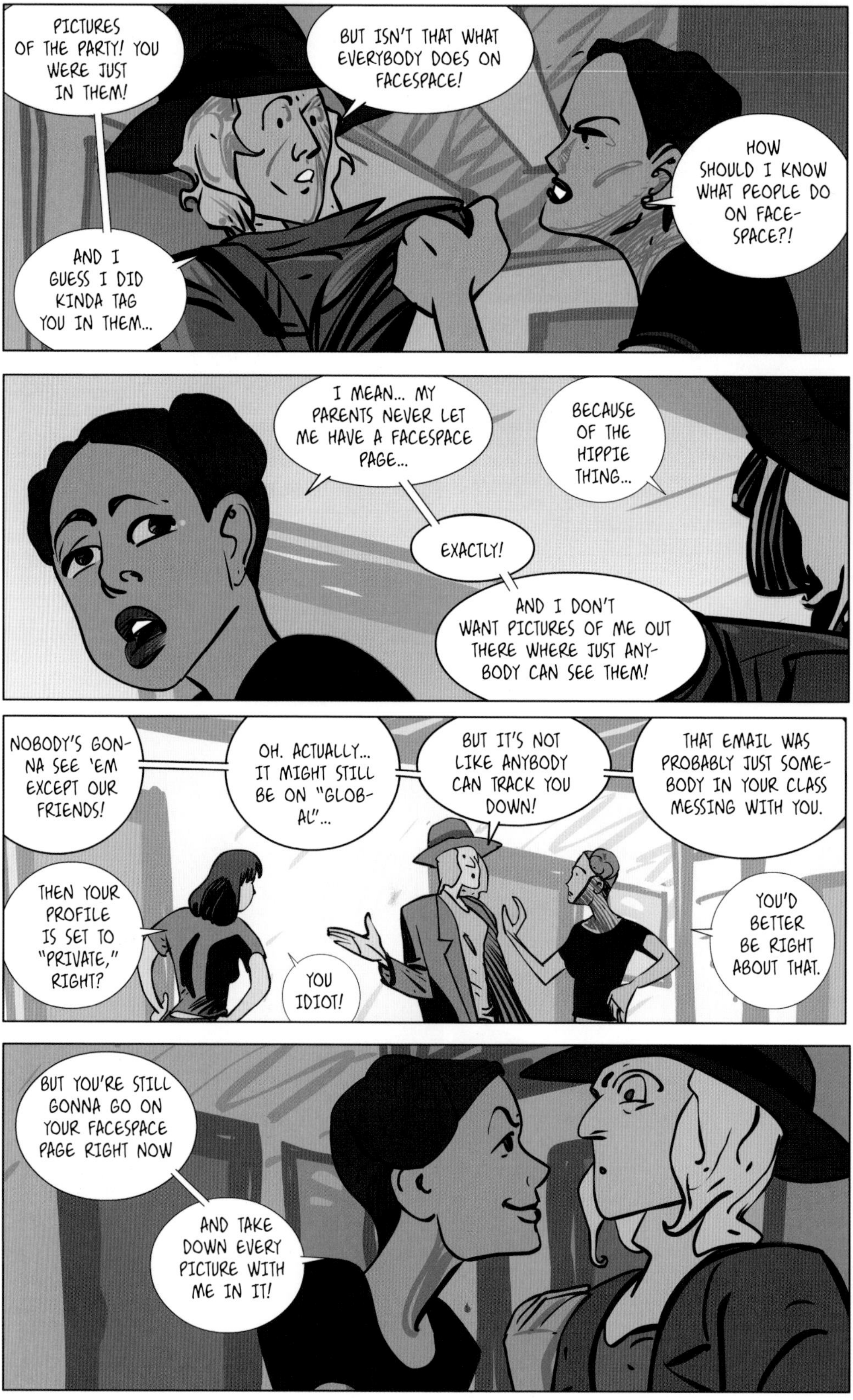
PICTURES OF THE PARTY! YOU WERE JUST IN THEM!
BUT ISN'T THAT WHAT EVERYBODY DOES ON FACESPACE!
AND I GUESS I DID KINDA TAG YOU IN THEM...
HOW SHOULD I KNOW WHAT PEOPLE DO ON FACE-SPACE?!
I MEAN... MY PARENTS NEVER LET ME HAVE A FACESPACE PAGE...
BECAUSE OF THE HIPPIE THING...
EXACTLY!
AND I DON'T WANT PICTURES OF ME OUT THERE WHERE JUST ANY-BODY CAN SEE THEM!
NOBODY'S GON-NA SEE 'EM EXCEPT OUR FRIENDS!
OH. ACTUALLY... IT MIGHT STILL BE ON "GLOB-AL"...
BUT IT'S NOT LIKE ANYBODY CAN TRACK YOU DOWN!
THAT EMAIL WAS PROBABLY JUST SOME-BODY IN YOUR CLASS MESSING WITH YOU.
THEN YOUR PROFILE IS SET TO "PRIVATE," RIGHT?
YOU IDIOT!
YOU'D BETTER BE RIGHT ABOUT THAT.
BUT YOU'RE STILL GONNA GO ON YOUR FACESPACE PAGE RIGHT NOW
AND TAKE DOWN EVERY PICTURE WITH ME IN IT!

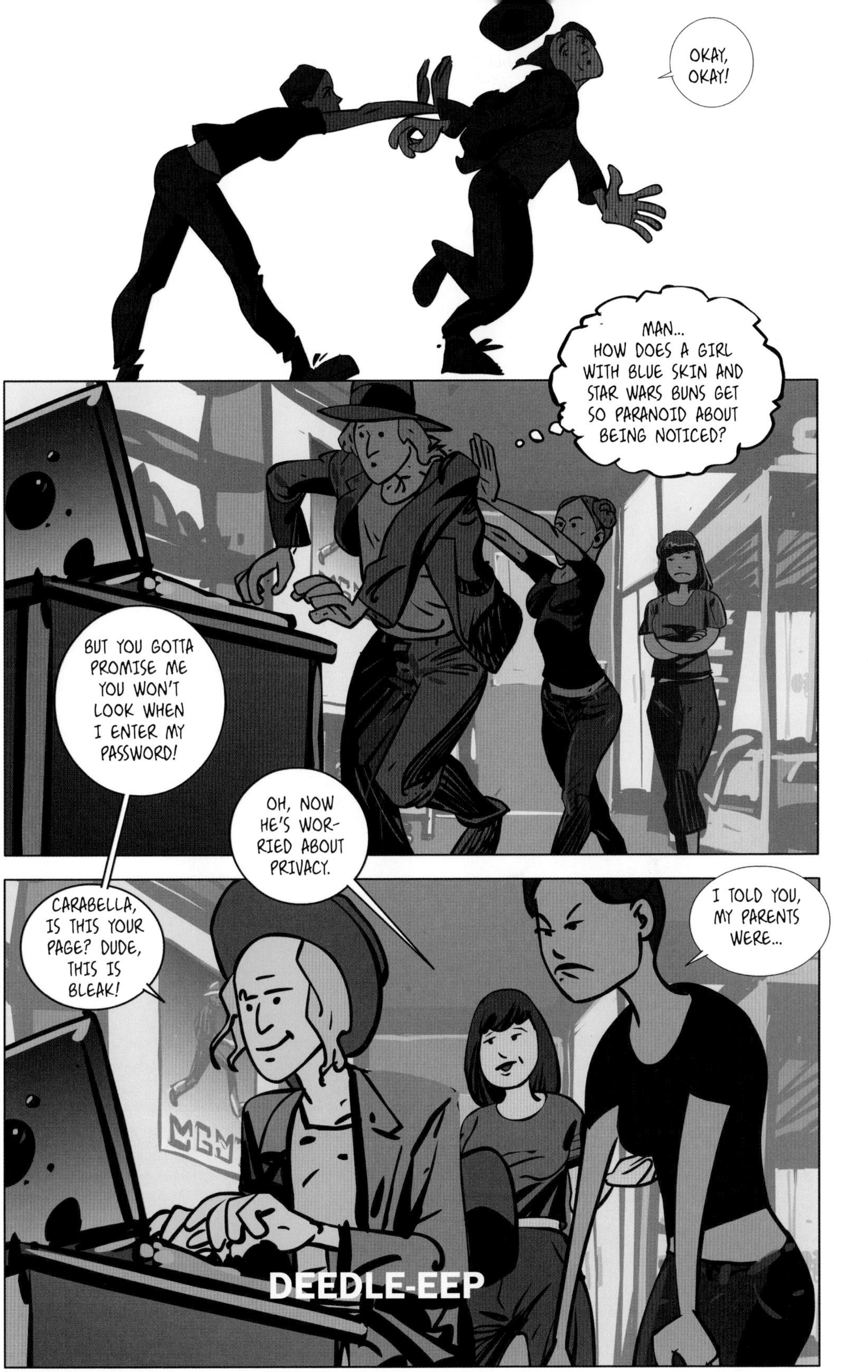
OKAY, OKAY!
MAN... HOW DOES A GIRL WITH BLUE SKIN AND STAR WARS BUNS GET SO PARANOID ABOUT BEING NOTICED?
BUT YOU GOTTA PROMISE ME YOU WON'T LOOK WHEN I ENTER MY PASSWORD!
OH, NOW HE'S WOR-RIED ABOUT PRIVACY.
CARABELLA, IS THIS YOUR PAGE? DUDE, THIS IS BLEAK!
I TOLD YOU, MY PARENTS WERE...
DEEDLE-EEP

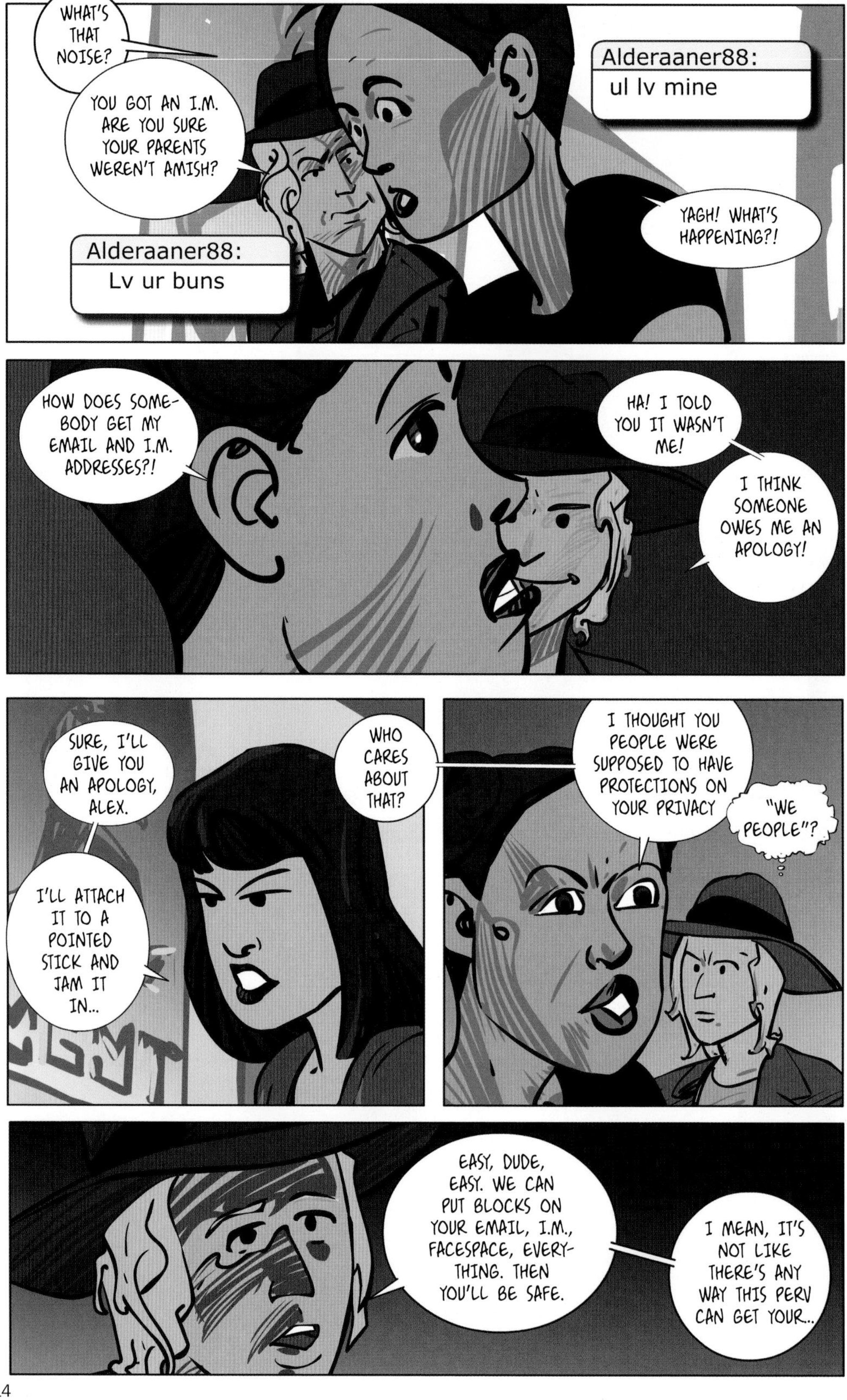
WHAT'S THAT NOISE?
YOU GOT AN I.M. ARE YOU SURE YOUR PARENTS WEREN'T AMISH?
Alderaaner88:
Lv ur buns
Alderaaner88:
ul lv mine
YAGH! WHAT'S HAPPENING?!
HOW DOES SOME-BODY GET MY EMAIL AND I.M. ADDRESSES?!
HA! I TOLD YOU IT WASN'T ME!
I THINK SOMEONE OWES ME AN APOLOGY!
SURE, I'LL GIVE YOU AN APOLOGY, ALEX.
I'LL ATTACH IT TO A POINTED STICK AND JAM IT IN...
WHO CARES ABOUT THAT?
I THOUGHT YOU PEOPLE WERE SUPPOSED TO HAVE PROTECTIONS ON YOUR PRIVACY
"WE PEOPLE"?
EASY, DUDE, EASY. WE CAN PUT BLOCKS ON YOUR EMAIL, I.M., FACESPACE, EVERY-THING. THEN YOU'LL BE SAFE.
I MEAN, IT'S NOT LIKE THERE'S ANY WAY THIS PERV CAN GET YOUR...

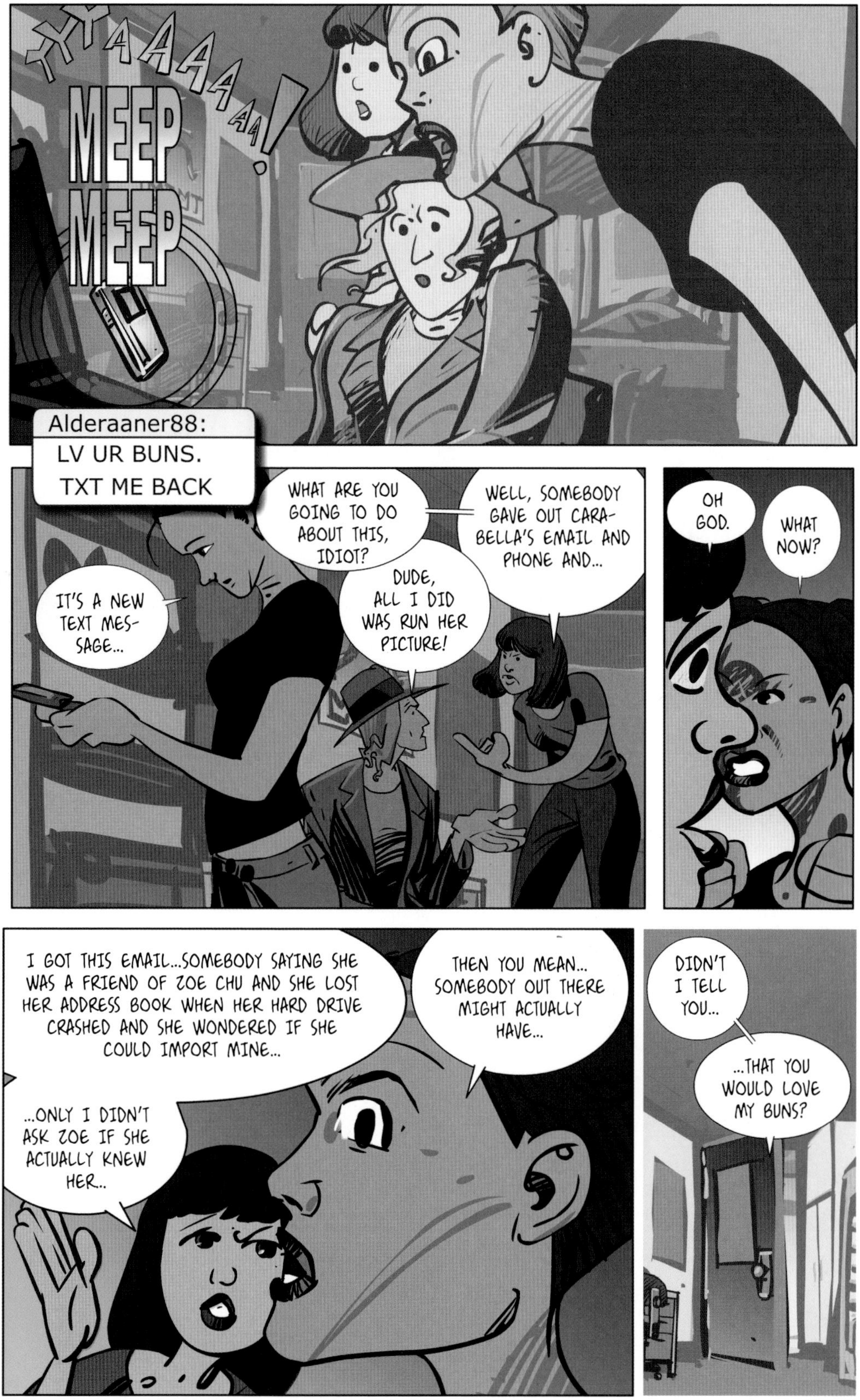
YYAAAAAAA!
MEEP MEEP
Alderaaner88: LV UR BUNS. TXT ME BACK
IT'S A NEW TEXT MES-SAGE...
WHAT ARE YOU GOING TO DO ABOUT THIS, IDIOT?
DUDE, ALL I DID WAS RUN HER PICTURE!
WELL, SOMEBODY GAVE OUT CARA-BELLA'S EMAIL AND PHONE AND...
OH GOD.
WHAT NOW?
I GOT THIS EMAIL...SOMEBODY SAYING SHE WAS A FRIEND OF ZOE CHU AND SHE LOST HER ADDRESS BOOK WHEN HER HARD DRIVE CRASHED AND SHE WONDERED IF SHE COULD IMPORT MINE...
...ONLY I DIDN'T ASK ZOE IF SHE ACTUALLY KNEW HER..
THEN YOU MEAN... SOMEBODY OUT THERE MIGHT ACTUALLY HAVE...
DIDN'T I TELL YOU...
...THAT YOU WOULD LOVE MY BUNS?

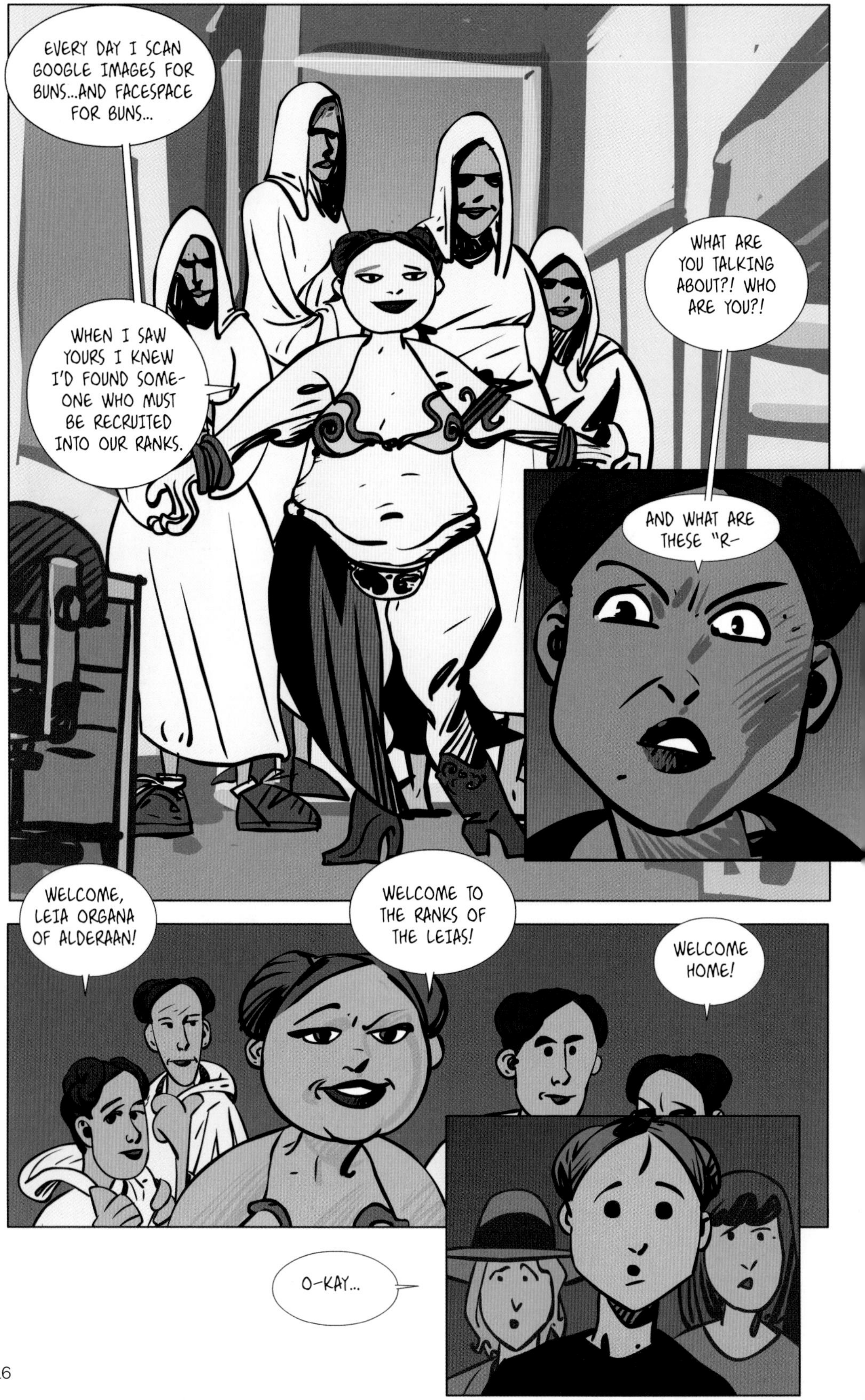
EVERY DAY I SCAN GOOGLE IMAGES FOR BUNS...AND FACESPACE FOR BUNS...
WHEN I SAW YOURS I KNEW I'D FOUND SOME-ONE WHO MUST BE RECRUITED INTO OUR RANKS.
WHAT ARE YOU TALKING ABOUT?! WHO ARE YOU?!
AND WHAT ARE THESE "R-
WELCOME, LEIA ORGANA OF ALDERAAN!
WELCOME TO THE RANKS OF THE LEIAS!
WELCOME HOME!
O-KAY...

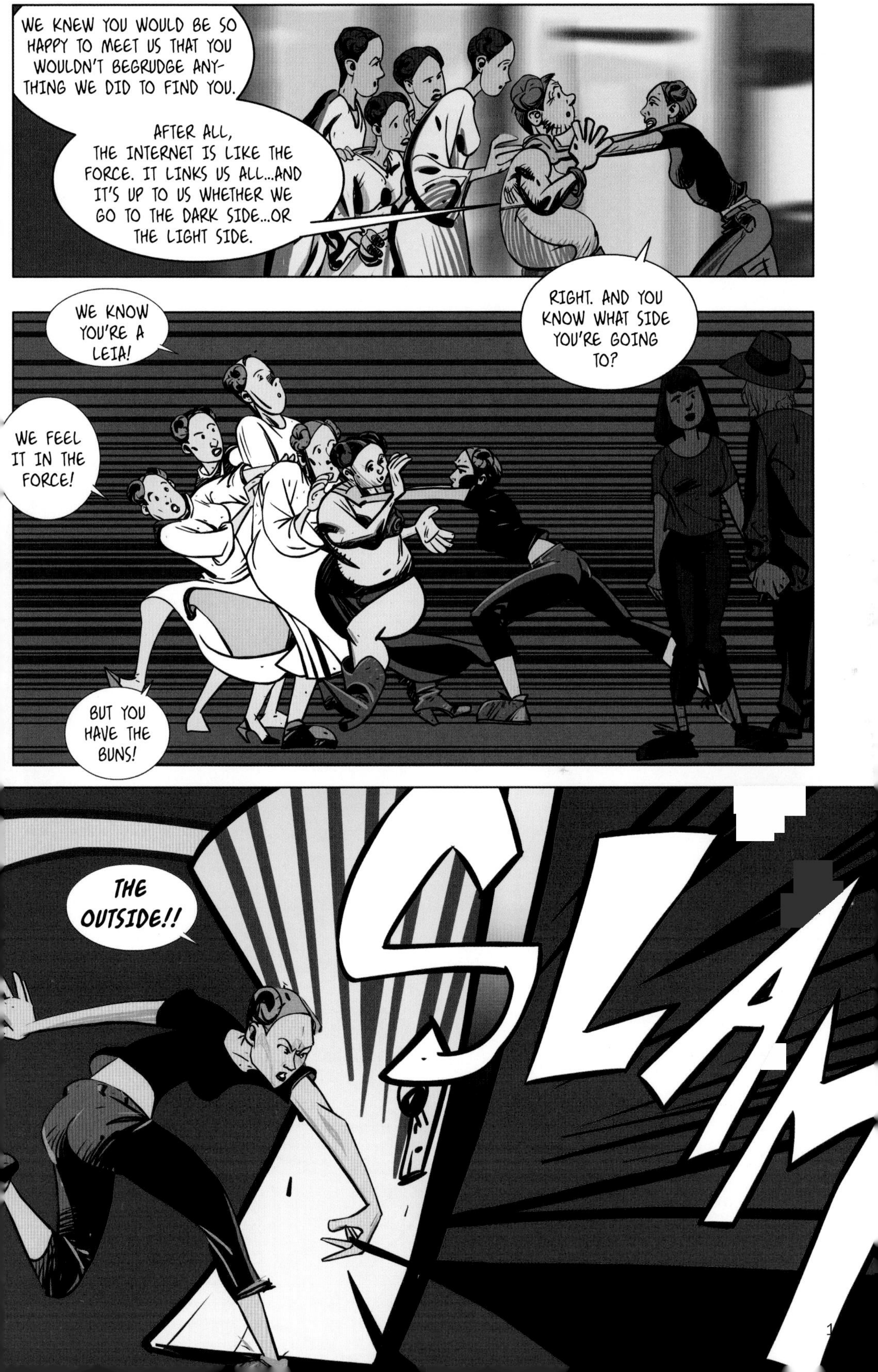
WE KNEW YOU WOULD BE SO HAPPY TO MEET US THAT YOU WOULDN'T BEGRUDGE ANY-THING WE DID TO FIND YOU.
AFTER ALL, THE INTERNET IS LIKE THE FORCE. IT LINKS US ALL...AND IT'S UP TO US WHETHER WE GO TO THE DARK SIDE...OR THE LIGHT SIDE.
RIGHT. AND YOU KNOW WHAT SIDE YOU'RE GOING TO?
WE KNOW YOU'RE A LEIA!
WE FEEL IT IN THE FORCE!
BUT YOU HAVE THE BUNS!
THE OUTSIDE!!
SLAM

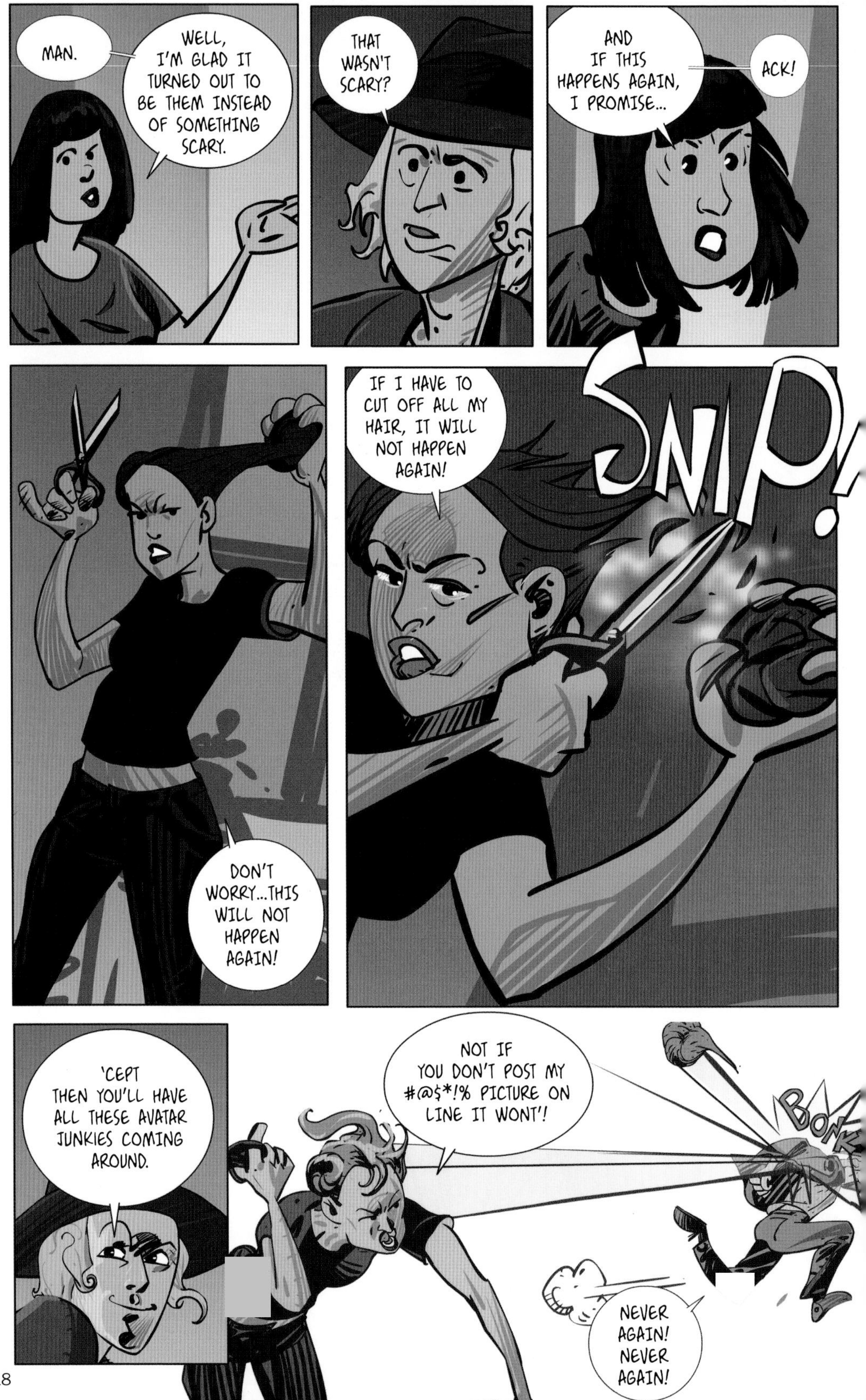
MAN.
WELL, I'M GLAD IT TURNED OUT TO BE THEM INSTEAD OF SOMETHING SCARY.
THAT WASN'T SCARY?
AND IF THIS HAPPENS AGAIN, I PROMISE...
ACK!
DON'T WORRY...THIS WILL NOT HAPPEN AGAIN!
IF I HAVE TO CUT OFF ALL MY HAIR, IT WILL NOT HAPPEN AGAIN!
SNIP!
'CEPT THEN YOU'LL HAVE ALL THESE AVATAR JUNKIES COMING AROUND.
NOT IF YOU DON'T POST MY #@$*!% PICTURE ON LINE IT WONT'!
BONK
NEVER AGAIN! NEVER AGAIN!

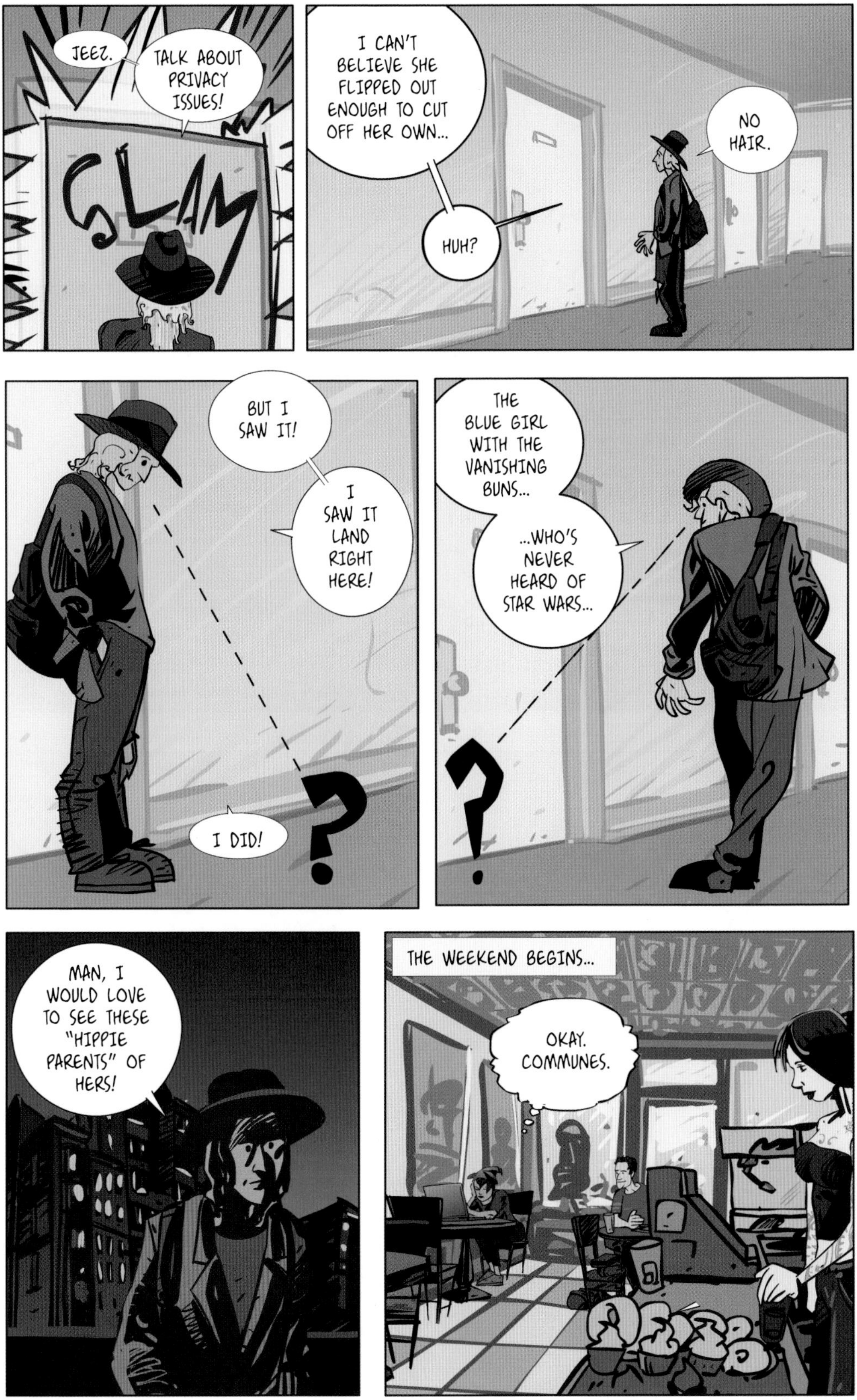
JEEZ.
TALK ABOUT PRIVACY ISSUES!
GLAM
I CAN'T BELIEVE SHE FLIPPED OUT ENOUGH TO CUT OFF HER OWN...
NO HAIR.
HUH?
BUT I SAW IT!
I SAW IT LAND RIGHT HERE!
I DID!
THE BLUE GIRL WITH THE VANISHING BUNS...
...WHO'S NEVER HEARD OF STAR WARS...
MAN, I WOULD LOVE TO SEE THESE "HIPPIE PARENTS" OF HERS!
THE WEEKEND BEGINS...
OKAY. COMMUNES.

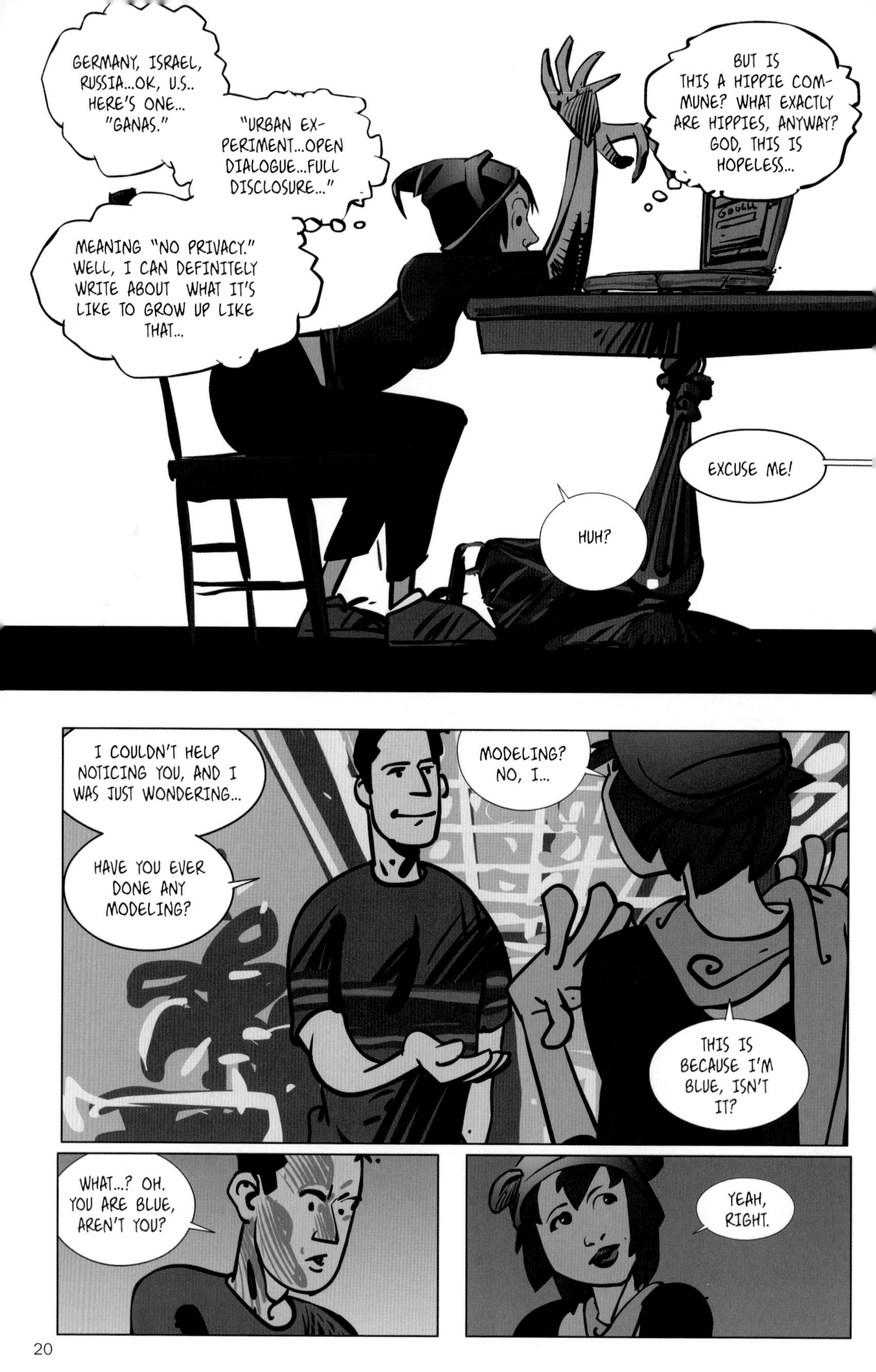
GERMANY, ISRAEL, RUSSIA...OK, U.S.. HERE'S ONE... "GANAS."
"URBAN EX-PERIMENT...OPEN DIALOGUE...FULL DISCLOSURE..."
MEANING "NO PRIVACY." WELL, I CAN DEFINITELY WRITE ABOUT WHAT IT'S LIKE TO GROW UP LIKE THAT...
BUT IS THIS A HIPPIE COM-MUNE? WHAT EXACTLY ARE HIPPIES, ANYWAY? GOD, THIS IS HOPELESS...
EXCUSE ME!
HUH?
I COULDN'T HELP NOTICING YOU, AND I WAS JUST WONDERING...
HAVE YOU EVER DONE ANY MODELING?
MODELING? NO, I...
THIS IS BECAUSE I'M BLUE, ISN'T IT?
WHAT...? OH. YOU ARE BLUE, AREN'T YOU?
YEAH, RIGHT.

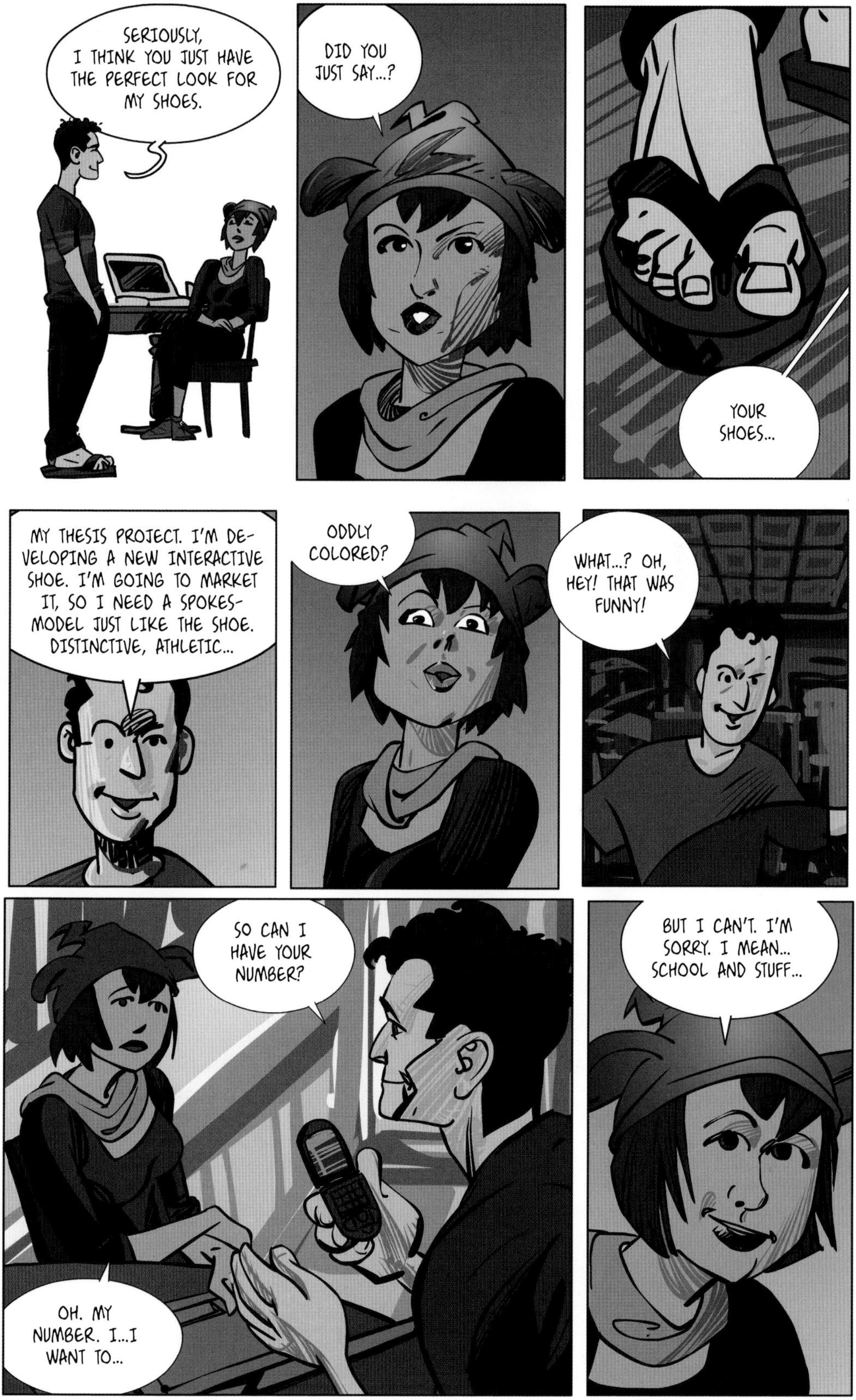
SERIOUSLY, I THINK YOU JUST HAVE THE PERFECT LOOK FOR MY SHOES.
DID YOU JUST SAY...?
YOUR SHOES...
MY THESIS PROJECT. I'M DE-VELOPING A NEW INTERACTIVE SHOE. I'M GOING TO MARKET IT, SO I NEED A SPOKES-MODEL JUST LIKE THE SHOE. DISTINCTIVE, ATHLETIC...
ODDLY COLORED?
WHAT...? OH, HEY! THAT WAS FUNNY!
SO CAN I HAVE YOUR NUMBER?
OH. MY NUMBER. I...I WANT TO...
BUT I CAN'T. I'M SORRY. I MEAN... SCHOOL AND STUFF...

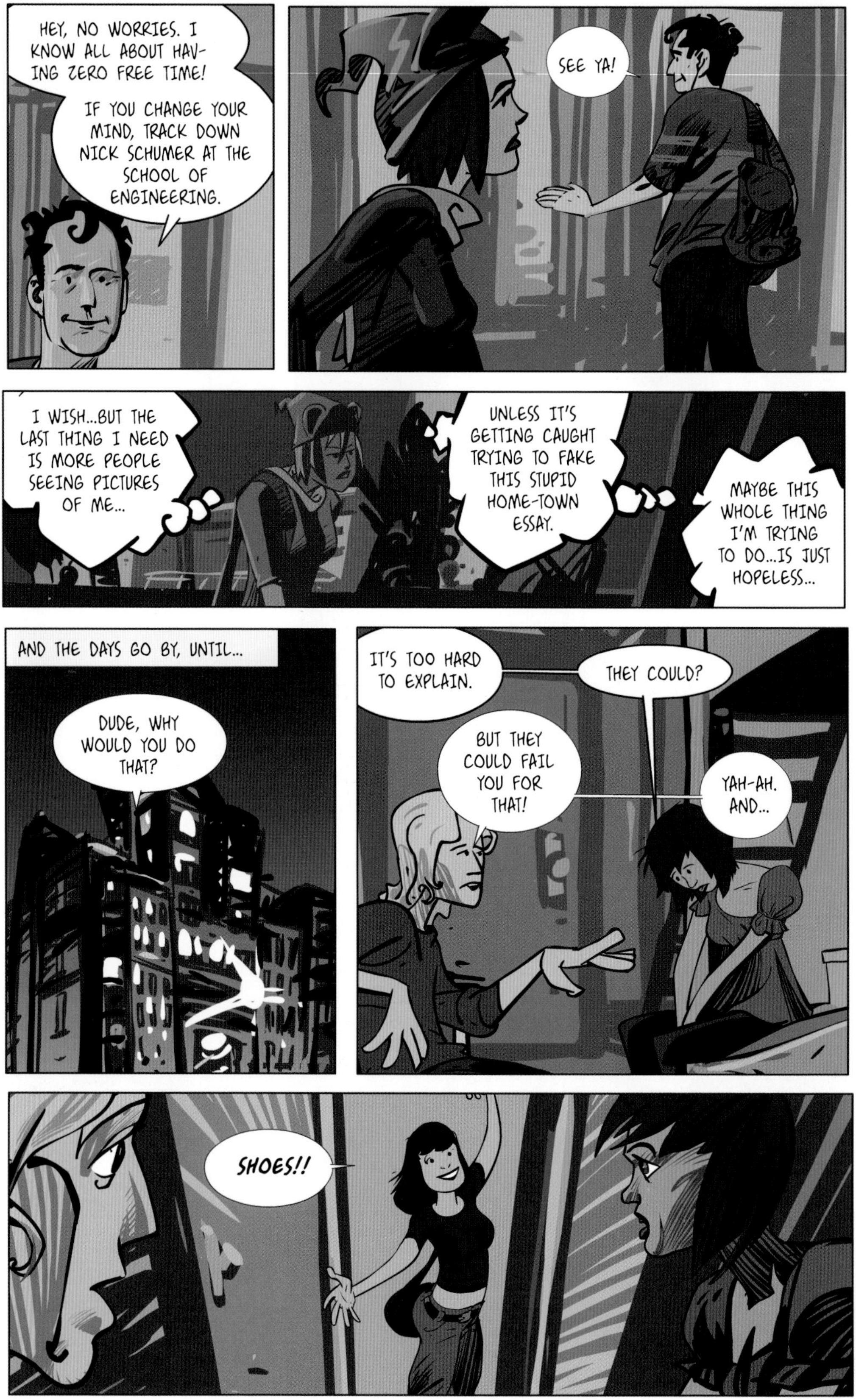
HEY, NO WORRIES. I KNOW ALL ABOUT HAV-ING ZERO FREE TIME!
IF YOU CHANGE YOUR MIND, TRACK DOWN NICK SCHUMER AT THE SCHOOL OF ENGINEERING.
SEE YA!
I WISH...BUT THE LAST THING I NEED IS MORE PEOPLE SEEING PICTURES OF ME...
UNLESS IT'S GETTING CAUGHT TRYING TO FAKE THIS STUPID HOME-TOWN ESSAY.
MAYBE THIS WHOLE THING I'M TRYING TO DO...IS JUST HOPELESS...
AND THE DAYS GO BY, UNTIL...
DUDE, WHY WOULD YOU DO THAT?
IT'S TOO HARD TO EXPLAIN.
THEY COULD?
BUT THEY COULD FAIL YOU FOR THAT!
YAH-AH. AND...
SHOES!!

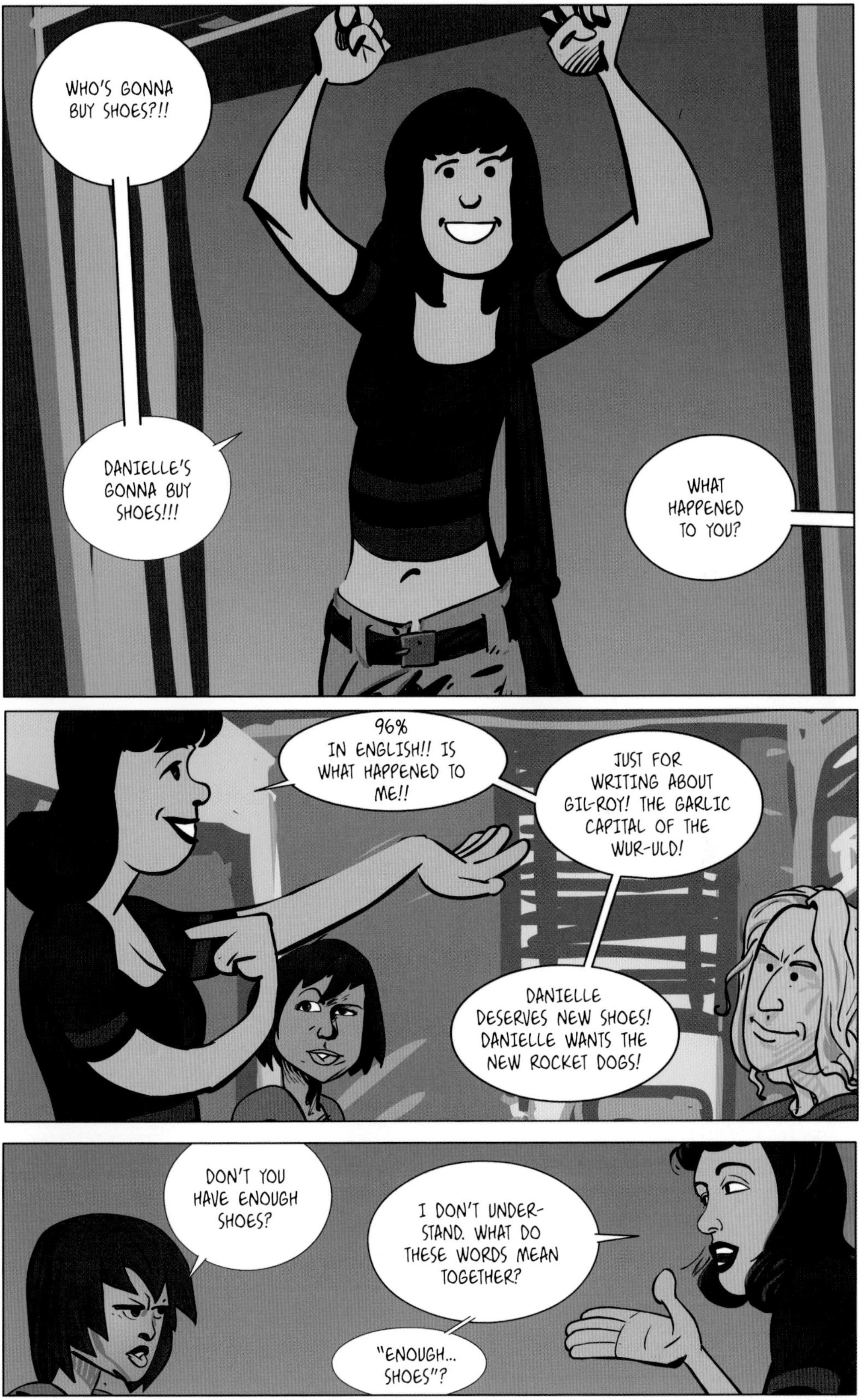
WHO'S GONNA BUY SHOES?!!
DANIELLE'S GONNA BUY SHOES!!!
WHAT HAPPENED TO YOU?
96% IN ENGLISH!! IS WHAT HAPPENED TO ME!!
JUST FOR WRITING ABOUT GIL-ROY! THE GARLIC CAPITAL OF THE WUR-ULD!
DANIELLE DESERVES NEW SHOES! DANIELLE WANTS THE NEW ROCKET DOGS!
DON'T YOU HAVE ENOUGH SHOES?
I DON'T UNDER-STAND. WHAT DO THESE WORDS MEAN TOGETHER?
"ENOUGH... SHOES"?

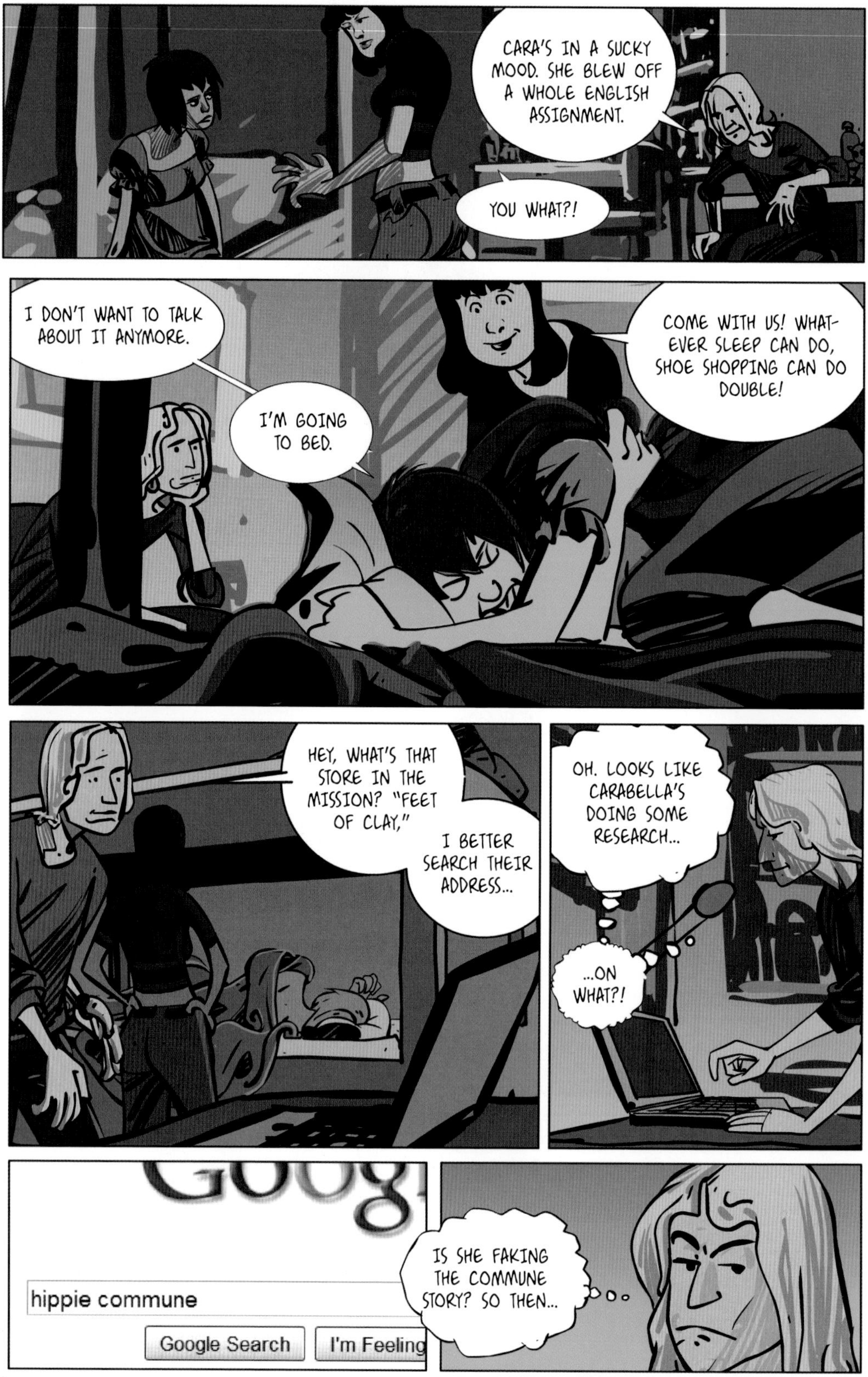
CARA'S IN A SUCKY MOOD. SHE BLEW OFF A WHOLE ENGLISH ASSIGNMENT.
YOU WHAT?!
I DON'T WANT TO TALK ABOUT IT ANYMORE.
I'M GOING TO BED.
COME WITH US! WHAT-EVER SLEEP CAN DO, SHOE SHOPPING CAN DO DOUBLE!
HEY, WHAT'S THAT STORE IN THE MISSION? "FEET OF CLAY,"
I BETTER SEARCH THEIR ADDRESS...
OH. LOOKS LIKE CARABELLA'S DOING SOME RESEARCH...
...ON WHAT?!
hippie commune
Google Search
I'm Feeling
IS SHE FAKING THE COMMUNE STORY? SO THEN...

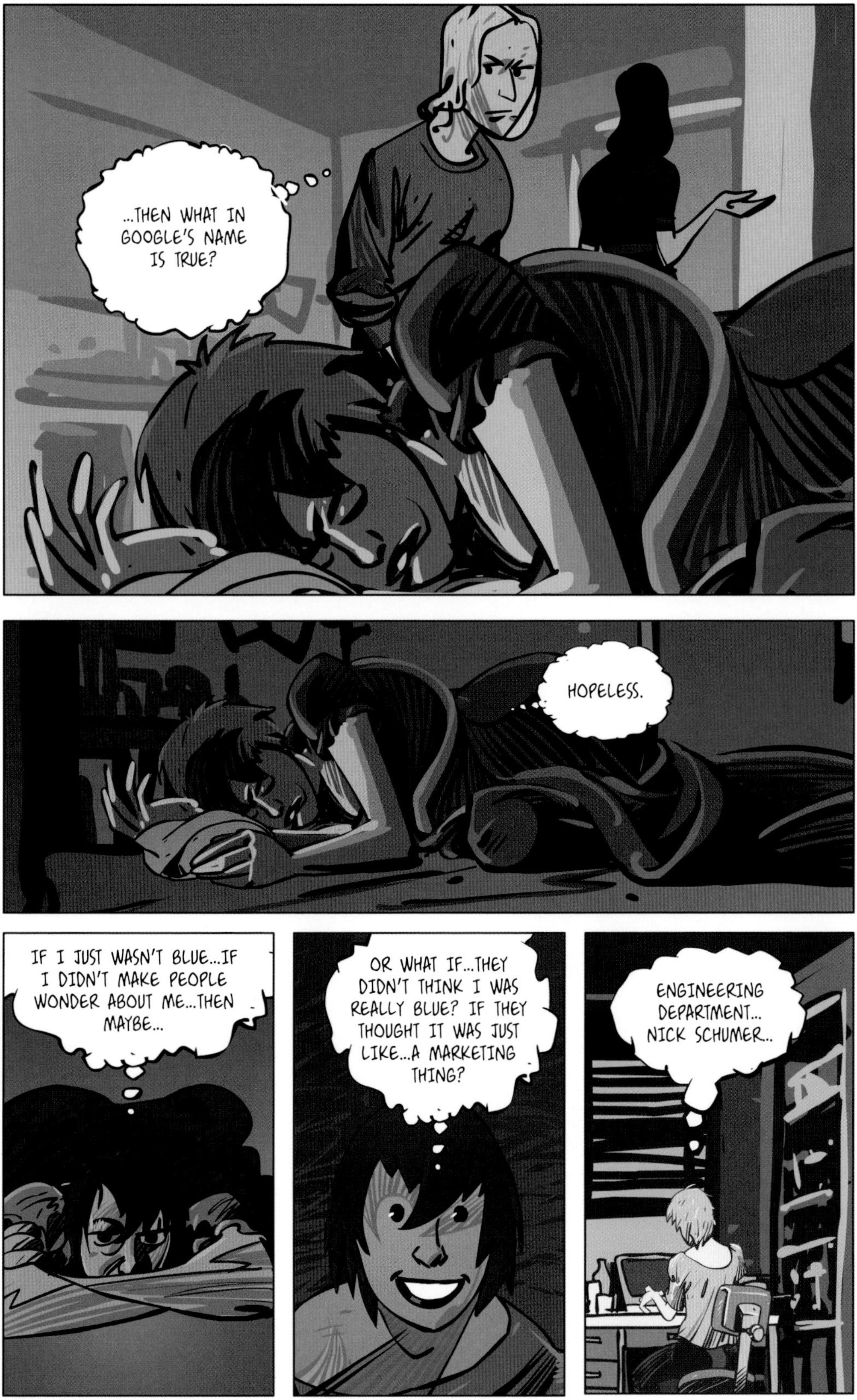
...THEN WHAT IN GOOGLE'S NAME IS TRUE?
HOPELESS.
IF I JUST WASN'T BLUE...IF I DIDN'T MAKE PEOPLE WONDER ABOUT ME...THEN MAYBE...
OR WHAT IF...THEY DIDN'T THINK I WAS REALLY BLUE? IF THEY THOUGHT IT WAS JUST LIKE...A MARKETING THING?
ENGINEERING DEPARTMENT... NICK SCHUMER...

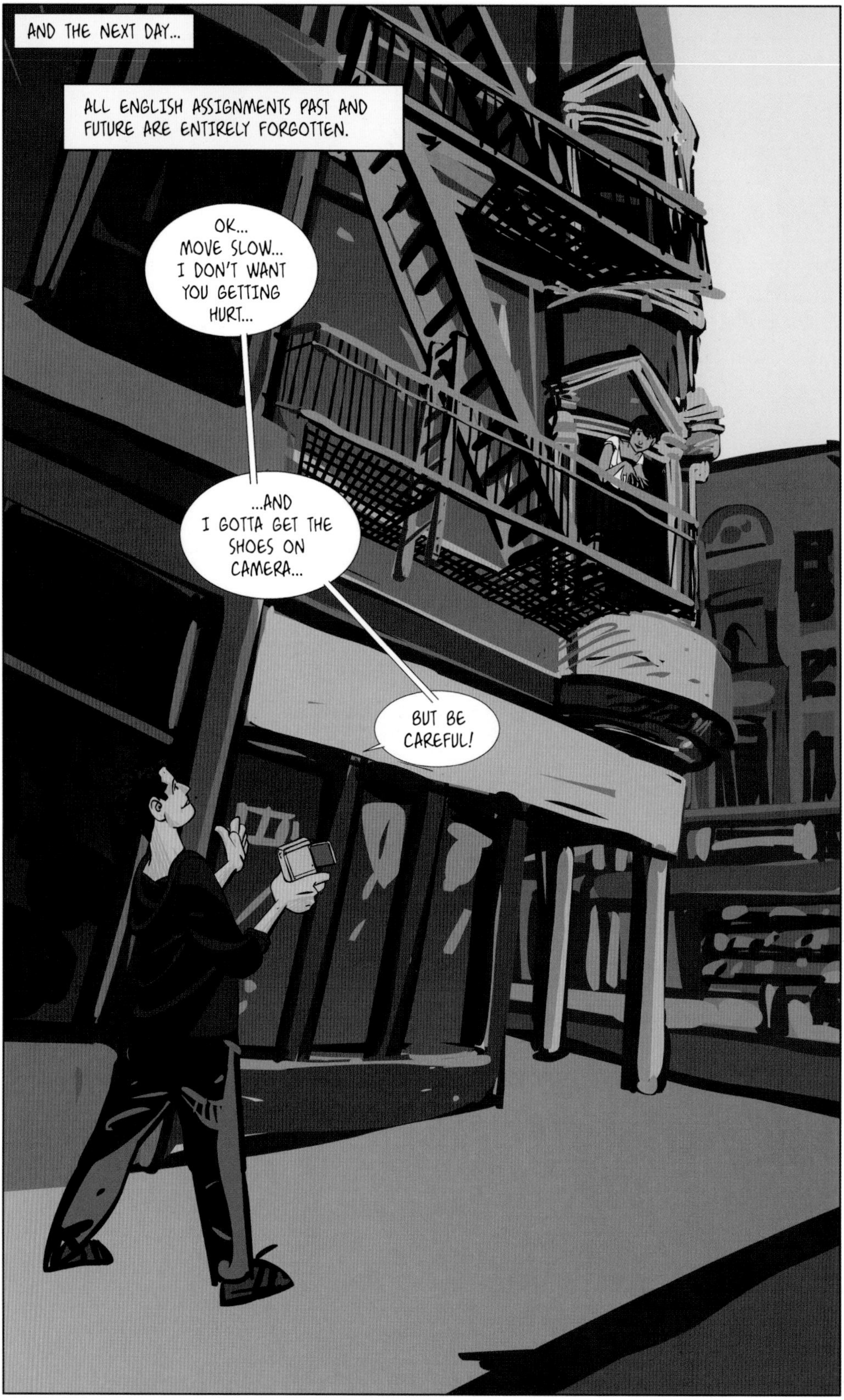
AND THE NEXT DAY...
ALL ENGLISH ASSIGNMENTS PAST AND FUTURE ARE ENTIRELY FORGOTTEN.
OK... MOVE SLOW... I DON'T WANT YOU GETTING HURT...
...AND I GOTTA GET THE SHOES ON CAMERA...
BUT BE CAREFUL!

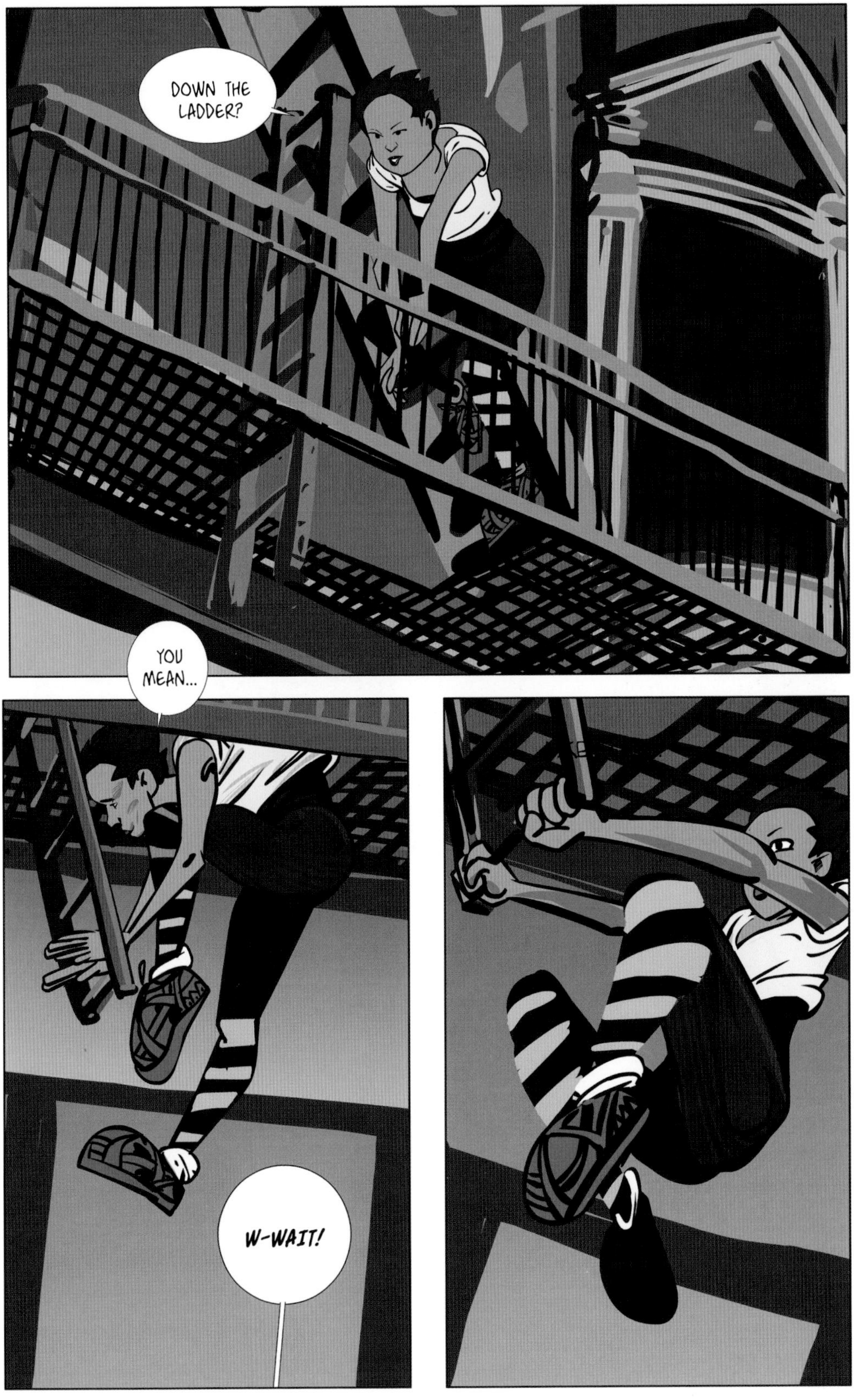
DOWN THE LADDER?
YOU MEAN...
W-WAIT!

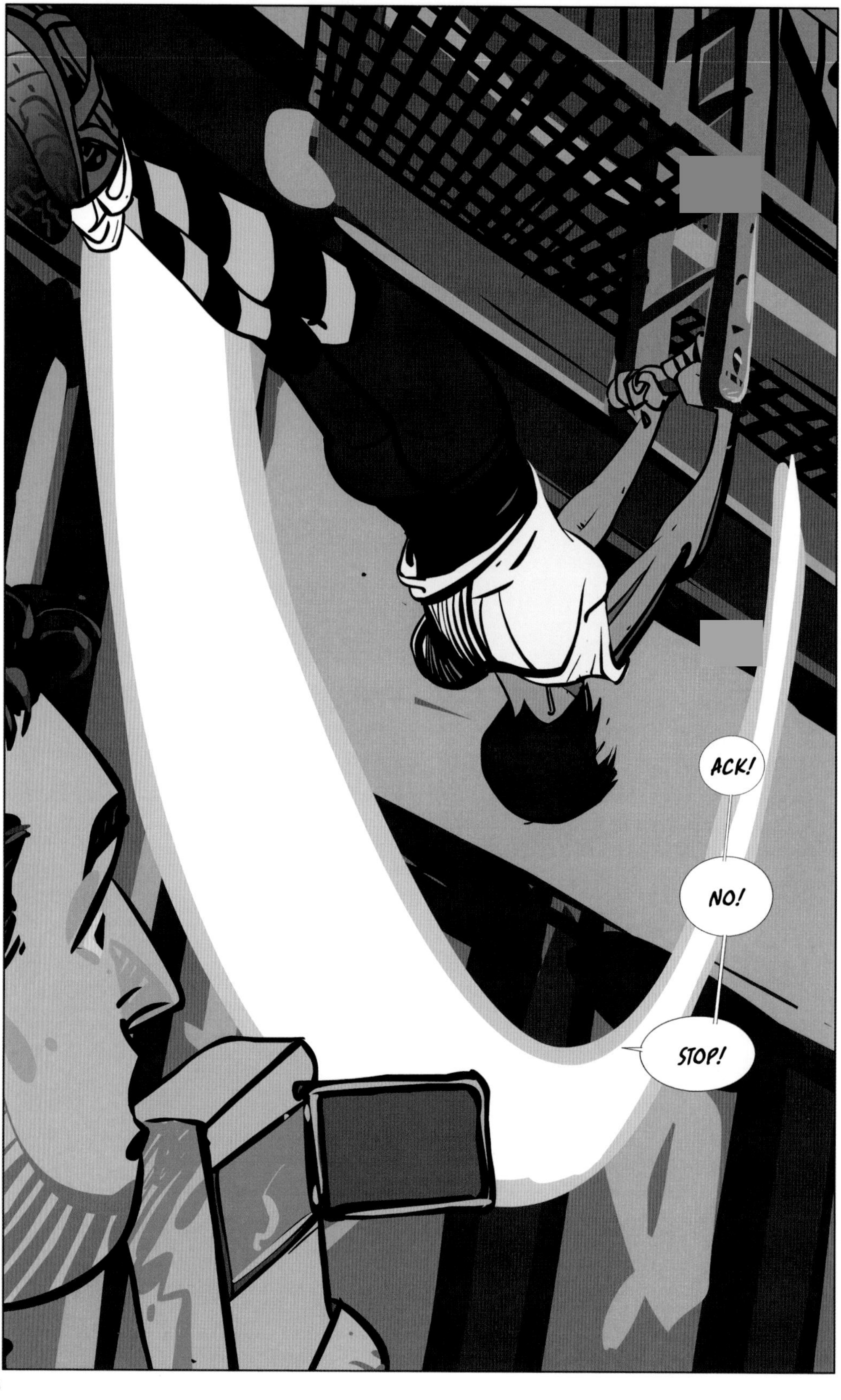
ACK!
NO!
STOP!

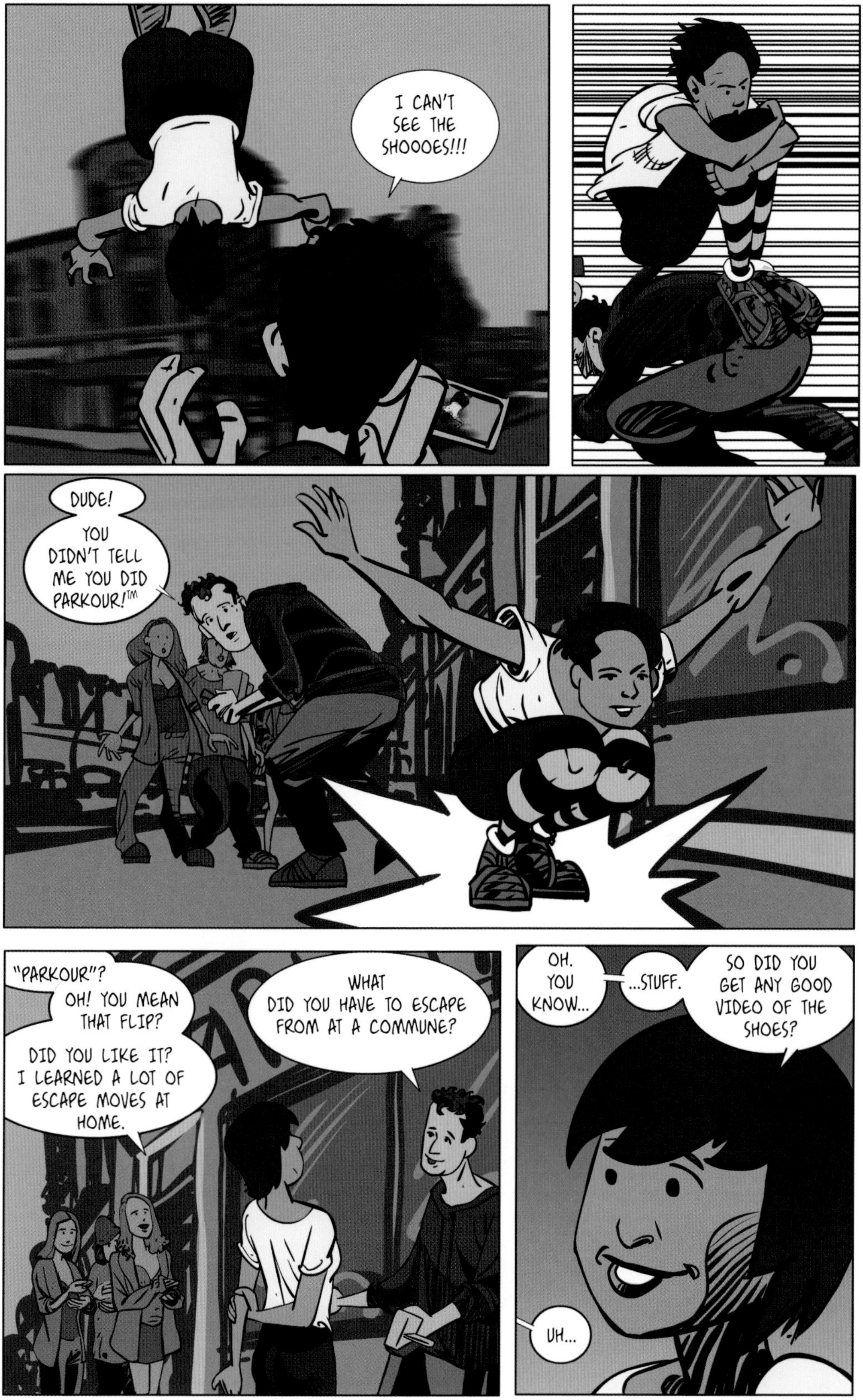
I CAN'T SEE THE SHOOOES!!!
DUDE!
YOU DIDN'T TELL ME YOU DID PARKOUR!™
"PARKOUR"?
OH! YOU MEAN THAT FLIP?
DID YOU LIKE IT? I LEARNED A LOT OF ESCAPE MOVES AT HOME.
WHAT DID YOU HAVE TO ESCAPE FROM AT A COMMUNE?
OH. YOU KNOW...
...STUFF.
SO DID YOU GET ANY GOOD VIDEO OF THE SHOES?
UH...

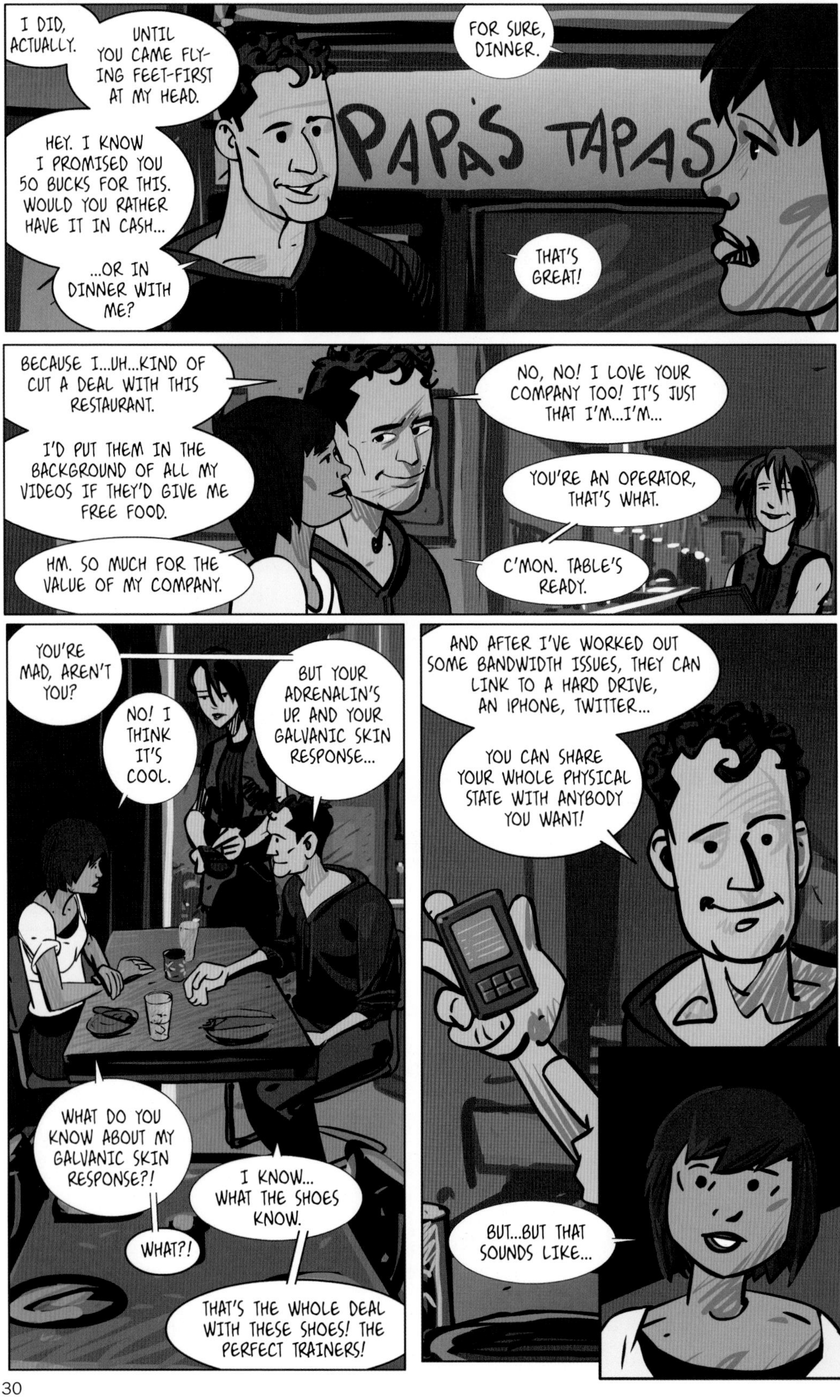
I DID, ACTUALLY.
UNTIL YOU CAME FLY-ING FEET-FIRST AT MY HEAD.
HEY. I KNOW I PROMISED YOU 50 BUCKS FOR THIS. WOULD YOU RATHER HAVE IT IN CASH...
...OR IN DINNER WITH ME?
FOR SURE, DINNER.
PAPA'S TAPAS
THAT'S GREAT!
BECAUSE I...UH...KIND OF CUT A DEAL WITH THIS RESTAURANT.
I'D PUT THEM IN THE BACKGROUND OF ALL MY VIDEOS IF THEY'D GIVE ME FREE FOOD.
HM. SO MUCH FOR THE VALUE OF MY COMPANY.
NO, NO! I LOVE YOUR COMPANY TOO! IT'S JUST THAT I'M...I'M...
YOU'RE AN OPERATOR, THAT'S WHAT.
C'MON. TABLE'S READY.
YOU'RE MAD, AREN'T YOU?
NO! I THINK IT'S COOL.
BUT YOUR ADRENALIN'S UP. AND YOUR GALVANIC SKIN RESPONSE...
WHAT DO YOU KNOW ABOUT MY GALVANIC SKIN RESPONSE?!
I KNOW... WHAT THE SHOES KNOW.
WHAT?!
THAT'S THE WHOLE DEAL WITH THESE SHOES! THE PERFECT TRAINERS!
AND AFTER I'VE WORKED OUT SOME BANDWIDTH ISSUES, THEY CAN LINK TO A HARD DRIVE, AN IPHONE, TWITTER...
YOU CAN SHARE YOUR WHOLE PHYSICAL STATE WITH ANYBODY YOU WANT!
BUT...BUT THAT SOUNDS LIKE...

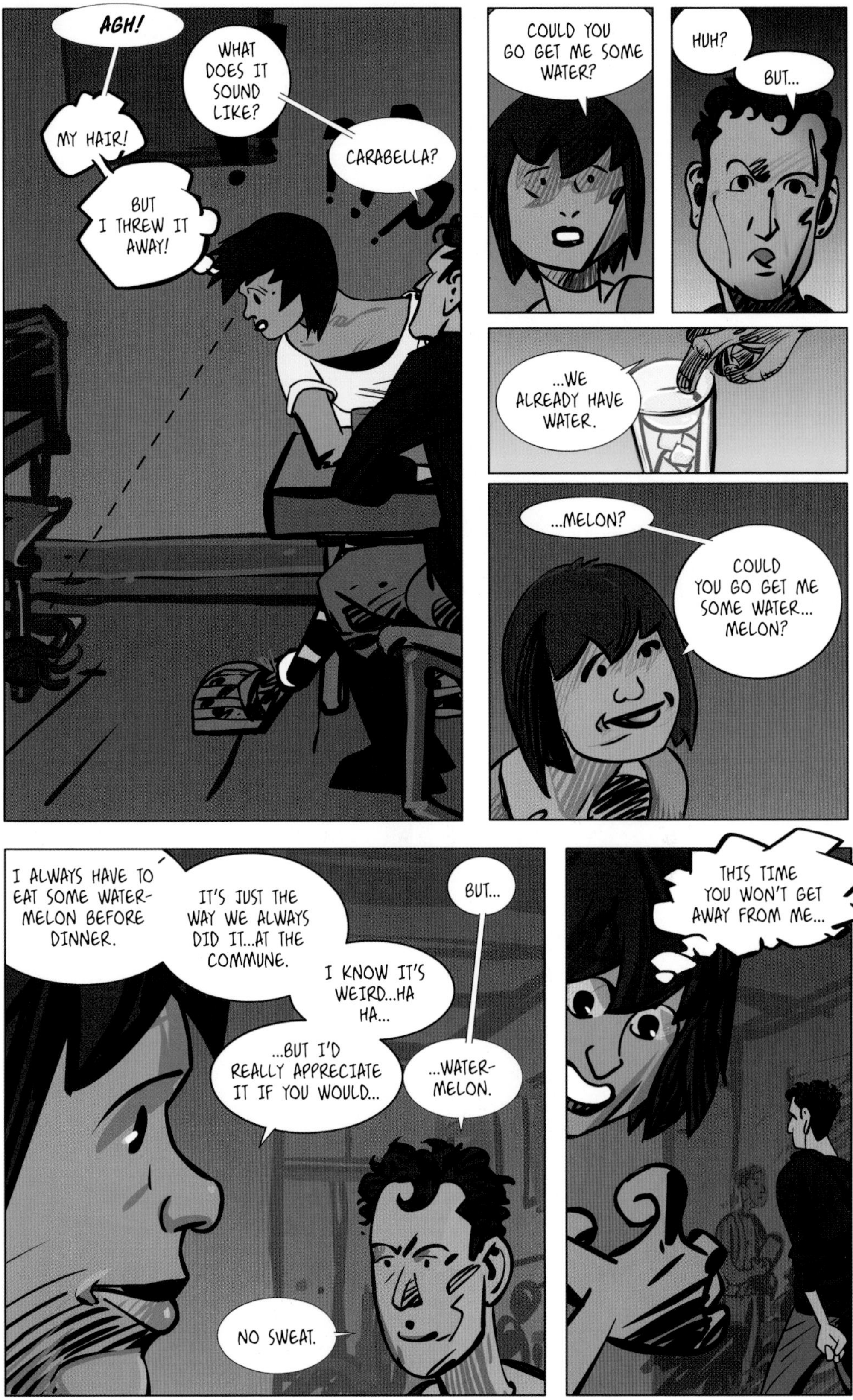
AGH!
MY HAIR!
BUT I THREW IT AWAY!
WHAT DOES IT SOUND LIKE?
CARABELLA?
COULD YOU GO GET ME SOME WATER?
HUH?
BUT...
...WE ALREADY HAVE WATER.
...MELON?
COULD YOU GO GET ME SOME WATER... MELON?
I ALWAYS HAVE TO EAT SOME WATER-MELON BEFORE DINNER.
IT'S JUST THE WAY WE ALWAYS DID IT...AT THE COMMUNE.
I KNOW IT'S WEIRD...HA HA...
...BUT I'D REALLY APPRECIATE IT IF YOU WOULD...
BUT...
...WATER-MELON.
NO SWEAT.
THIS TIME YOU WON'T GET AWAY FROM ME...

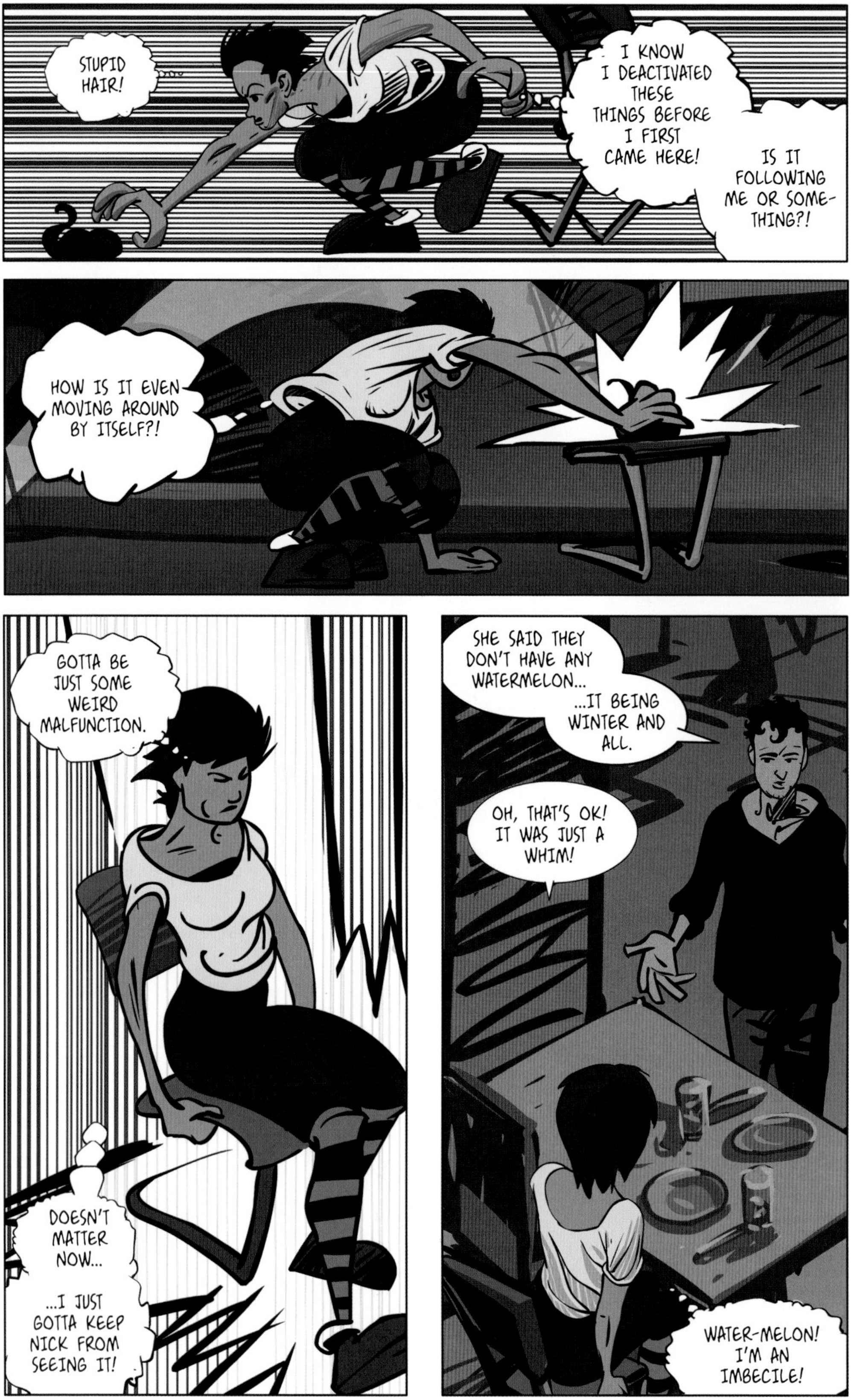
STUPID HAIR!
I KNOW I DEACTIVATED THESE THINGS BEFORE I FIRST CAME HERE!
IS IT FOLLOWING ME OR SOME-THING?!
HOW IS IT EVEN MOVING AROUND BY ITSELF?!
GOTTA BE JUST SOME WEIRD MALFUNCTION.
DOESN'T MATTER NOW...
...I JUST GOTTA KEEP NICK FROM SEEING IT!
SHE SAID THEY DON'T HAVE ANY WATERMELON...
...IT BEING WINTER AND ALL.
OH, THAT'S OK! IT WAS JUST A WHIM!
WATER-MELON! I'M AN IMBECILE!

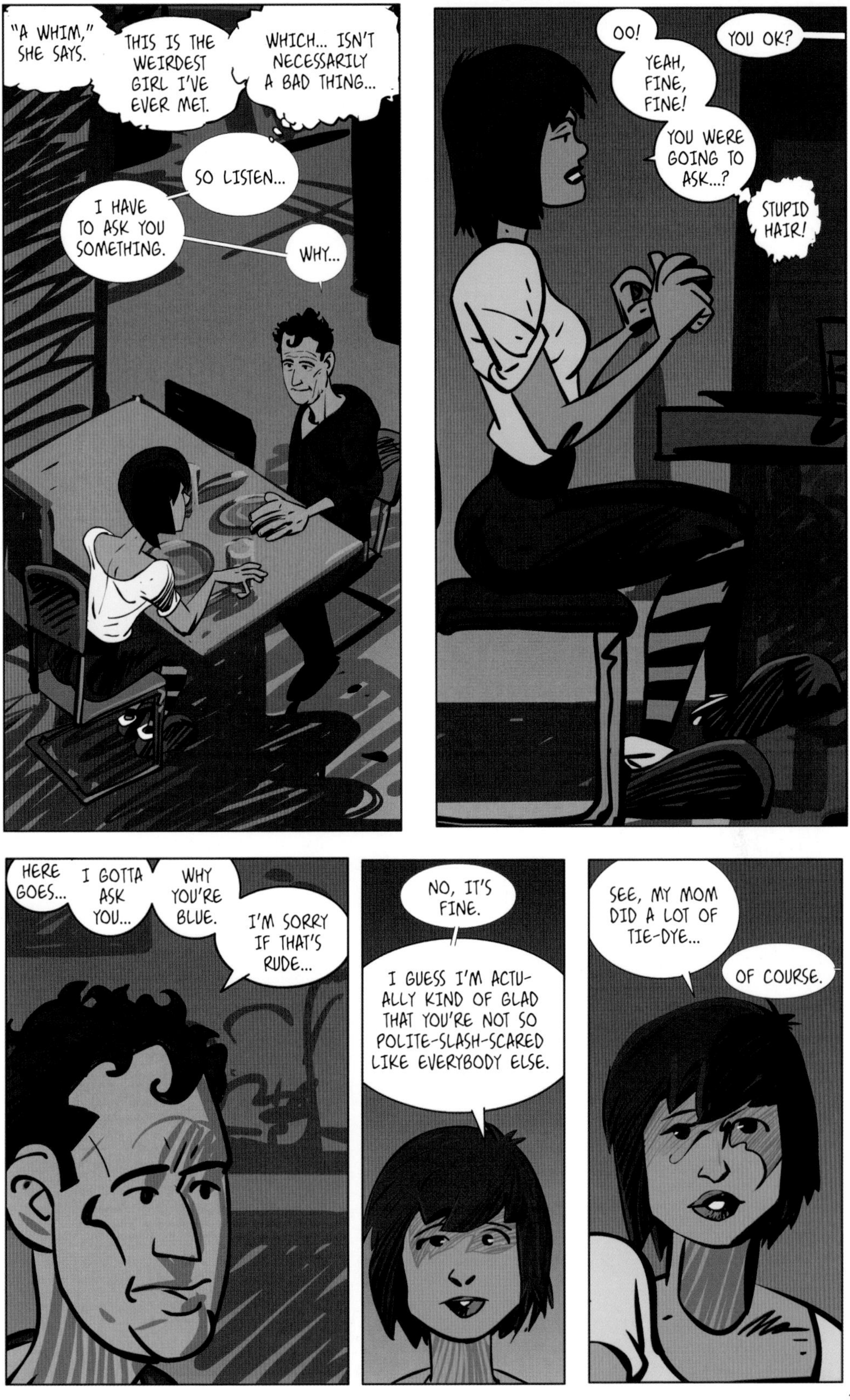
"A WHIM," SHE SAYS.
THIS IS THE WEIRDEST GIRL I'VE EVER MET.
WHICH... ISN'T NECESSARILY A BAD THING...
SO LISTEN...
I HAVE TO ASK YOU SOMETHING.
WHY...
YOU OK?
OO!
YEAH, FINE, FINE!
YOU WERE GOING TO ASK...?
STUPID HAIR!
HERE GOES...
I GOTTA ASK YOU...
WHY YOU'RE BLUE.
I'M SORRY IF THAT'S RUDE...
NO, IT'S FINE.
I GUESS I'M ACTUALLY KIND OF GLAD THAT YOU'RE NOT SO POLITE-SLASH-SCARED LIKE EVERYBODY ELSE.
SEE, MY MOM DID A LOT OF TIE-DYE...
OF COURSE.

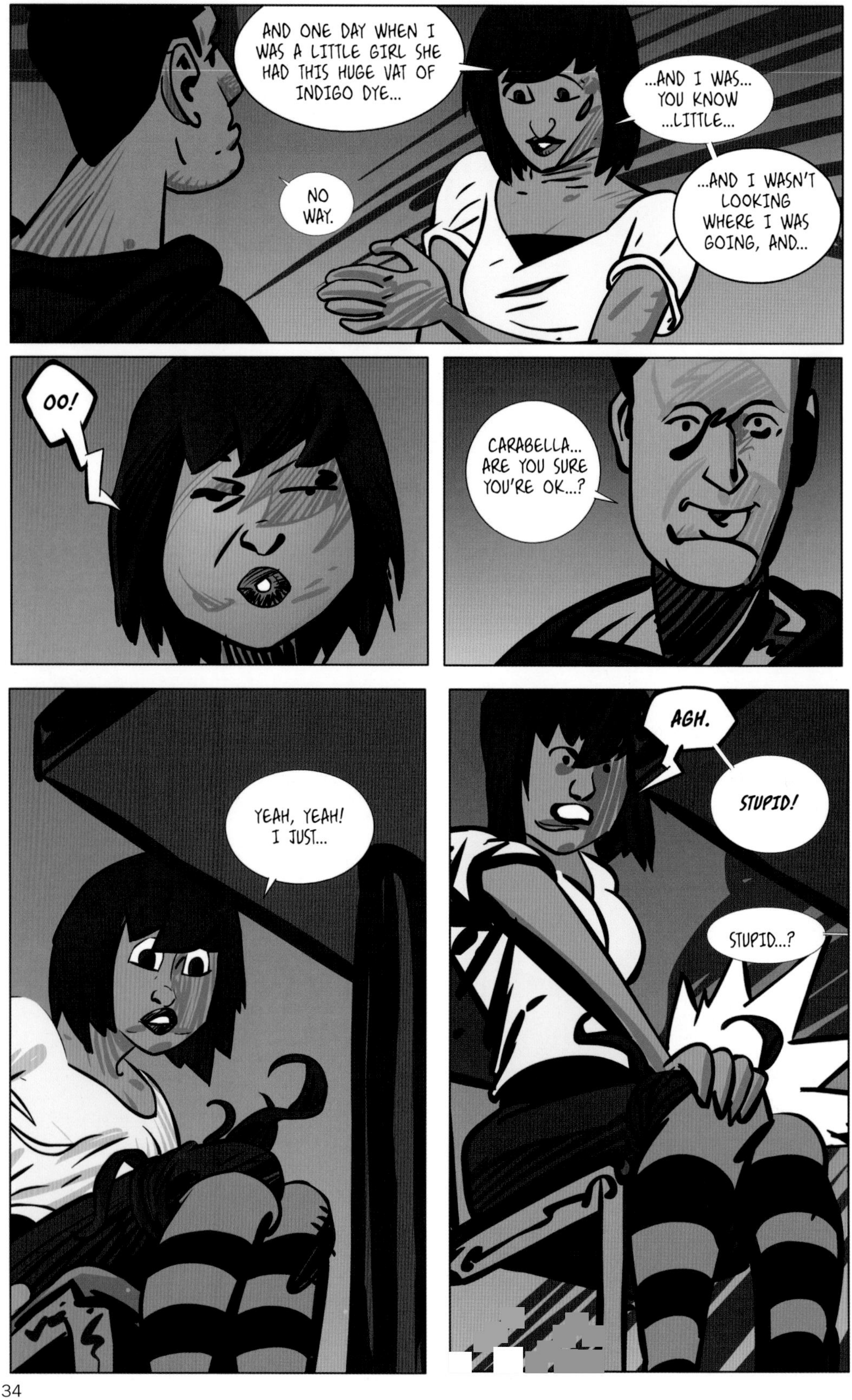
AND ONE DAY WHEN I WAS A LITTLE GIRL SHE HAD THIS HUGE VAT OF INDIGO DYE...
...AND I WAS... YOU KNOW ...LITTLE...
NO WAY.
...AND I WASN'T LOOKING WHERE I WAS GOING, AND...
OO!
CARABELLA... ARE YOU SURE YOU'RE OK...?
YEAH, YEAH! I JUST...
AGH.
STUPID!
STUPID...?

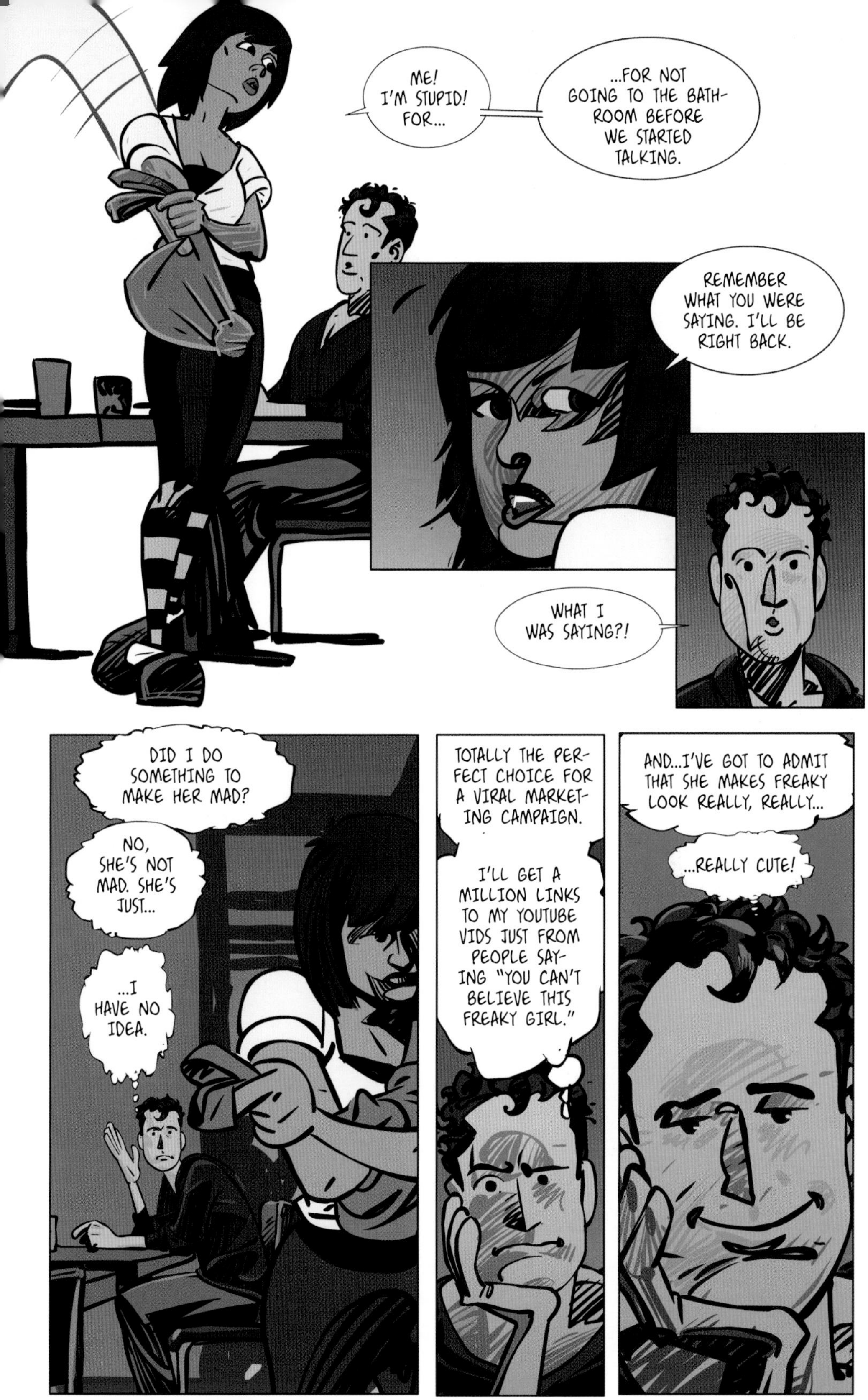
ME! I'M STUPID! FOR...
...FOR NOT GOING TO THE BATH-ROOM BEFORE WE STARTED TALKING.
REMEMBER WHAT YOU WERE SAYING. I'LL BE RIGHT BACK.
WHAT I WAS SAYING?!
DID I DO SOMETHING TO MAKE HER MAD?
NO, SHE'S NOT MAD. SHE'S JUST...
...I HAVE NO IDEA.
TOTALLY THE PER-FECT CHOICE FOR A VIRAL MARKET-ING CAMPAIGN.
I'LL GET A MILLION LINKS TO MY YOUTUBE VIDS JUST FROM PEOPLE SAY-ING "YOU CAN'T BELIEVE THIS FREAKY GIRL."
AND...I'VE GOT TO ADMIT THAT SHE MAKES FREAKY LOOK REALLY, REALLY...
...REALLY CUTE!

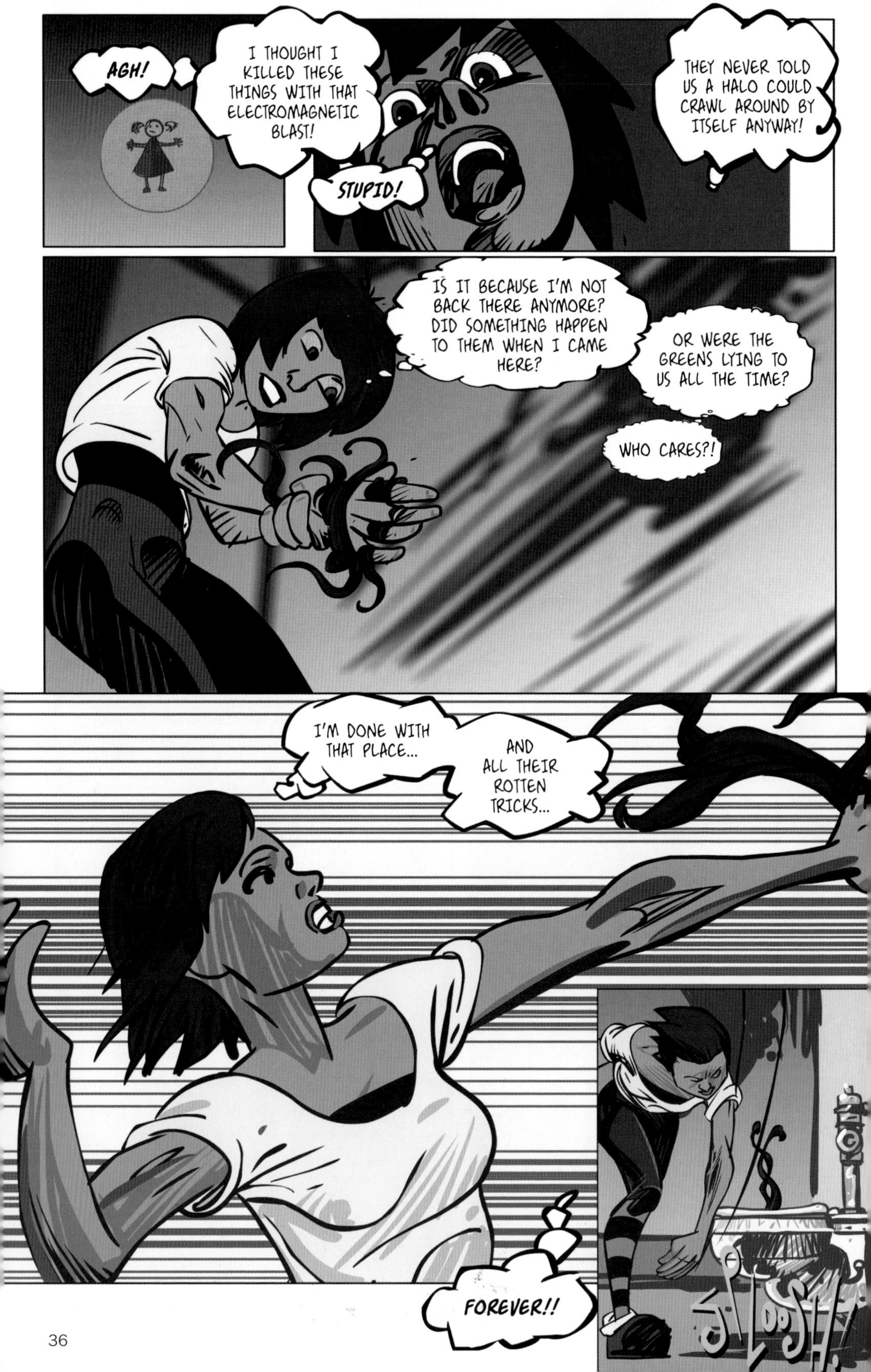
AGH!
I THOUGHT I KILLED THESE THINGS WITH THAT ELECTROMAGNETIC BLAST!
STUPID!
THEY NEVER TOLD US A HALO COULD CRAWL AROUND BY ITSELF ANYWAY!
IS IT BECAUSE I'M NOT BACK THERE ANYMORE? DID SOMETHING HAPPEN TO THEM WHEN I CAME HERE?
OR WERE THE GREENS LYING TO US ALL THE TIME?
WHO CARES?!
I'M DONE WITH THAT PLACE...
AND ALL THEIR ROTTEN TRICKS...
FOREVER!!
SPLOOSH!

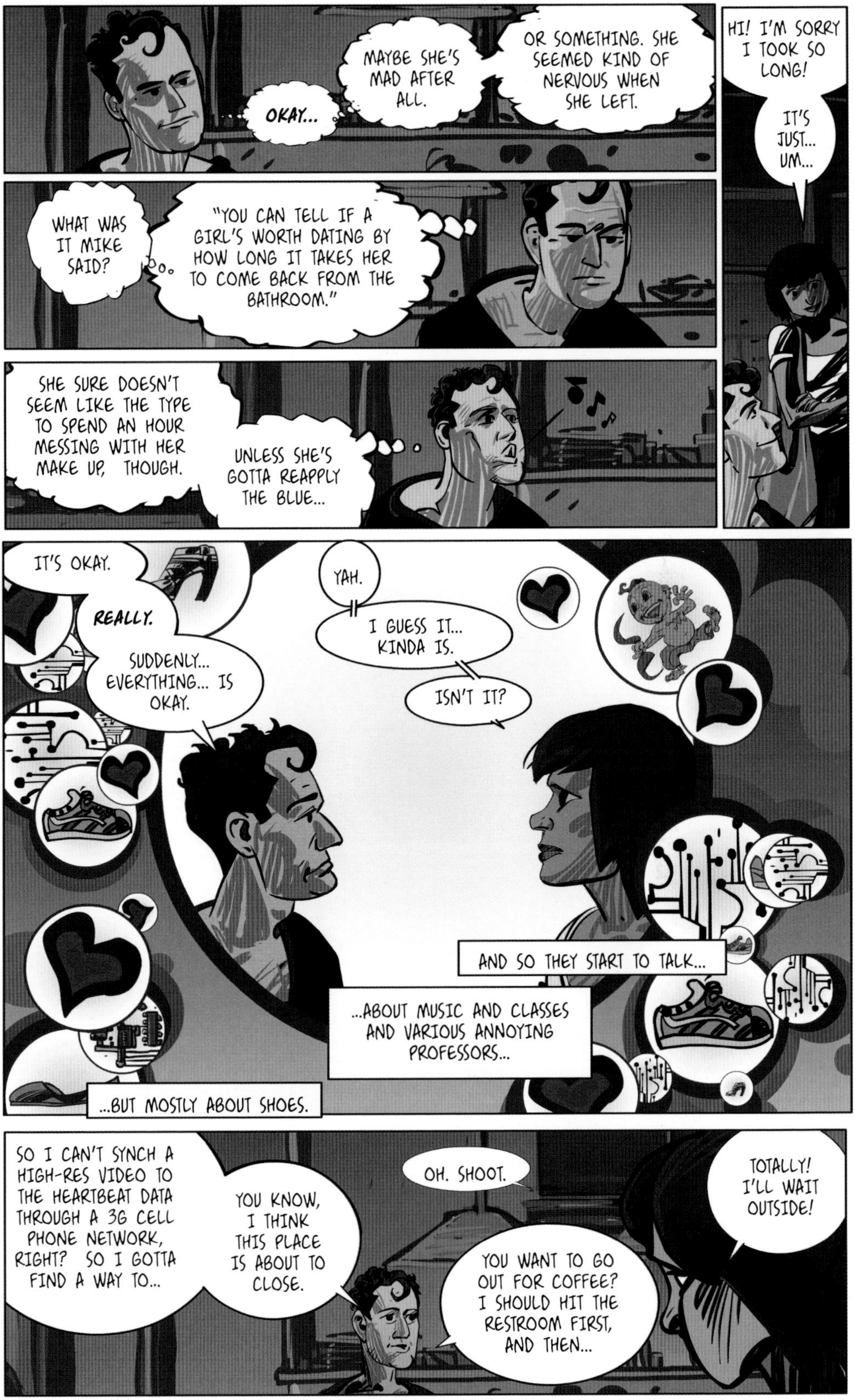
OKAY...
MAYBE SHE'S MAD AFTER ALL.
OR SOMETHING. SHE SEEMED KIND OF NERVOUS WHEN SHE LEFT.
WHAT WAS IT MIKE SAID?
"YOU CAN TELL IF A GIRL'S WORTH DATING BY HOW LONG IT TAKES HER TO COME BACK FROM THE BATHROOM."
SHE SURE DOESN'T SEEM LIKE THE TYPE TO SPEND AN HOUR MESSING WITH HER MAKE UP, THOUGH.
UNLESS SHE'S GOTTA REAPPLY THE BLUE...
HI! I'M SORRY I TOOK SO LONG!
IT'S JUST... UM...
IT'S OKAY.
REALLY.
SUDDENLY... EVERYTHING... IS OKAY.
YAH.
I GUESS IT... KINDA IS.
ISN'T IT?
AND SO THEY START TO TALK...
...ABOUT MUSIC AND CLASSES AND VARIOUS ANNOYING PROFESSORS...
...BUT MOSTLY ABOUT SHOES.
SO I CAN'T SYNCH A HIGH-RES VIDEO TO THE HEARTBEAT DATA THROUGH A 3G CELL PHONE NETWORK, RIGHT? SO I GOTTA FIND A WAY TO...
YOU KNOW, I THINK THIS PLACE IS ABOUT TO CLOSE.
OH. SHOOT.
YOU WANT TO GO OUT FOR COFFEE? I SHOULD HIT THE RESTROOM FIRST, AND THEN...
TOTALLY! I'LL WAIT OUTSIDE!

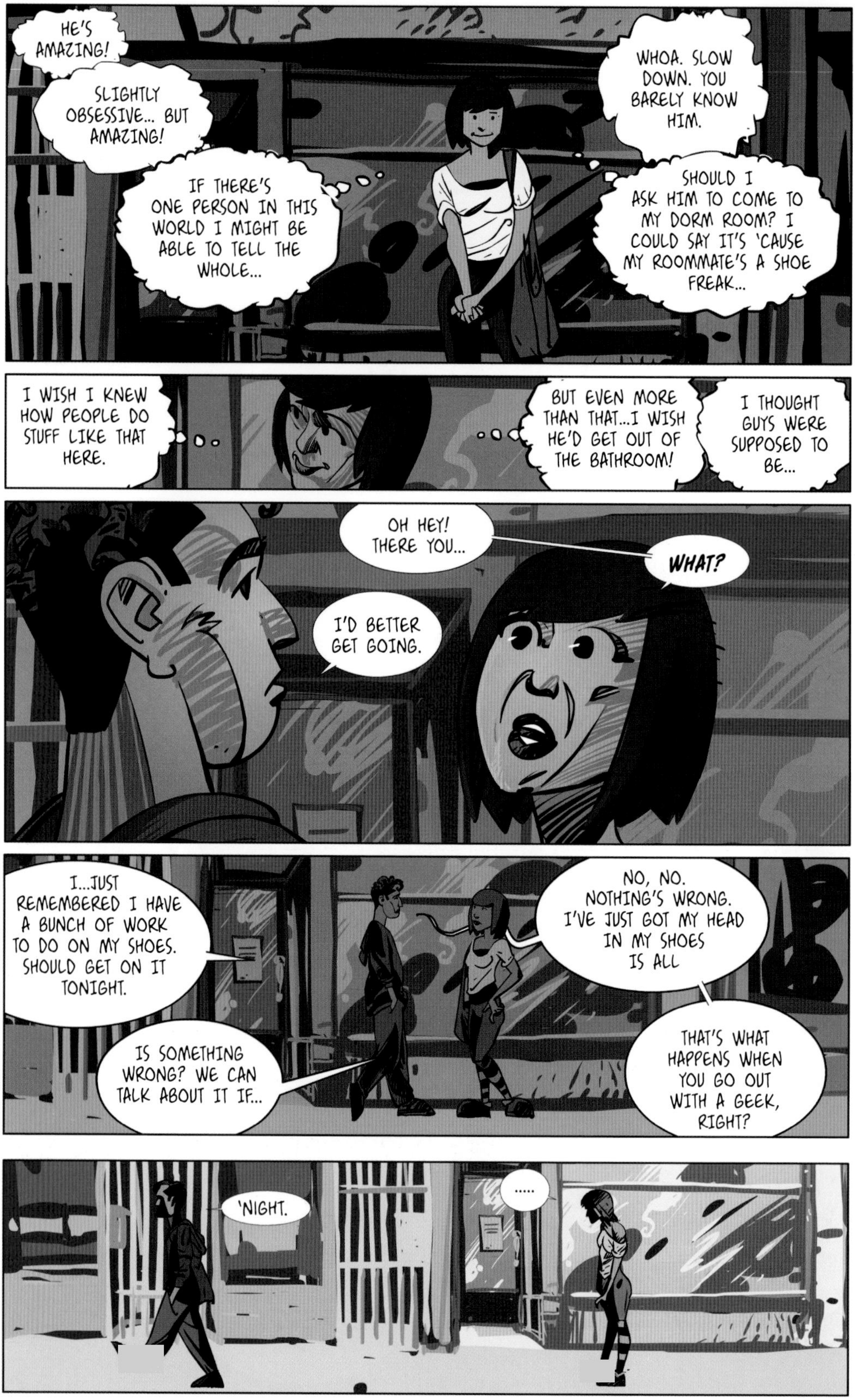
HE'S AMAZING!
SLIGHTLY OBSESSIVE... BUT AMAZING!
IF THERE'S ONE PERSON IN THIS WORLD I MIGHT BE ABLE TO TELL THE WHOLE...
WHOA. SLOW DOWN. YOU BARELY KNOW HIM.
SHOULD I ASK HIM TO COME TO MY DORM ROOM? I COULD SAY IT'S 'CAUSE MY ROOMMATE'S A SHOE FREAK...
I WISH I KNEW HOW PEOPLE DO STUFF LIKE THAT HERE.
BUT EVEN MORE THAN THAT...I WISH HE'D GET OUT OF THE BATHROOM!
I THOUGHT GUYS WERE SUPPOSED TO BE...
OH HEY! THERE YOU...
WHAT?
I'D BETTER GET GOING.
I...JUST REMEMBERED I HAVE A BUNCH OF WORK TO DO ON MY SHOES. SHOULD GET ON IT TONIGHT.
IS SOMETHING WRONG? WE CAN TALK ABOUT IT IF...
NO, NO. NOTHING'S WRONG. I'VE JUST GOT MY HEAD IN MY SHOES IS ALL
THAT'S WHAT HAPPENS WHEN YOU GO OUT WITH A GEEK, RIGHT?
'NIGHT.
.....

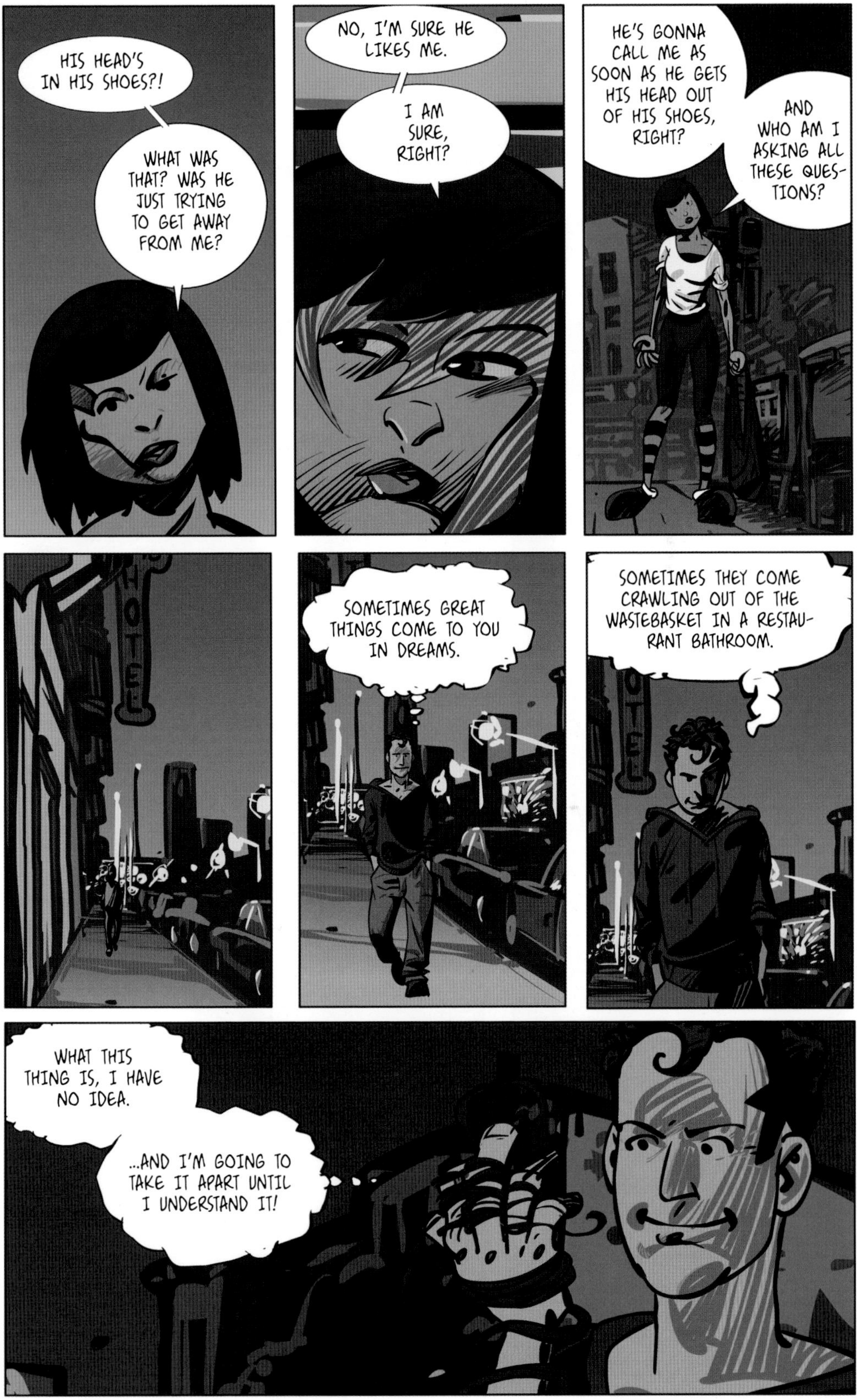
HIS HEAD'S IN HIS SHOES?!
WHAT WAS THAT? WAS HE JUST TRYING TO GET AWAY FROM ME?
NO, I'M SURE HE LIKES ME.
I AM SURE, RIGHT?
HE'S GONNA CALL ME AS SOON AS HE GETS HIS HEAD OUT OF HIS SHOES, RIGHT?
AND WHO AM I ASKING ALL THESE QUES-TIONS?
HOTEL
SOMETIMES GREAT THINGS COME TO YOU IN DREAMS.
SOMETIMES THEY COME CRAWLING OUT OF THE WASTEBASKET IN A RESTAU-RANT BATHROOM.
WHAT THIS THING IS, I HAVE NO IDEA.
...AND I'M GOING TO TAKE IT APART UNTIL I UNDERSTAND IT!

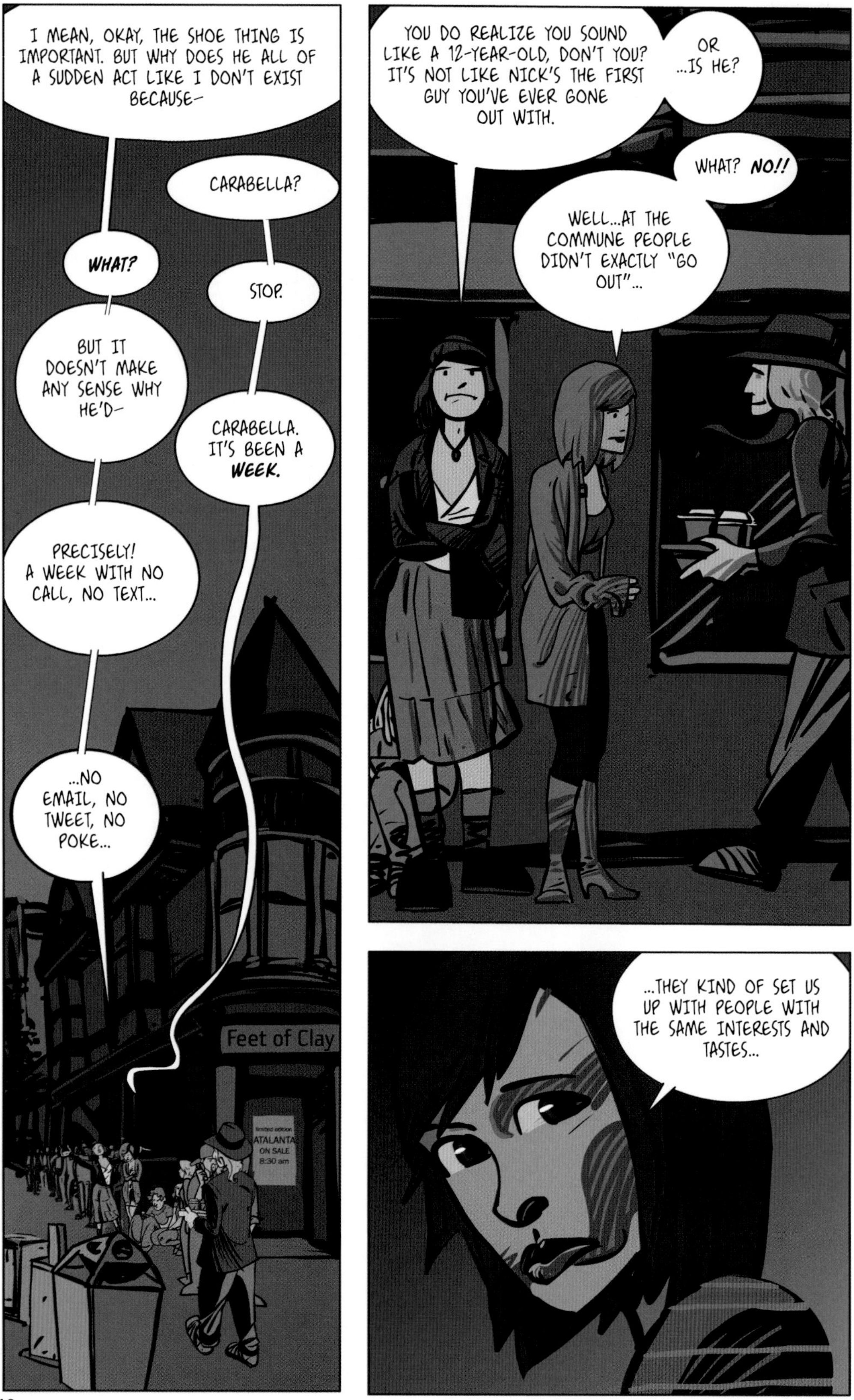
I MEAN, OKAY, THE SHOE THING IS IMPORTANT. BUT WHY DOES HE ALL OF A SUDDEN ACT LIKE I DON'T EXIST BECAUSE–
CARABELLA?
WHAT?
STOP.
BUT IT DOESN'T MAKE ANY SENSE WHY HE'D–
CARABELLA. IT'S BEEN A WEEK.
PRECISELY! A WEEK WITH NO CALL, NO TEXT...
...NO EMAIL, NO TWEET, NO POKE...
Feet of Clay
limited edition ATALANTA ON SALE 8:30 am
YOU DO REALIZE YOU SOUND LIKE A 12-YEAR-OLD, DON'T YOU? IT'S NOT LIKE NICK'S THE FIRST GUY YOU'VE EVER GONE OUT WITH.
OR ...IS HE?
WHAT? NO!!
WELL...AT THE COMMUNE PEOPLE DIDN'T EXACTLY "GO OUT"...
...THEY KIND OF SET US UP WITH PEOPLE WITH THE SAME INTERESTS AND TASTES...

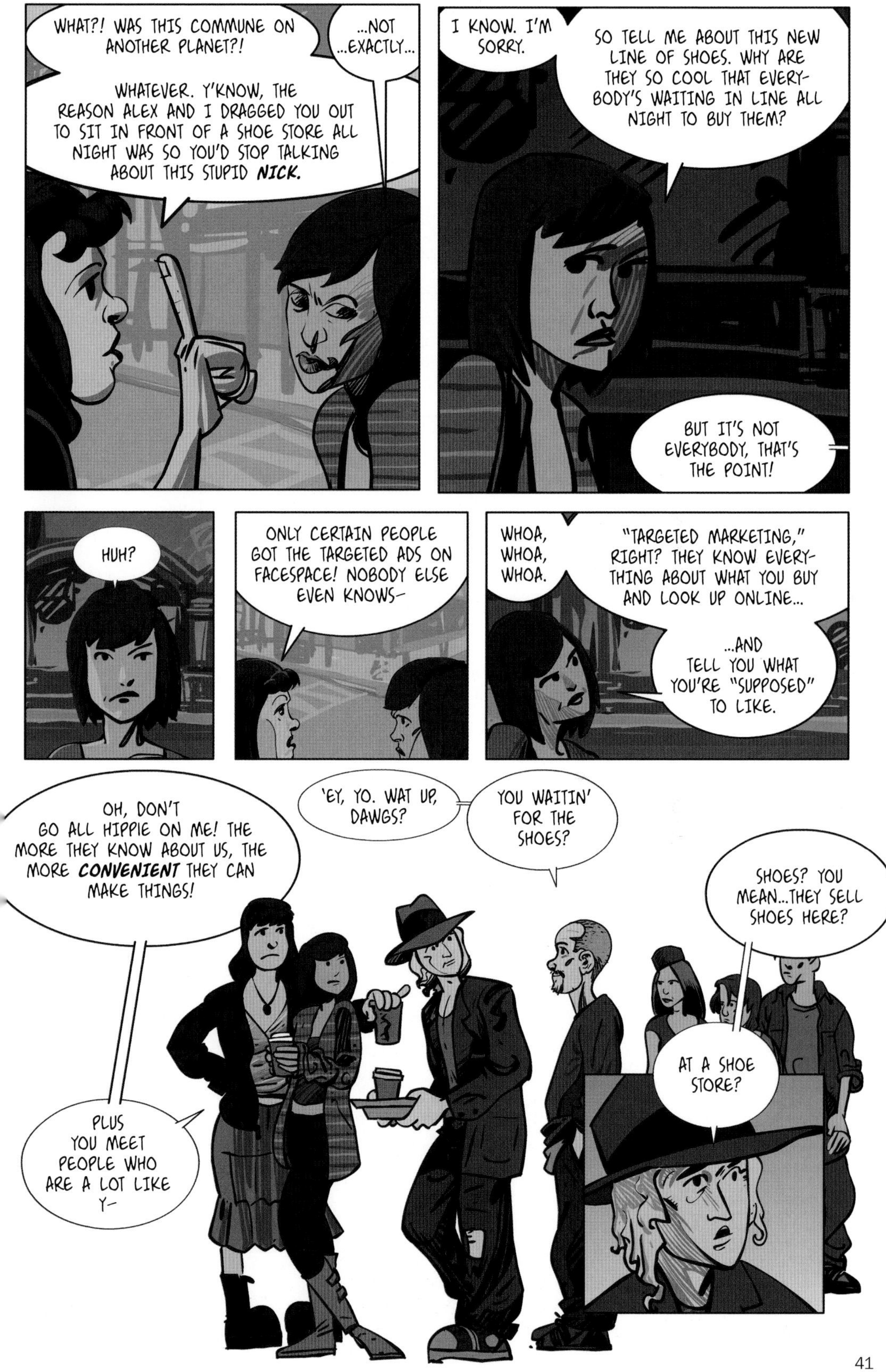
WHAT?! WAS THIS COMMUNE ON ANOTHER PLANET?!
...NOT ...EXACTLY...
WHATEVER. Y'KNOW, THE REASON ALEX AND I DRAGGED YOU OUT TO SIT IN FRONT OF A SHOE STORE ALL NIGHT WAS SO YOU'D STOP TALKING ABOUT THIS STUPID ***NICK.***
I KNOW. I'M SORRY.
SO TELL ME ABOUT THIS NEW LINE OF SHOES. WHY ARE THEY SO COOL THAT EVERYBODY'S WAITING IN LINE ALL NIGHT TO BUY THEM?
BUT IT'S NOT EVERYBODY, THAT'S THE POINT!
HUH?
ONLY CERTAIN PEOPLE GOT THE TARGETED ADS ON FACESPACE! NOBODY ELSE EVEN KNOWS–
WHOA, WHOA, WHOA.
"TARGETED MARKETING," RIGHT? THEY KNOW EVERYTHING ABOUT WHAT YOU BUY AND LOOK UP ONLINE...
...AND TELL YOU WHAT YOU'RE "SUPPOSED" TO LIKE.
OH, DON'T GO ALL HIPPIE ON ME! THE MORE THEY KNOW ABOUT US, THE MORE ***CONVENIENT*** THEY CAN MAKE THINGS!
'EY, YO. WAT UP, DAWGS?
YOU WAITIN' FOR THE SHOES?
SHOES? YOU MEAN...THEY SELL SHOES HERE?
PLUS YOU MEET PEOPLE WHO ARE A LOT LIKE Y–
AT A SHOE STORE?

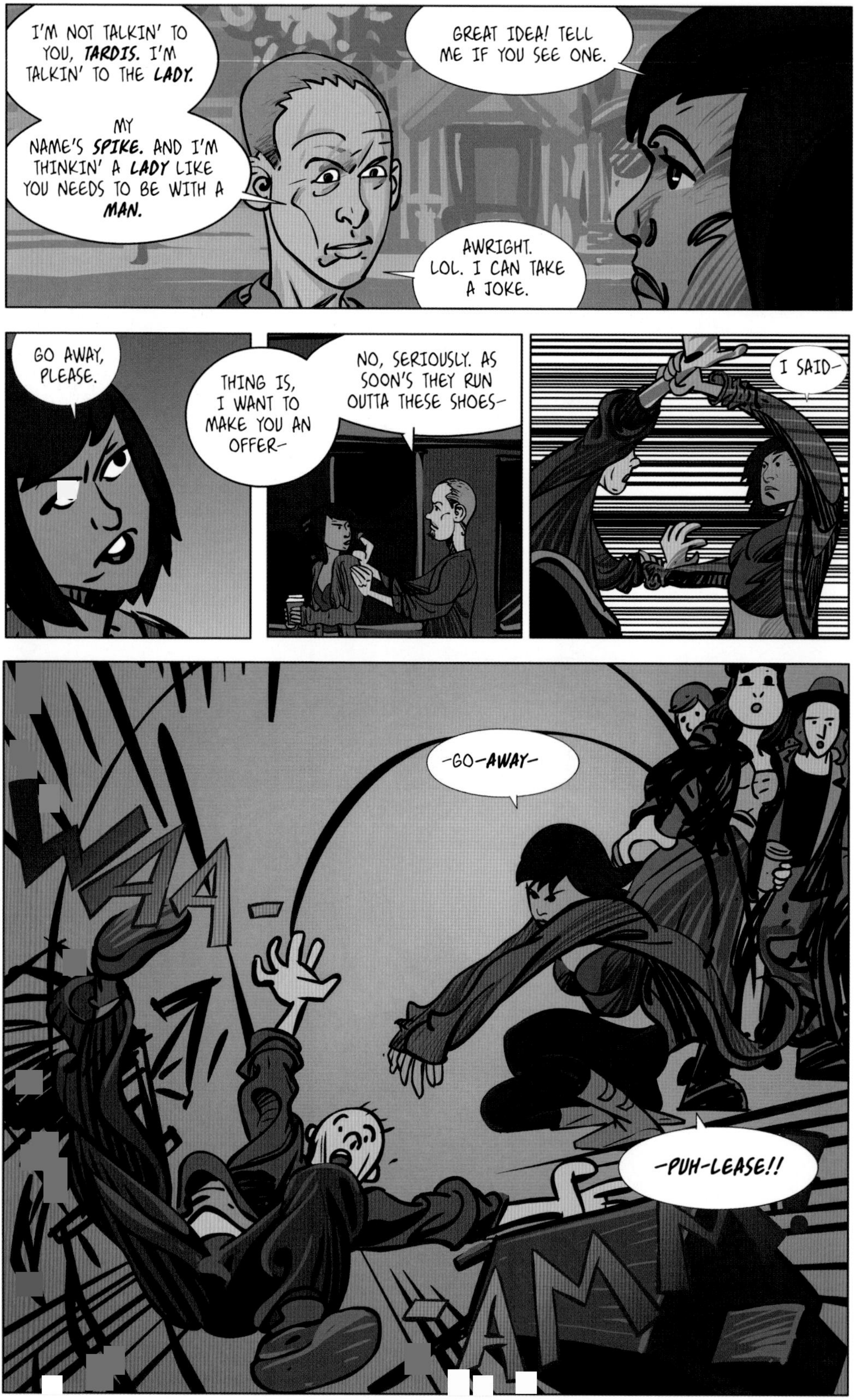
I'M NOT TALKIN' TO YOU, TARDIS. I'M TALKIN' TO THE LADY.
MY NAME'S SPIKE. AND I'M THINKIN' A LADY LIKE YOU NEEDS TO BE WITH A MAN.
GREAT IDEA! TELL ME IF YOU SEE ONE.
AWRIGHT. LOL. I CAN TAKE A JOKE.
GO AWAY, PLEASE.
NO, SERIOUSLY. AS SOON'S THEY RUN OUTTA THESE SHOES–
THING IS, I WANT TO MAKE YOU AN OFFER–
I SAID–
–GO–AWAY–
–PUH-LEASE!!

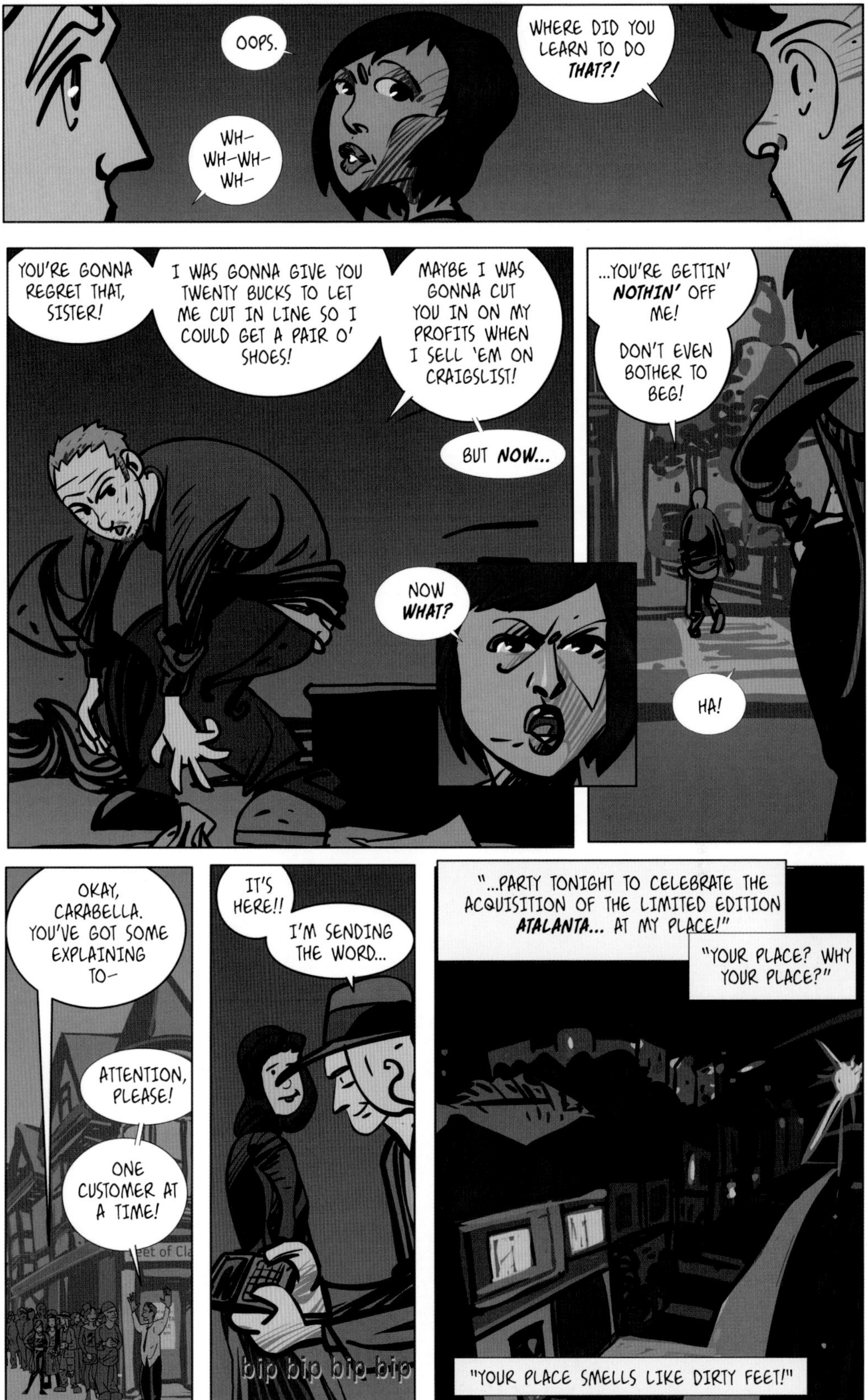
OOPS.
WH- WH-WH- WH-
WHERE DID YOU LEARN TO DO **THAT?!**
YOU'RE GONNA REGRET THAT, SISTER!
I WAS GONNA GIVE YOU TWENTY BUCKS TO LET ME CUT IN LINE SO I COULD GET A PAIR O' SHOES!
MAYBE I WAS GONNA CUT YOU IN ON MY PROFITS WHEN I SELL 'EM ON CRAIGSLIST!
BUT **NOW...**
NOW **WHAT?**
...YOU'RE GETTIN' **NOTHIN'** OFF ME!
DON'T EVEN BOTHER TO BEG!
HA!
OKAY, CARABELLA. YOU'VE GOT SOME EXPLAINING TO-
ATTENTION, PLEASE!
ONE CUSTOMER AT A TIME!
IT'S HERE!!
I'M SENDING THE WORD...
bip bip bip bip
"...PARTY TONIGHT TO CELEBRATE THE ACQUISITION OF THE LIMITED EDITION ***ATALANTA...*** AT MY PLACE!"
"YOUR PLACE? WHY YOUR PLACE?"
"YOUR PLACE SMELLS LIKE DIRTY FEET!"

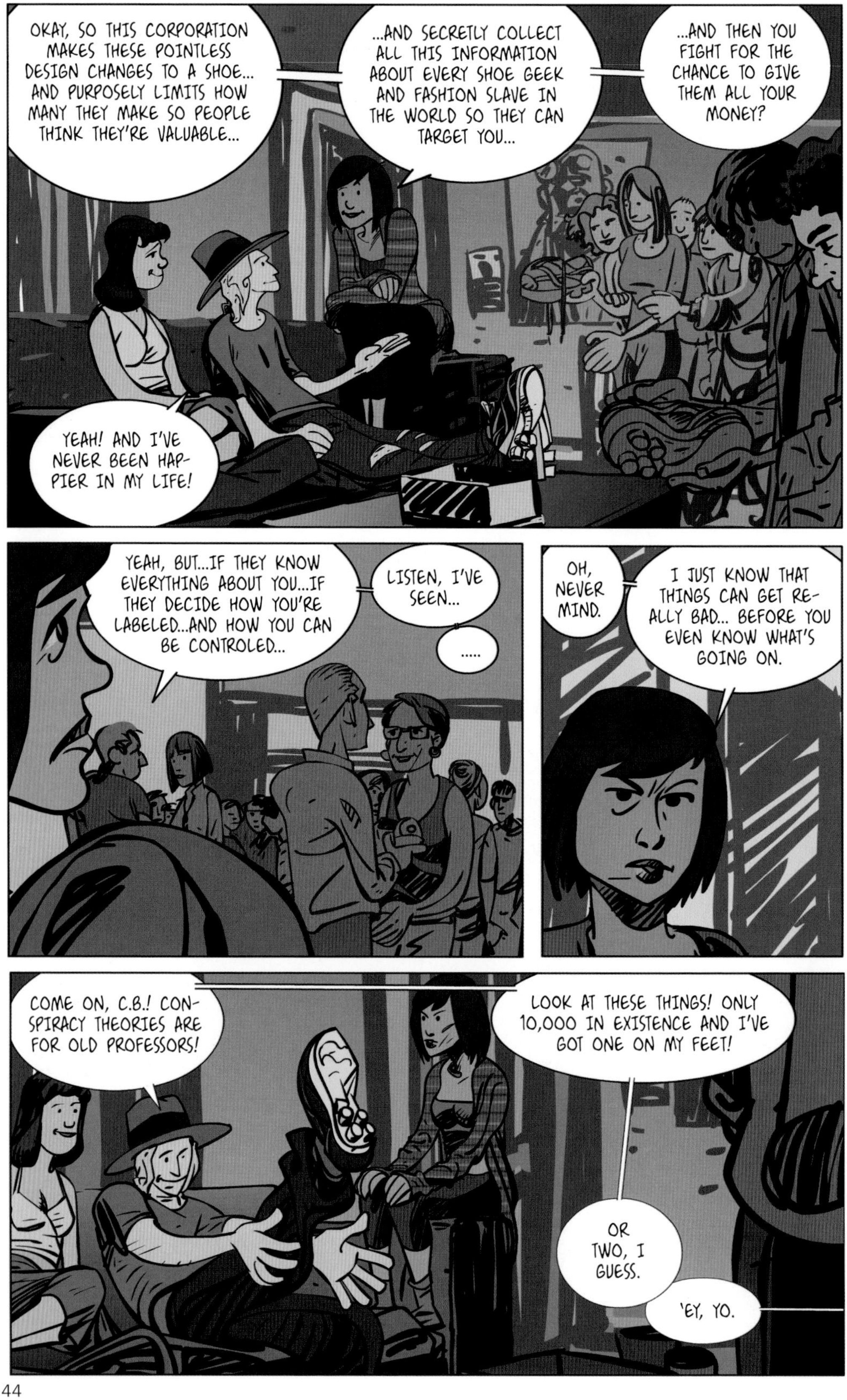
OKAY, SO THIS CORPORATION MAKES THESE POINTLESS DESIGN CHANGES TO A SHOE... AND PURPOSELY LIMITS HOW MANY THEY MAKE SO PEOPLE THINK THEY'RE VALUABLE...
...AND SECRETLY COLLECT ALL THIS INFORMATION ABOUT EVERY SHOE GEEK AND FASHION SLAVE IN THE WORLD SO THEY CAN TARGET YOU...
...AND THEN YOU FIGHT FOR THE CHANCE TO GIVE THEM ALL YOUR MONEY?
YEAH! AND I'VE NEVER BEEN HAP-PIER IN MY LIFE!
YEAH, BUT...IF THEY KNOW EVERYTHING ABOUT YOU...IF THEY DECIDE HOW YOU'RE LABELED...AND HOW YOU CAN BE CONTROLED...
LISTEN, I'VE SEEN...
.....
OH, NEVER MIND.
I JUST KNOW THAT THINGS CAN GET RE-ALLY BAD... BEFORE YOU EVEN KNOW WHAT'S GOING ON.
COME ON, C.B.! CON-SPIRACY THEORIES ARE FOR OLD PROFESSORS!
LOOK AT THESE THINGS! ONLY 10,000 IN EXISTENCE AND I'VE GOT ONE ON MY FEET!
OR TWO, I GUESS.
'EY, YO.

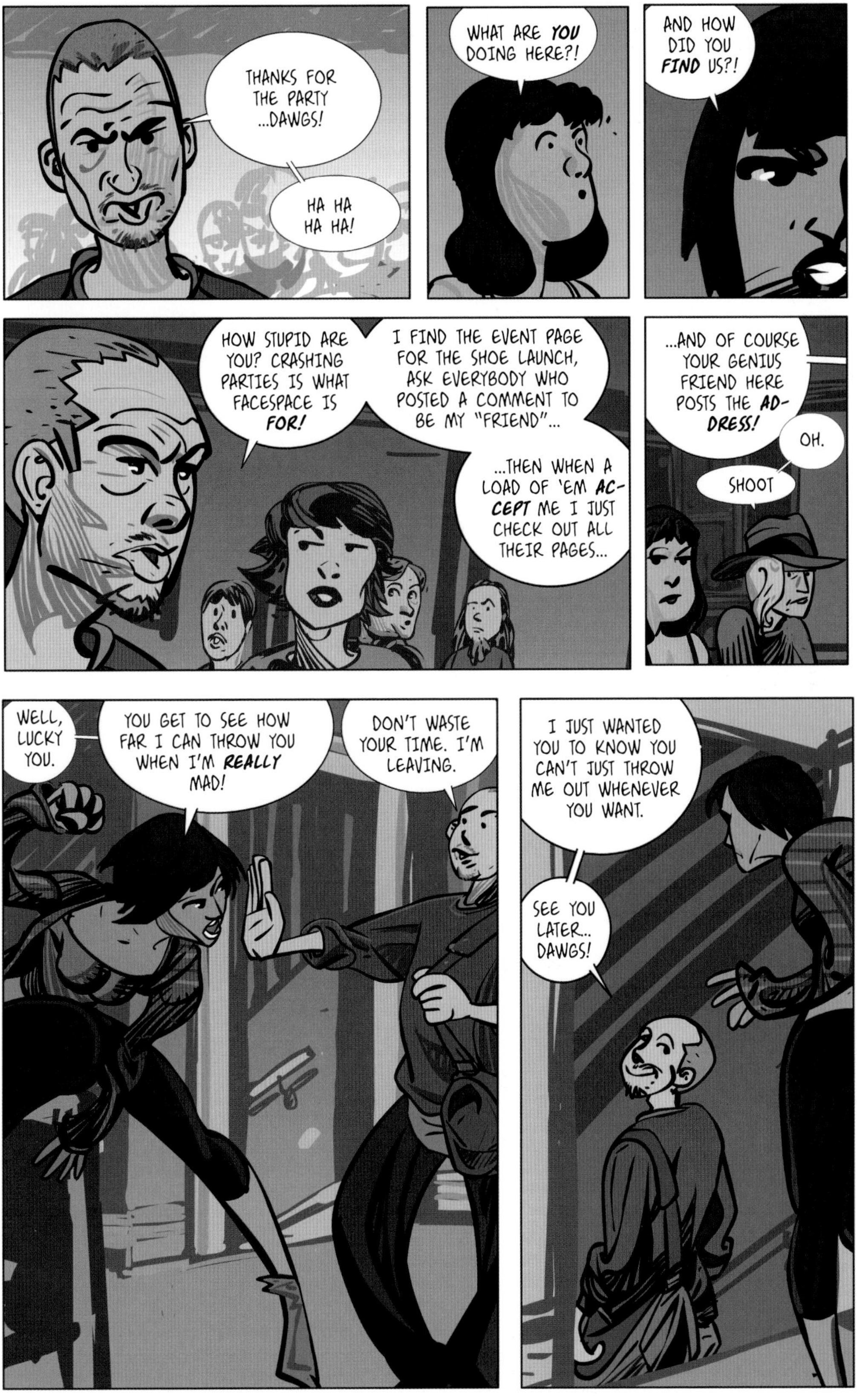
THANKS FOR THE PARTY ...DAWGS!
HA HA HA HA!
WHAT ARE YOU DOING HERE?!
AND HOW DID YOU FIND US?!
HOW STUPID ARE YOU? CRASHING PARTIES IS WHAT FACESPACE IS FOR!
I FIND THE EVENT PAGE FOR THE SHOE LAUNCH, ASK EVERYBODY WHO POSTED A COMMENT TO BE MY "FRIEND"...
...THEN WHEN A LOAD OF 'EM ACCEPT ME I JUST CHECK OUT ALL THEIR PAGES...
...AND OF COURSE YOUR GENIUS FRIEND HERE POSTS THE ADDRESS!
OH.
SHOOT
WELL, LUCKY YOU.
YOU GET TO SEE HOW FAR I CAN THROW YOU WHEN I'M REALLY MAD!
DON'T WASTE YOUR TIME. I'M LEAVING.
I JUST WANTED YOU TO KNOW YOU CAN'T JUST THROW ME OUT WHENEVER YOU WANT.
SEE YOU LATER... DAWGS!

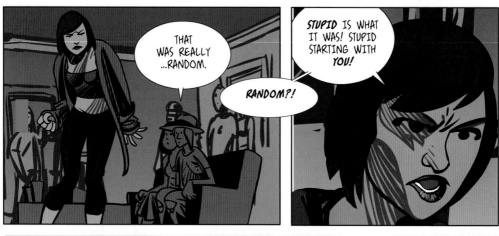

THAT WAS REALLY ...RANDOM.

RANDOM?!

STUPID IS WHAT IT WAS! STUPID STARTING WITH YOU!

HEY...WHERE ARE MY NEW SHOES...?

YEAH... MINE TOO...

THE SHOES!

HE STOLE THE SHOES!

...WELL, THAT WAS A CRUMMY DAY.

I HOPE ALEX IS RIGHT THAT THE POLICE CATCH THAT JERK.

SUDDENLY I ALMOST WISH THE COPS HERE WERE MORE LIKE THE COPS WHERE I CAME FROM.

POOR ALEX. YEAH, HE WAS DUMB, BUT...IF I HADN'T FLIPPED THE GUY IN THE FIRST PLACE...

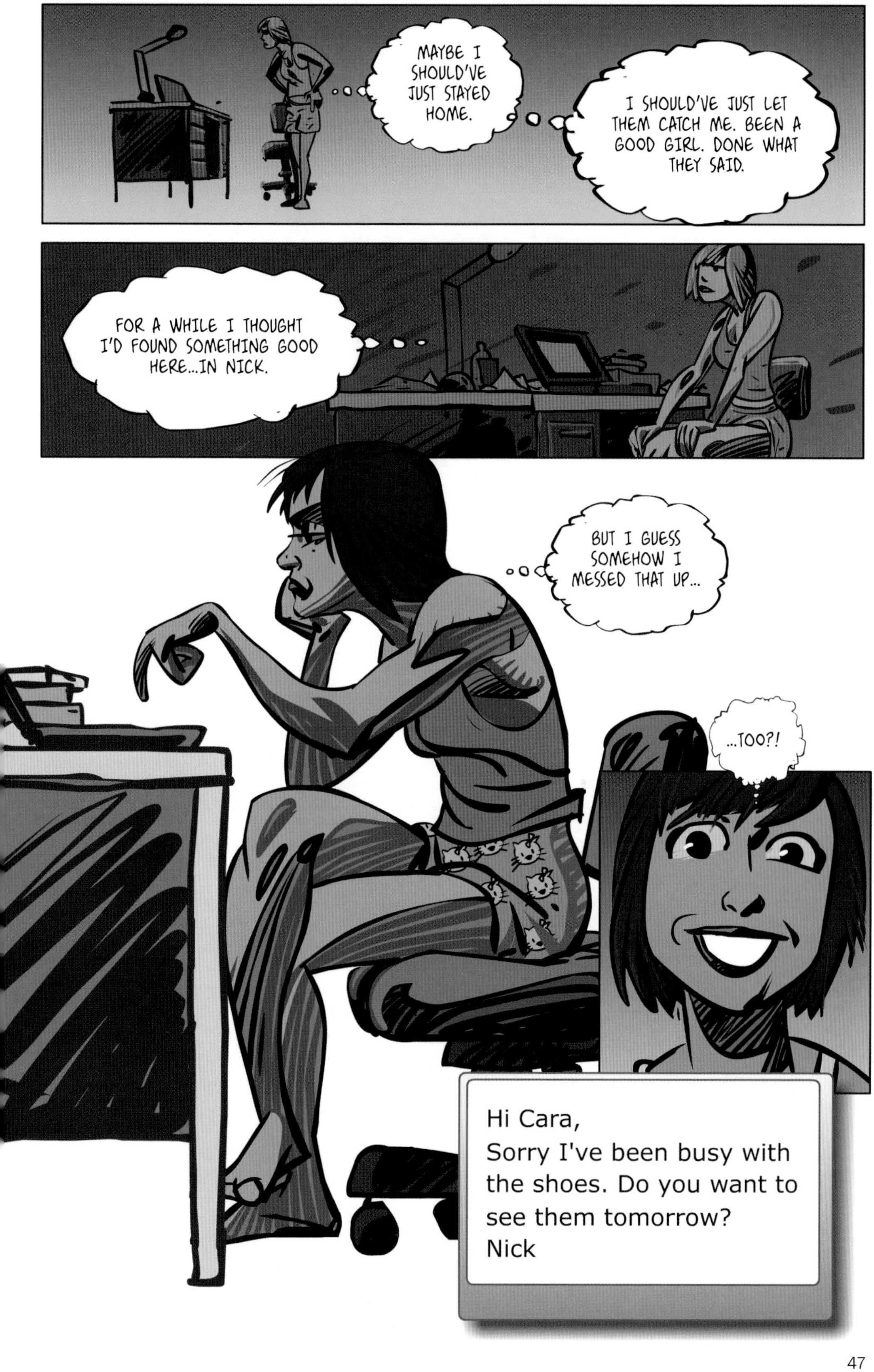
MAYBE I SHOULD'VE JUST STAYED HOME.
I SHOULD'VE JUST LET THEM CATCH ME. BEEN A GOOD GIRL. DONE WHAT THEY SAID.
FOR A WHILE I THOUGHT I'D FOUND SOMETHING GOOD HERE...IN NICK.
BUT I GUESS SOMEHOW I MESSED THAT UP...
...TOO?!
Hi Cara,
Sorry I've been busy with the shoes. Do you want to see them tomorrow?
Nick

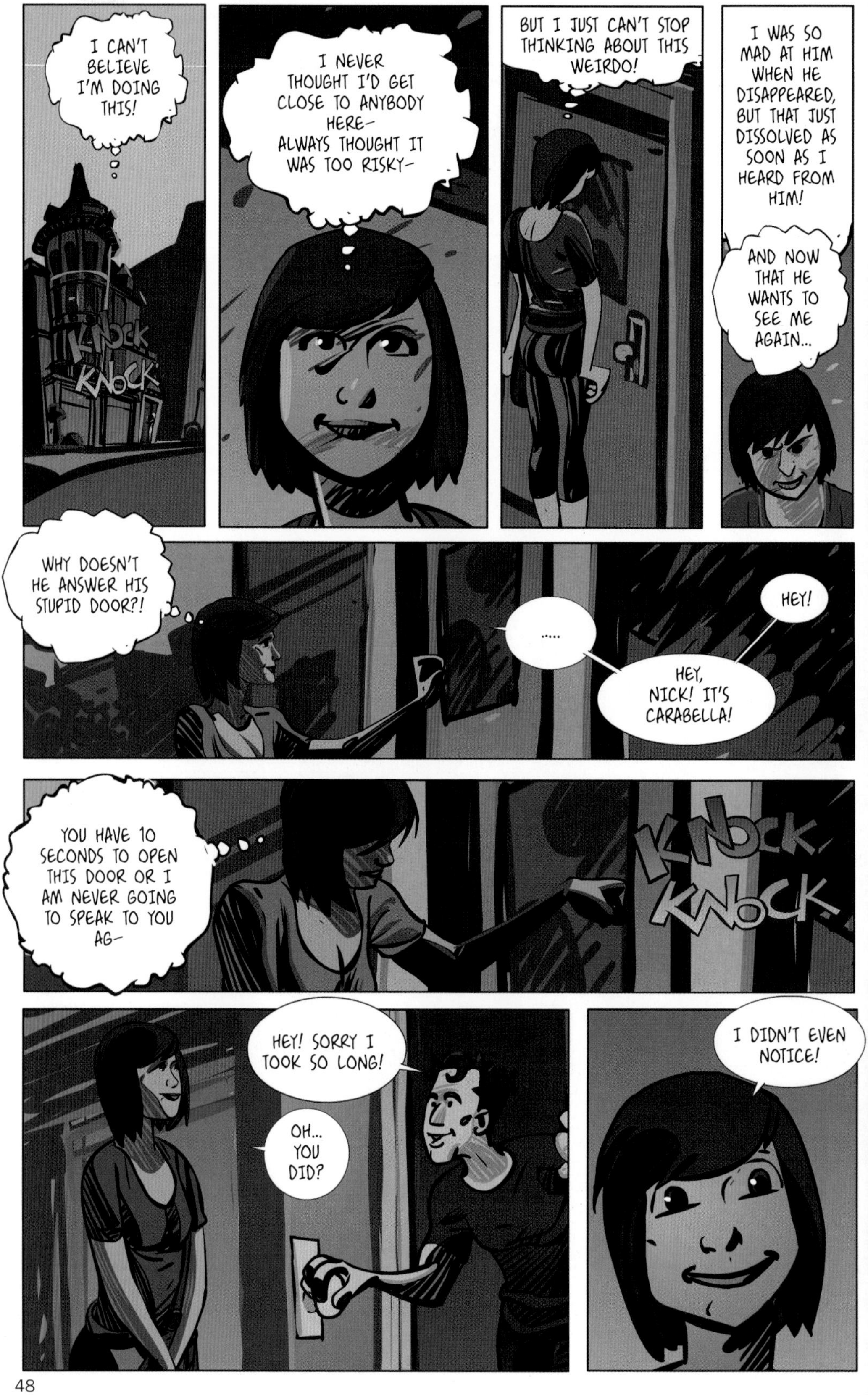
I CAN'T BELIEVE I'M DOING THIS!
KNOCK KNOCK
I NEVER THOUGHT I'D GET CLOSE TO ANYBODY HERE- ALWAYS THOUGHT IT WAS TOO RISKY-
BUT I JUST CAN'T STOP THINKING ABOUT THIS WEIRDO!
I WAS SO MAD AT HIM WHEN HE DISAPPEARED, BUT THAT JUST DISSOLVED AS SOON AS I HEARD FROM HIM!
AND NOW THAT HE WANTS TO SEE ME AGAIN...
WHY DOESN'T HE ANSWER HIS STUPID DOOR?!
.....
HEY!
HEY, NICK! IT'S CARABELLA!
YOU HAVE 10 SECONDS TO OPEN THIS DOOR OR I AM NEVER GOING TO SPEAK TO YOU AG-
KNOCK KNOCK
HEY! SORRY I TOOK SO LONG!
OH... YOU DID?
I DIDN'T EVEN NOTICE!

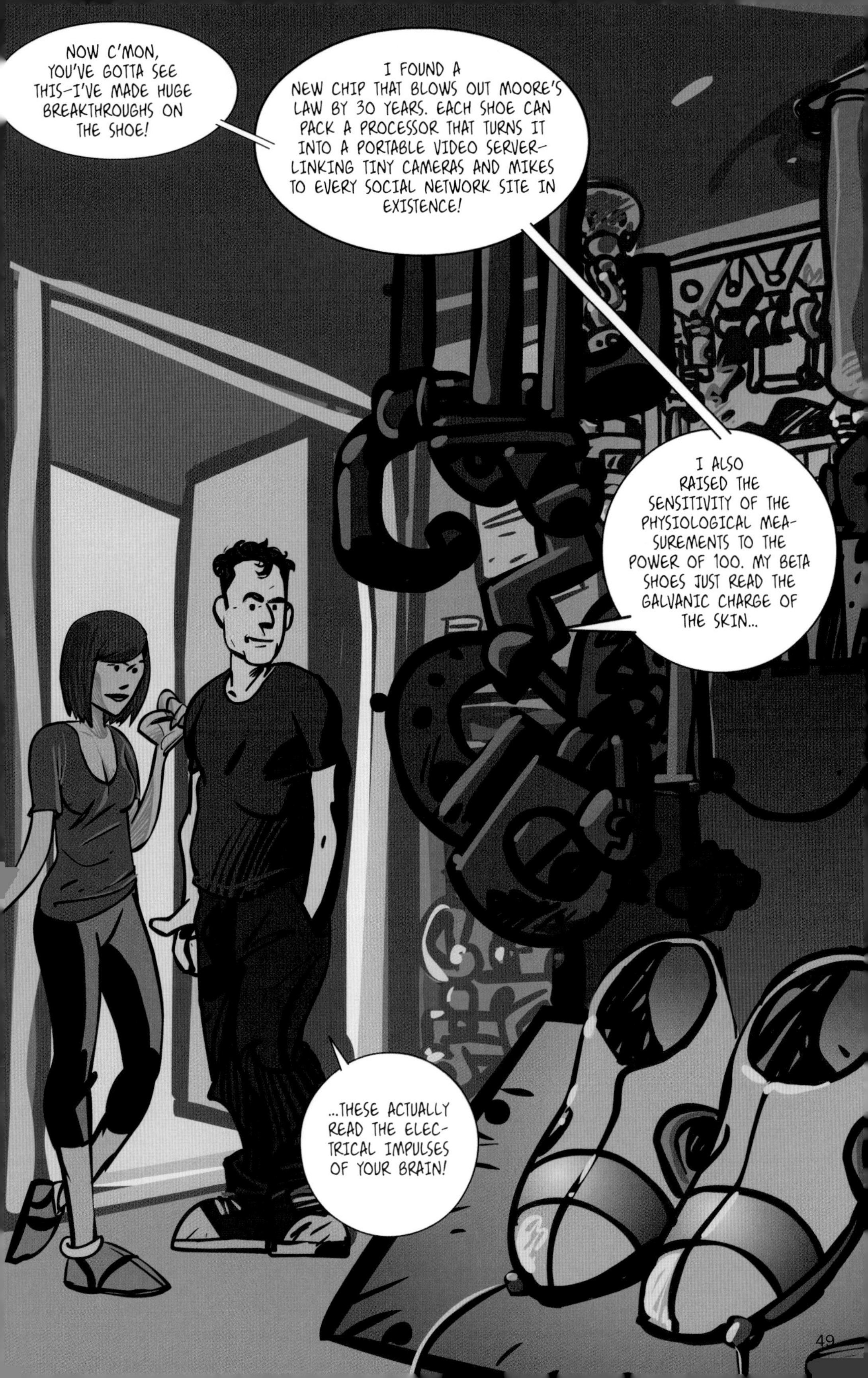
NOW C'MON, YOU'VE GOTTA SEE THIS—I'VE MADE HUGE BREAKTHROUGHS ON THE SHOE!
I FOUND A NEW CHIP THAT BLOWS OUT MOORE'S LAW BY 30 YEARS. EACH SHOE CAN PACK A PROCESSOR THAT TURNS IT INTO A PORTABLE VIDEO SERVER-LINKING TINY CAMERAS AND MIKES TO EVERY SOCIAL NETWORK SITE IN EXISTENCE!
I ALSO RAISED THE SENSITIVITY OF THE PHYSIOLOGICAL MEA-SUREMENTS TO THE POWER OF 100. MY BETA SHOES JUST READ THE GALVANIC CHARGE OF THE SKIN...
...THESE ACTUALLY READ THE ELEC-TRICAL IMPULSES OF YOUR BRAIN!

—AND I'M JUST GETTING STARTED.

BUT...

...HOW DID YOU DO ALL THAT SO FAST? I MEAN, WHERE'D YOU COME UP WITH THE NEW PROCESSOR AND EVERYTHING?

WELL...YOU KNOW.

SOMETIMES YOU JUST KIND OF...STUMBLE ONTO THINGS.

BUT WHAT DO YOU THINK OF THEM?

...UH...

OH...

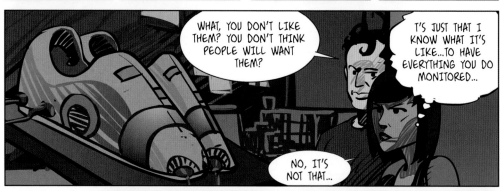

WHAT, YOU DON'T LIKE THEM? YOU DON'T THINK PEOPLE WILL WANT THEM?

T'S JUST THAT I KNOW WHAT IT'S LIKE...TO HAVE EVERYTHING YOU DO MONITORED...

NO, IT'S NOT THAT...

BUT WHAT'S THAT GOT TO DO WITH THIS? THAT'S OVER!

THIS IS NICK'S CREATION!

I DON'T KNOW WHAT TO SAY, NICK. THEY'RE INCREDIBLE...

...AND I KNOW THEY'RE NOTHING LIKE THE HALOES I HAD TO WEAR..

PERFECT! BECAUSE I NEED YOU TO HELP ME PROMOTE THEM!

HERE'S THE PLAN I'VE WORKED UP...

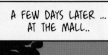

A FEW DAYS LATER ...
AT THE MALL..
WE SHOULD BE LIVE...
I'VE GOT US!
ALEX! CAN YOU SEE US?
YUP. SHOE'S EYE VIEW.
THE RESOLUTION'S FANTASTIC, CARA! I'VE NEVER SEEN ANYTHING LIKE THIS ON THE WEB!

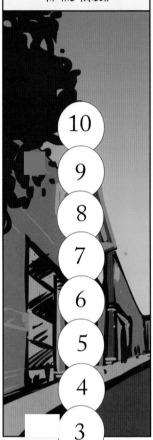

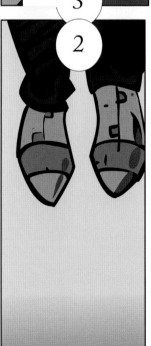

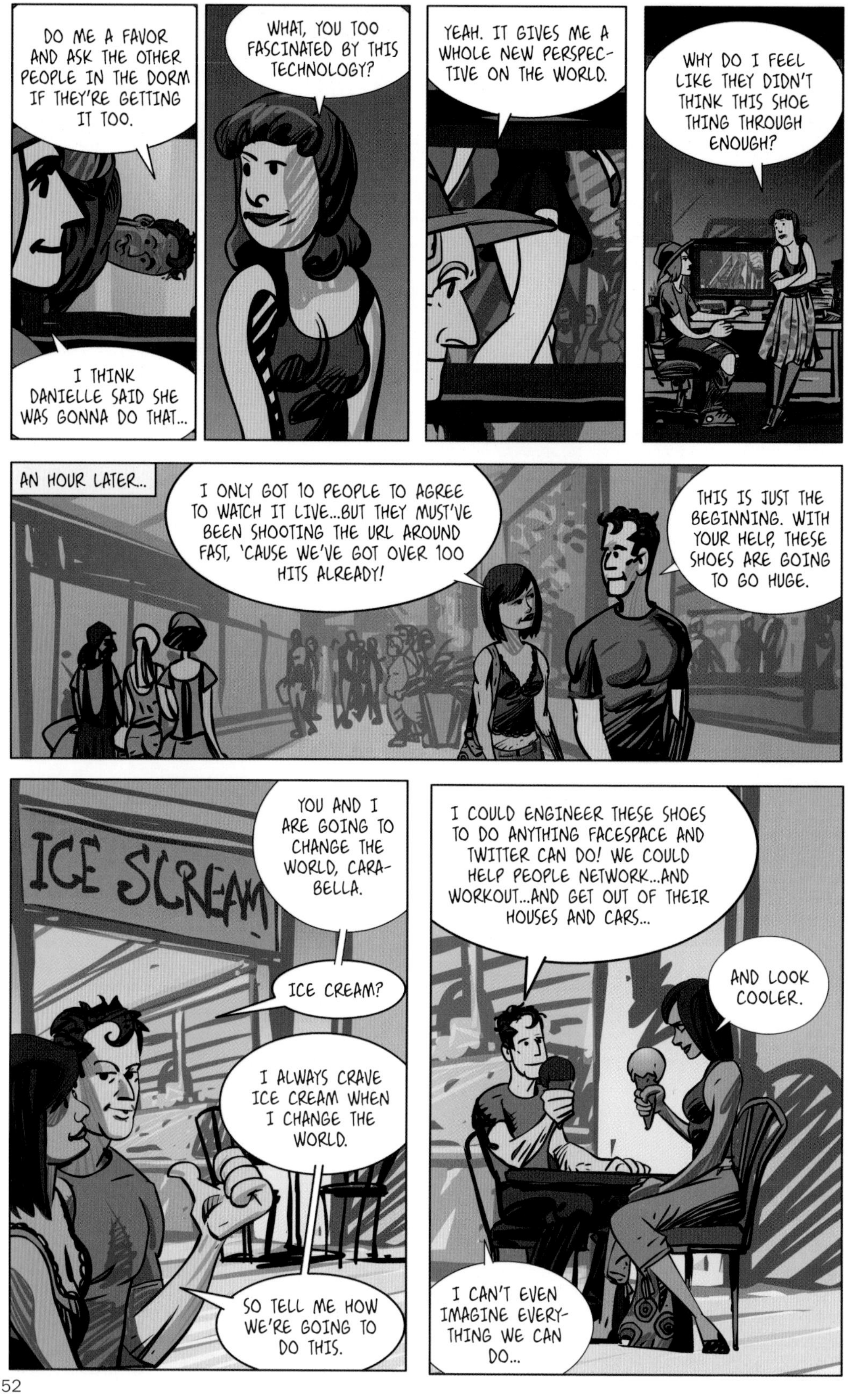
DO ME A FAVOR AND ASK THE OTHER PEOPLE IN THE DORM IF THEY'RE GETTING IT TOO.
I THINK DANIELLE SAID SHE WAS GONNA DO THAT...
WHAT, YOU TOO FASCINATED BY THIS TECHNOLOGY?
YEAH. IT GIVES ME A WHOLE NEW PERSPEC-TIVE ON THE WORLD.
WHY DO I FEEL LIKE THEY DIDN'T THINK THIS SHOE THING THROUGH ENOUGH?
AN HOUR LATER..
I ONLY GOT 10 PEOPLE TO AGREE TO WATCH IT LIVE...BUT THEY MUST'VE BEEN SHOOTING THE URL AROUND FAST, 'CAUSE WE'VE GOT OVER 100 HITS ALREADY!
THIS IS JUST THE BEGINNING. WITH YOUR HELP, THESE SHOES ARE GOING TO GO HUGE.
ICE SCREAM
YOU AND I ARE GOING TO CHANGE THE WORLD, CARA-BELLA.
ICE CREAM?
I ALWAYS CRAVE ICE CREAM WHEN I CHANGE THE WORLD.
SO TELL ME HOW WE'RE GOING TO DO THIS.
I COULD ENGINEER THESE SHOES TO DO ANYTHING FACESPACE AND TWITTER CAN DO! WE COULD HELP PEOPLE NETWORK...AND WORKOUT...AND GET OUT OF THEIR HOUSES AND CARS...
AND LOOK COOLER.
I CAN'T EVEN IMAGINE EVERY-THING WE CAN DO...

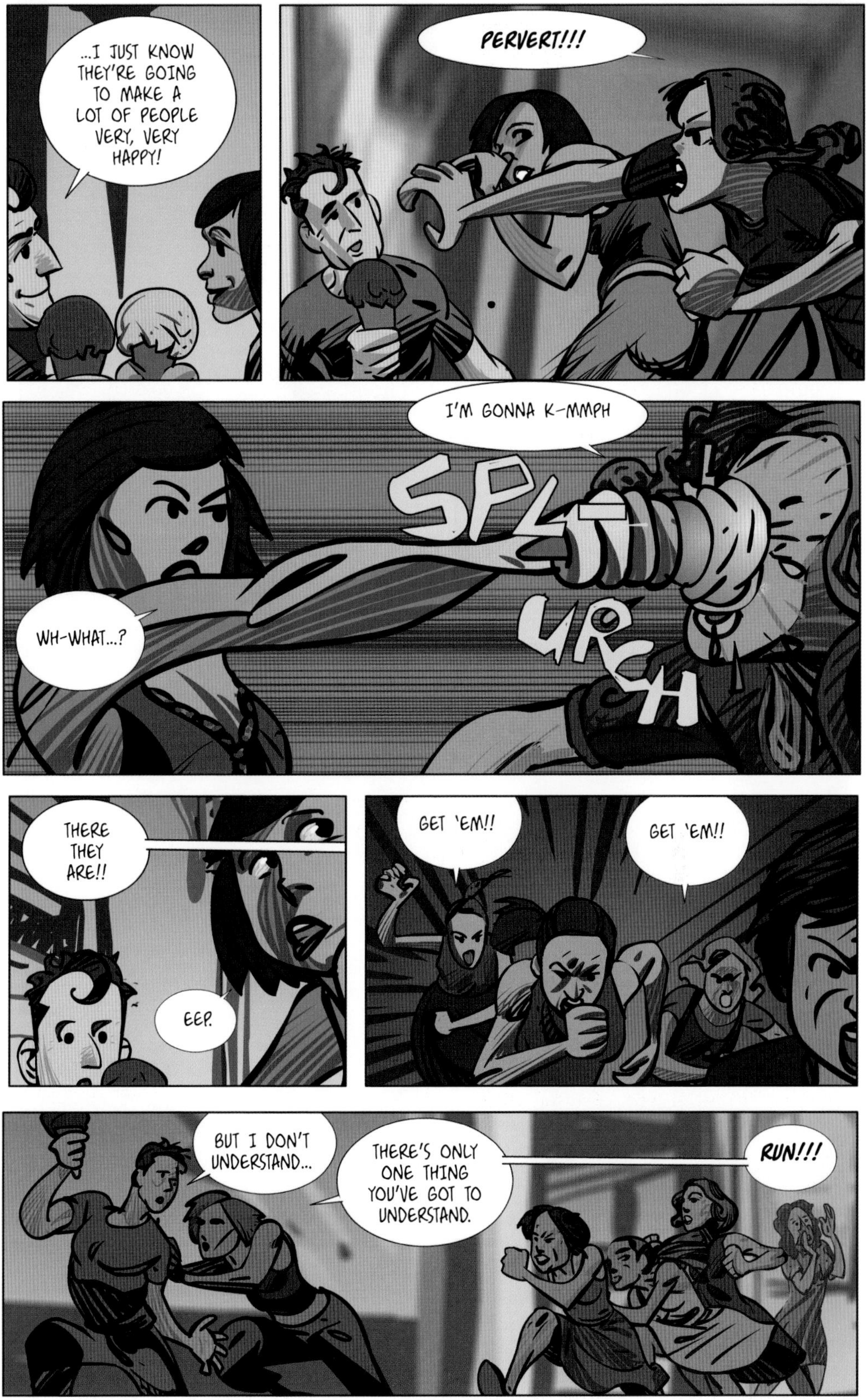
...I JUST KNOW THEY'RE GOING TO MAKE A LOT OF PEOPLE VERY, VERY HAPPY!
PERVERT!!!
I'M GONNA K-MMPH
SPL-
URCH
WH-WHAT...?
THERE THEY ARE!!
EEP.
GET 'EM!!
GET 'EM!!
BUT I DON'T UNDERSTAND...
THERE'S ONLY ONE THING YOU'VE GOT TO UNDERSTAND.
RUN!!!

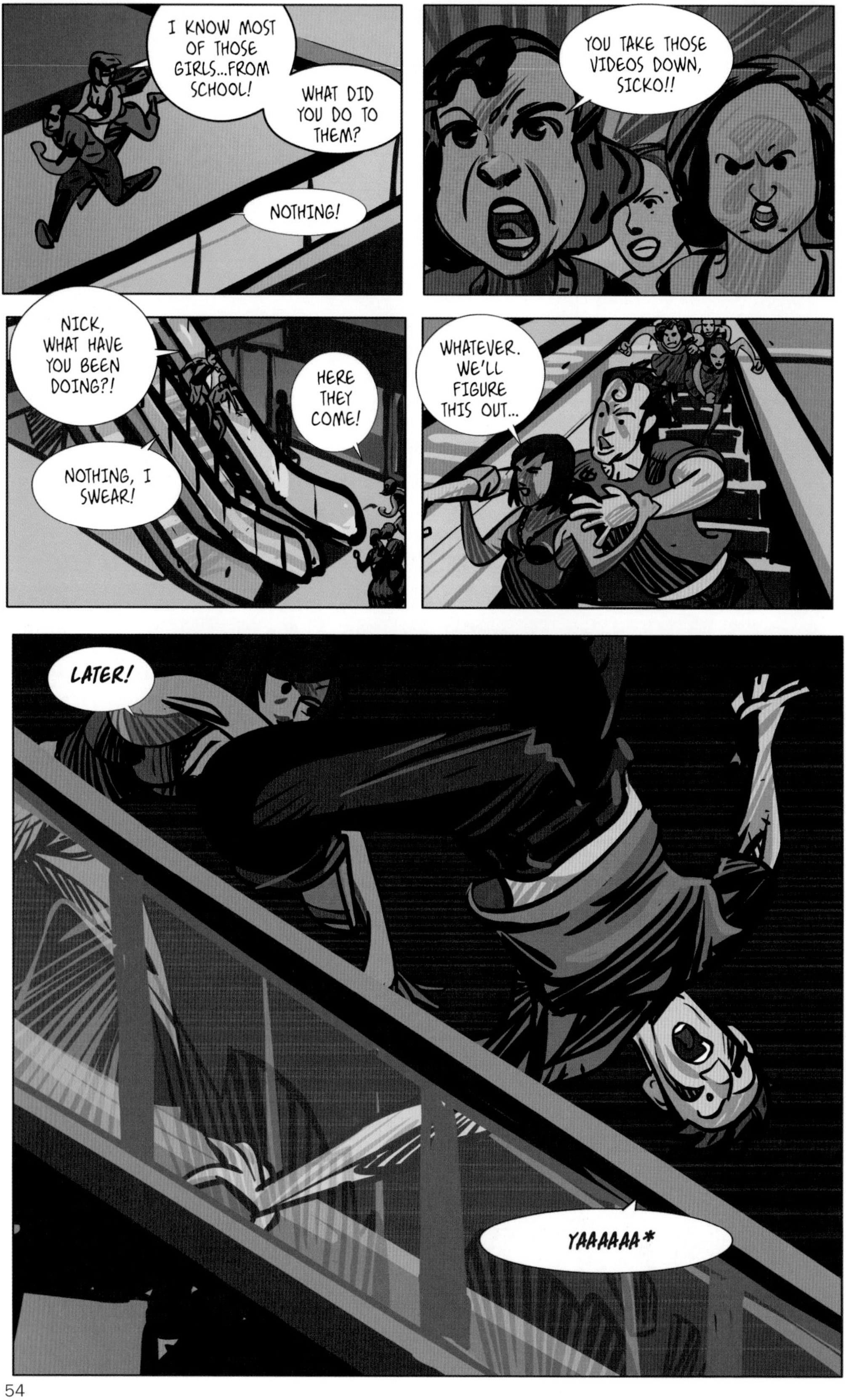
I KNOW MOST OF THOSE GIRLS...FROM SCHOOL!
WHAT DID YOU DO TO THEM?
NOTHING!
YOU TAKE THOSE VIDEOS DOWN, SICKO!!
NICK, WHAT HAVE YOU BEEN DOING?!
NOTHING, I SWEAR!
HERE THEY COME!
WHATEVER. WE'LL FIGURE THIS OUT...
LATER!
YAAAAAA*

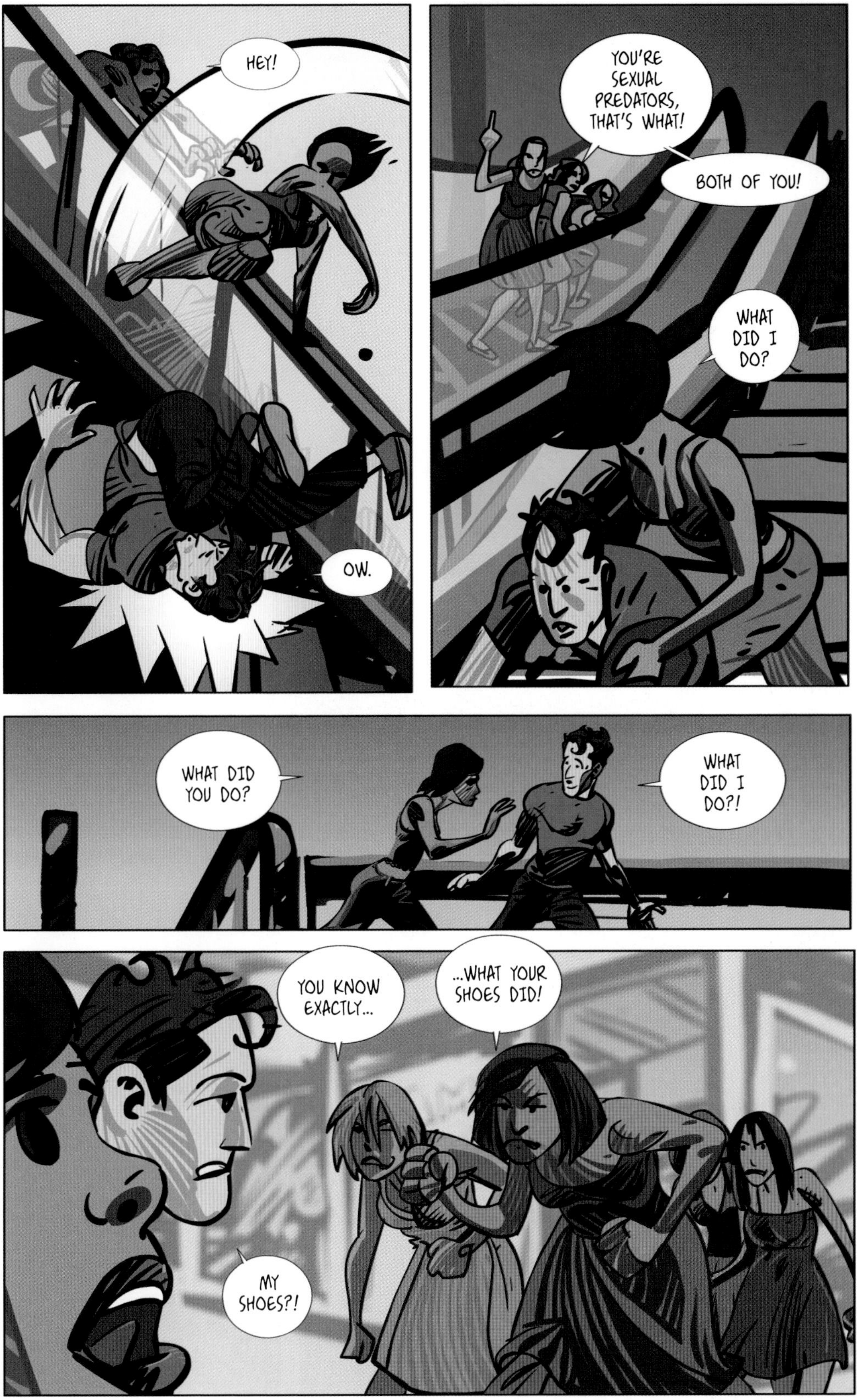
HEY!
OW.
YOU'RE SEXUAL PREDATORS, THAT'S WHAT!
BOTH OF YOU!
WHAT DID I DO?
WHAT DID YOU DO?
WHAT DID I DO?!
YOU KNOW EXACTLY...
...WHAT YOUR SHOES DID!
MY SHOES?!

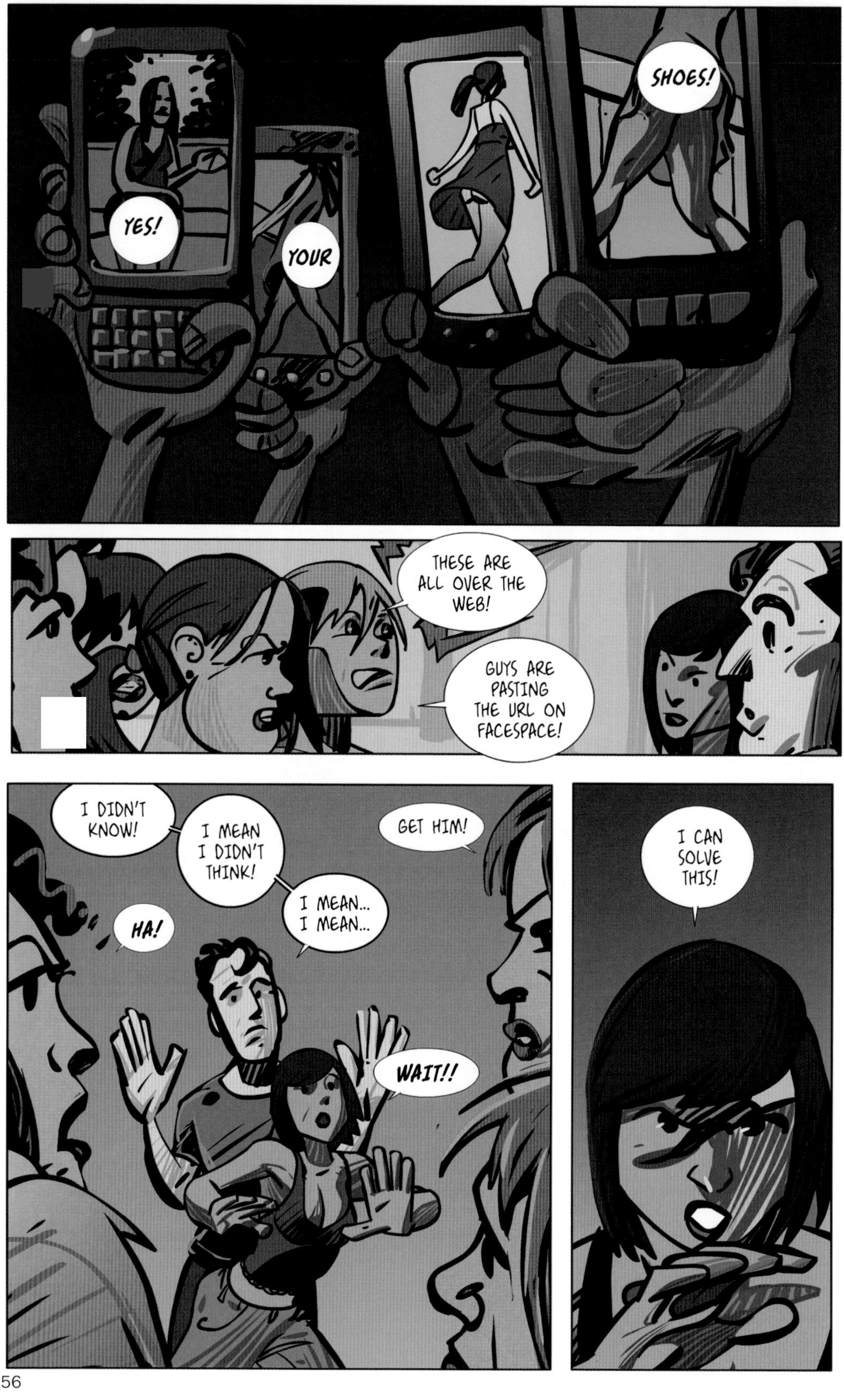
YES!
YOUR
SHOES!
THESE ARE ALL OVER THE WEB!
GUYS ARE PASTING THE URL ON FACESPACE!
I DIDN'T KNOW!
I MEAN I DIDN'T THINK!
I MEAN... I MEAN...
GET HIM!
HA!
WAIT!!
I CAN SOLVE THIS!

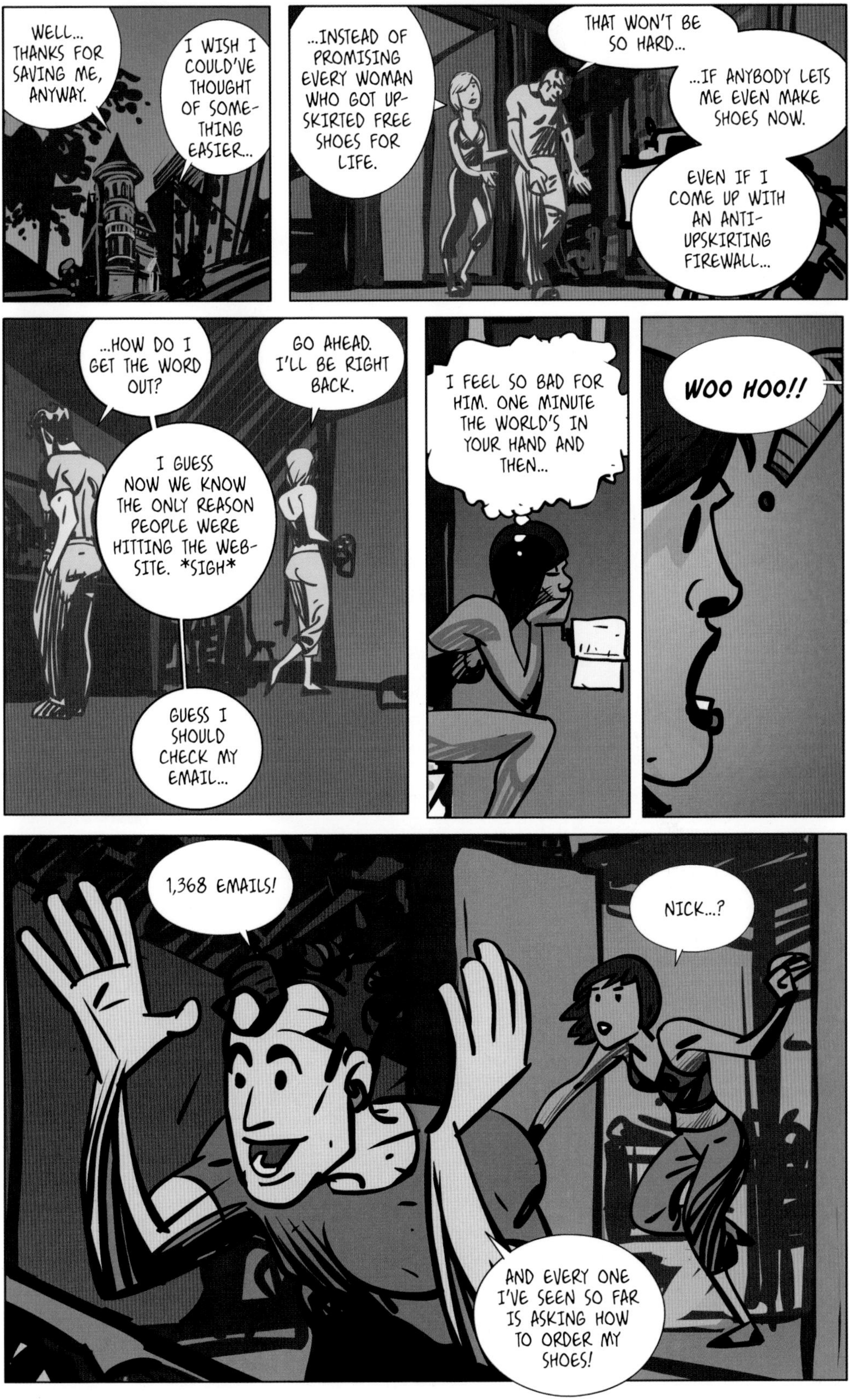
WELL... THANKS FOR SAVING ME, ANYWAY.
I WISH I COULD'VE THOUGHT OF SOMETHING EASIER...
...INSTEAD OF PROMISING EVERY WOMAN WHO GOT UPSKIRTED FREE SHOES FOR LIFE.
THAT WON'T BE SO HARD...
...IF ANYBODY LETS ME EVEN MAKE SHOES NOW.
EVEN IF I COME UP WITH AN ANTI-UPSKIRTING FIREWALL...
...HOW DO I GET THE WORD OUT?
GO AHEAD. I'LL BE RIGHT BACK.
I GUESS NOW WE KNOW THE ONLY REASON PEOPLE WERE HITTING THE WEBSITE. *SIGH*
GUESS I SHOULD CHECK MY EMAIL...
I FEEL SO BAD FOR HIM. ONE MINUTE THE WORLD'S IN YOUR HAND AND THEN...
WOO HOO!!
1,368 EMAILS!
NICK...?
AND EVERY ONE I'VE SEEN SO FAR IS ASKING HOW TO ORDER MY SHOES!

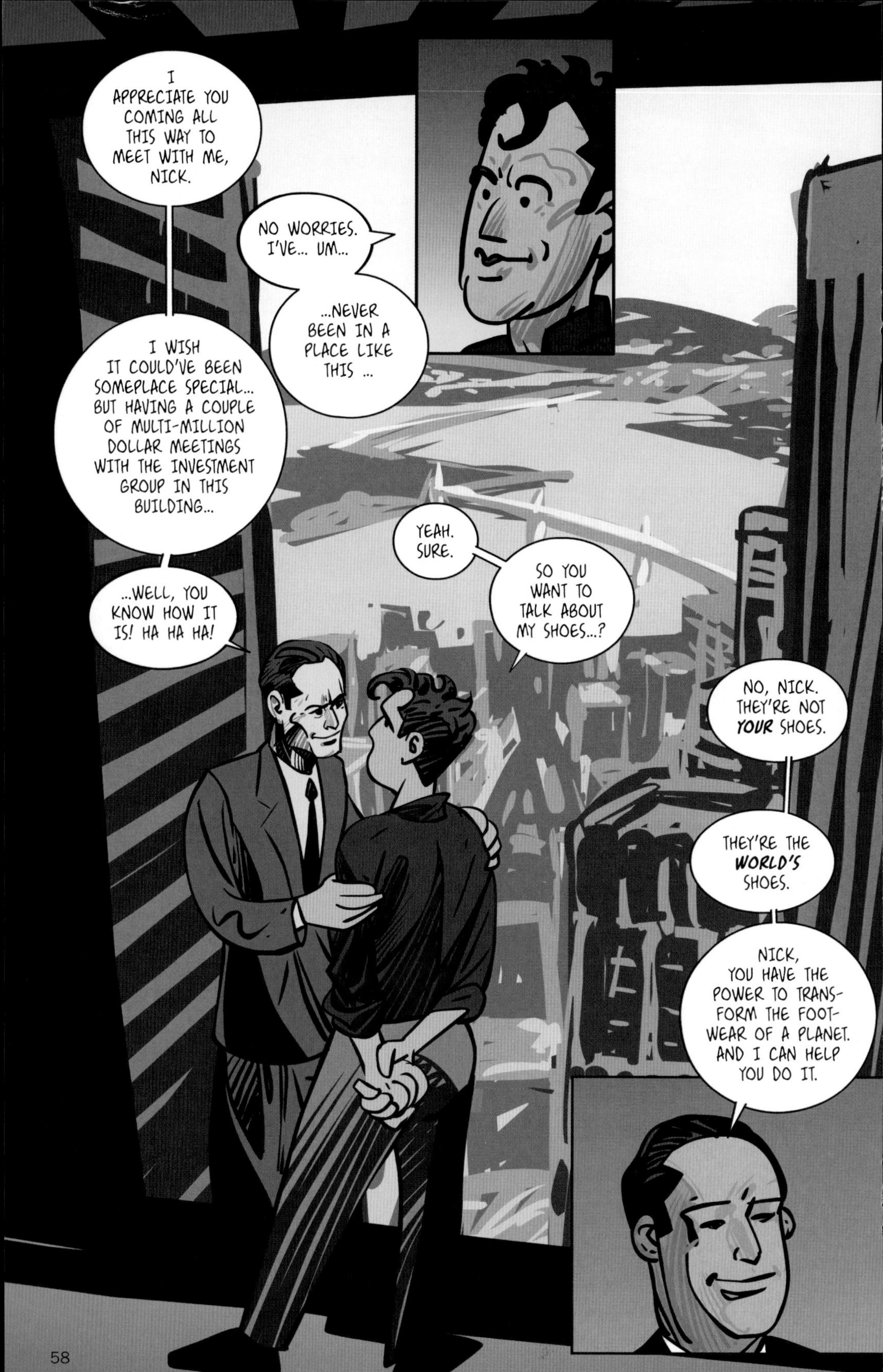
I APPRECIATE YOU COMING ALL THIS WAY TO MEET WITH ME, NICK.
NO WORRIES. I'VE... UM...
...NEVER BEEN IN A PLACE LIKE THIS ...
I WISH IT COULD'VE BEEN SOMEPLACE SPECIAL... BUT HAVING A COUPLE OF MULTI-MILLION DOLLAR MEETINGS WITH THE INVESTMENT GROUP IN THIS BUILDING...
...WELL, YOU KNOW HOW IT IS! HA HA HA!
YEAH. SURE.
SO YOU WANT TO TALK ABOUT MY SHOES...?
NO, NICK. THEY'RE NOT YOUR SHOES.
THEY'RE THE WORLD'S SHOES.
NICK, YOU HAVE THE POWER TO TRANS-FORM THE FOOT-WEAR OF A PLANET. AND I CAN HELP YOU DO IT.

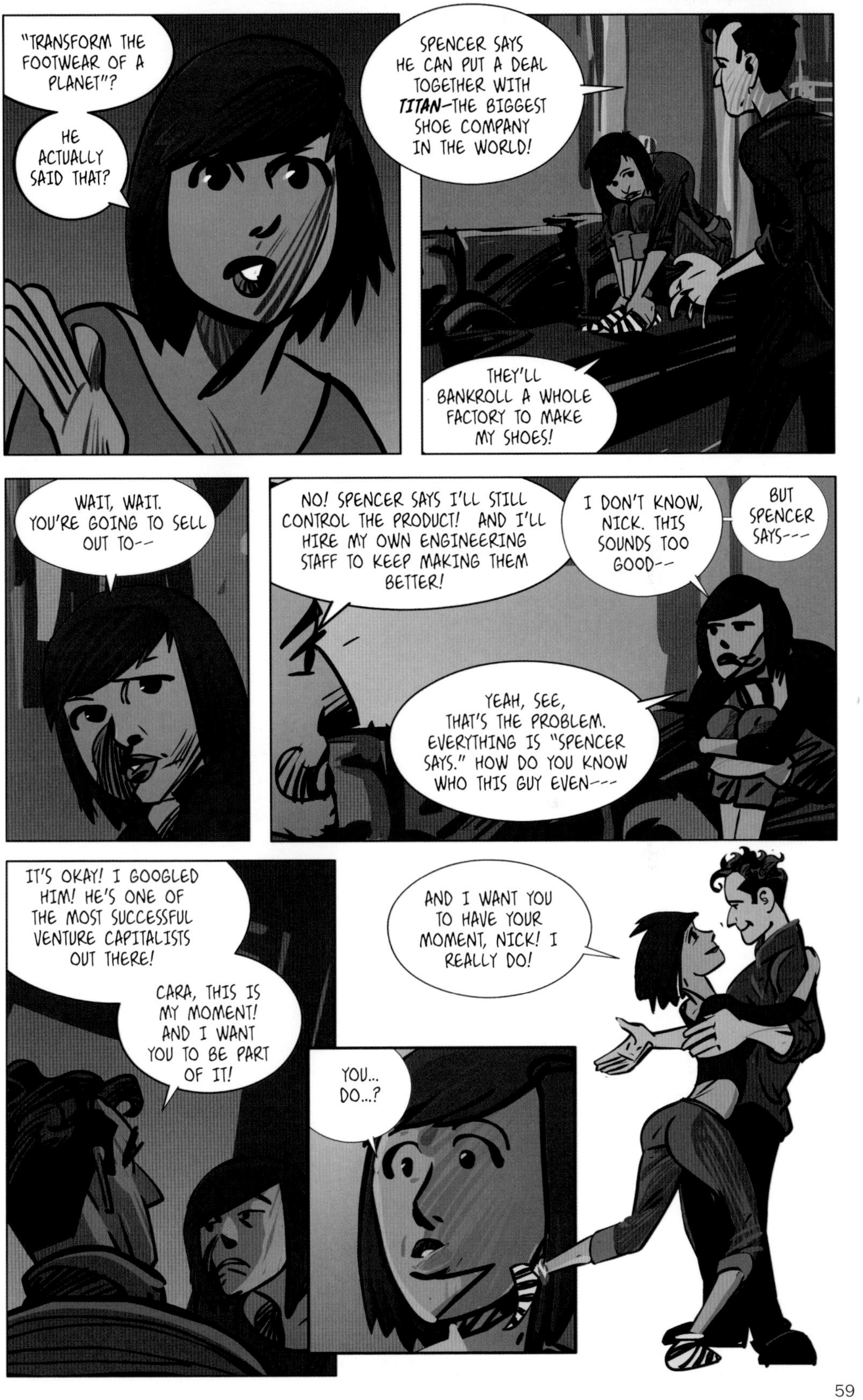
"TRANSFORM THE FOOTWEAR OF A PLANET"?
HE ACTUALLY SAID THAT?
SPENCER SAYS HE CAN PUT A DEAL TOGETHER WITH TITAN—THE BIGGEST SHOE COMPANY IN THE WORLD!
THEY'LL BANKROLL A WHOLE FACTORY TO MAKE MY SHOES!
WAIT, WAIT. YOU'RE GOING TO SELL OUT TO--
NO! SPENCER SAYS I'LL STILL CONTROL THE PRODUCT! AND I'LL HIRE MY OWN ENGINEERING STAFF TO KEEP MAKING THEM BETTER!
I DON'T KNOW, NICK. THIS SOUNDS TOO GOOD--
BUT SPENCER SAYS---
YEAH, SEE, THAT'S THE PROBLEM. EVERYTHING IS "SPENCER SAYS." HOW DO YOU KNOW WHO THIS GUY EVEN---
IT'S OKAY! I GOOGLED HIM! HE'S ONE OF THE MOST SUCCESSFUL VENTURE CAPITALISTS OUT THERE!
CARA, THIS IS MY MOMENT! AND I WANT YOU TO BE PART OF IT!
YOU... DO...?
AND I WANT YOU TO HAVE YOUR MOMENT, NICK! I REALLY DO!

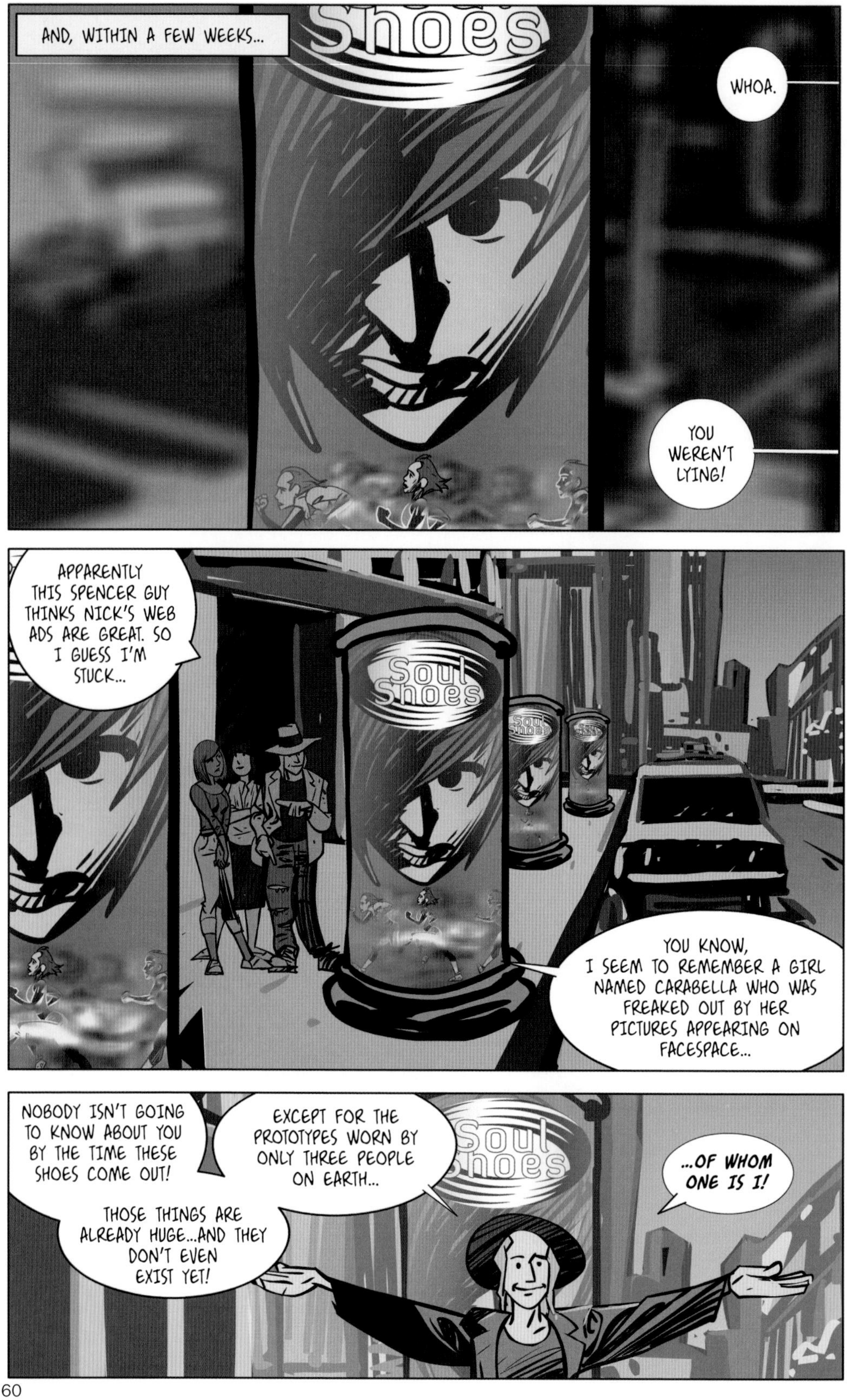
AND, WITHIN A FEW WEEKS...
Shoes
WHOA.
YOU WEREN'T LYING!
APPARENTLY THIS SPENCER GUY THINKS NICK'S WEB ADS ARE GREAT. SO I GUESS I'M STUCK...
Soul Shoes
YOU KNOW, I SEEM TO REMEMBER A GIRL NAMED CARABELLA WHO WAS FREAKED OUT BY HER PICTURES APPEARING ON FACESPACE...
NOBODY ISN'T GOING TO KNOW ABOUT YOU BY THE TIME THESE SHOES COME OUT!
THOSE THINGS ARE ALREADY HUGE...AND THEY DON'T EVEN EXIST YET!
EXCEPT FOR THE PROTOTYPES WORN BY ONLY THREE PEOPLE ON EARTH...
Soul Shoes
...OF WHOM ONE IS I!

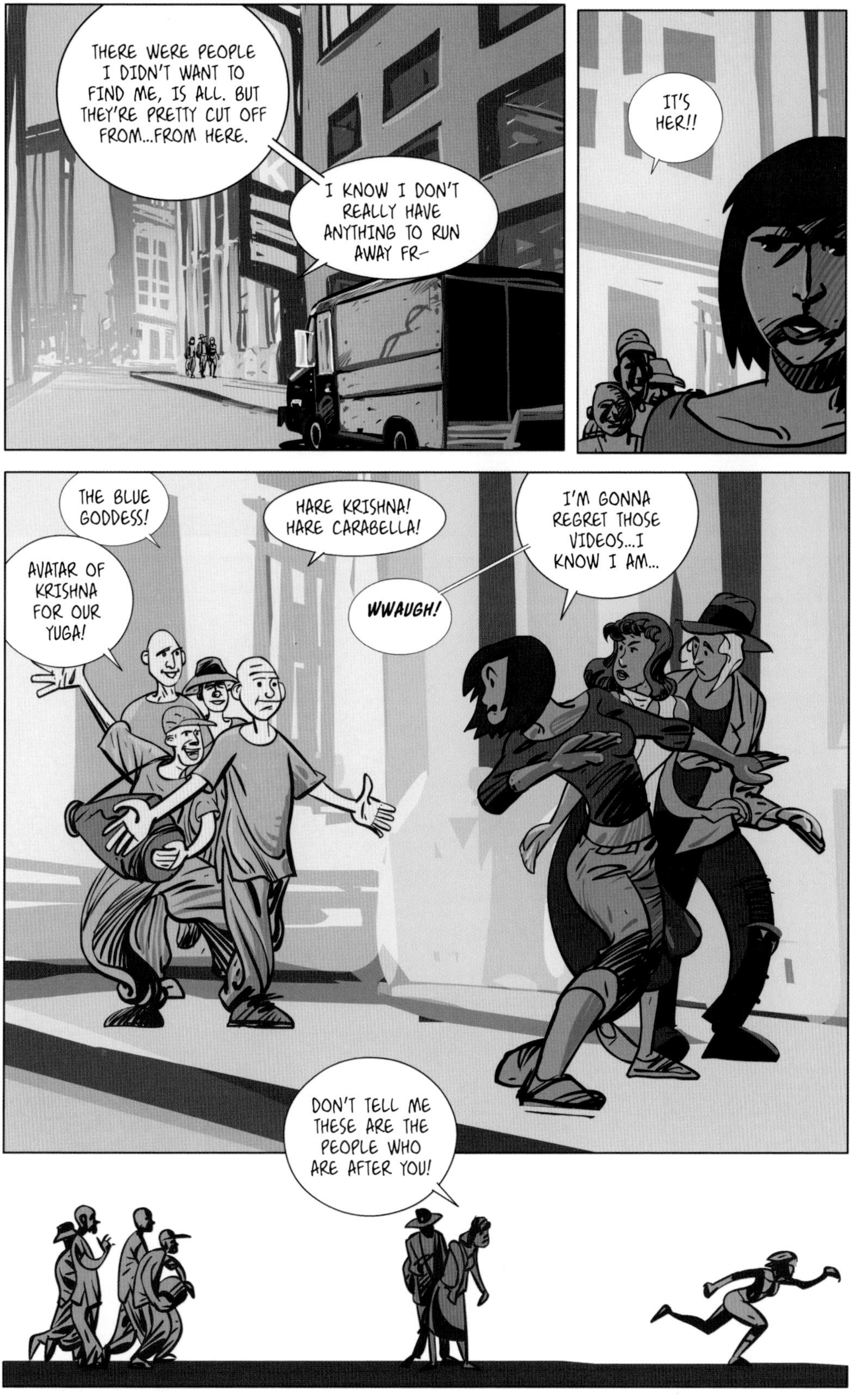
THERE WERE PEOPLE I DIDN'T WANT TO FIND ME, IS ALL. BUT THEY'RE PRETTY CUT OFF FROM...FROM HERE.
I KNOW I DON'T REALLY HAVE ANYTHING TO RUN AWAY FR–
IT'S HER!!
THE BLUE GODDESS!
AVATAR OF KRISHNA FOR OUR YUGA!
HARE KRISHNA! HARE CARABELLA!
I'M GONNA REGRET THOSE VIDEOS...I KNOW I AM...
WWAUGH!
DON'T TELL ME THESE ARE THE PEOPLE WHO ARE AFTER YOU!

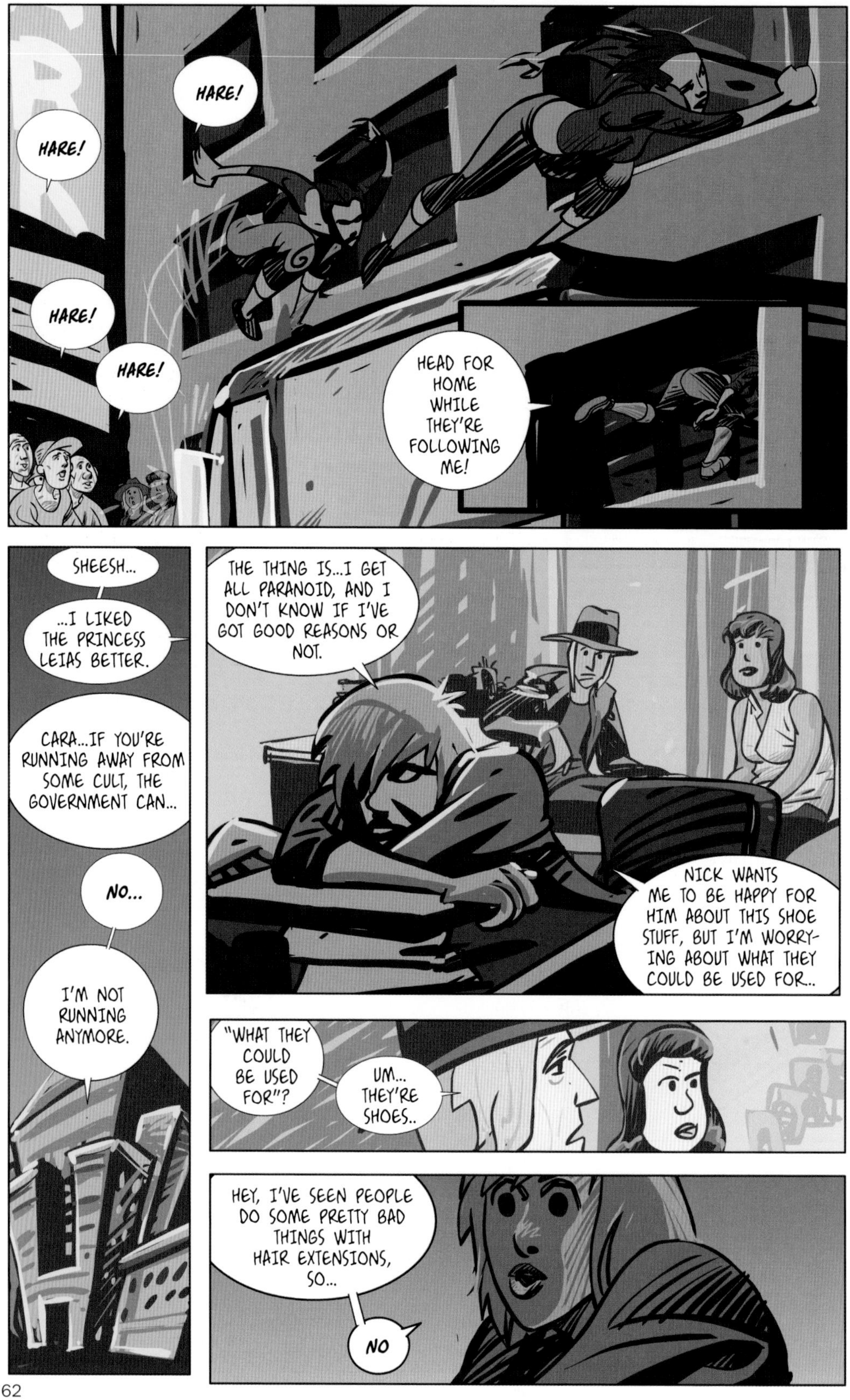

HARE!
HARE!
HARE!
HARE!
HEAD FOR HOME WHILE THEY'RE FOLLOWING ME!
SHEESH...
...I LIKED THE PRINCESS LEIAS BETTER.
THE THING IS...I GET ALL PARANOID, AND I DON'T KNOW IF I'VE GOT GOOD REASONS OR NOT.
NICK WANTS ME TO BE HAPPY FOR HIM ABOUT THIS SHOE STUFF, BUT I'M WORRY-ING ABOUT WHAT THEY COULD BE USED FOR..
CARA...IF YOU'RE RUNNING AWAY FROM SOME CULT, THE GOVERNMENT CAN...
NO...
I'M NOT RUNNING ANYMORE.
"WHAT THEY COULD BE USED FOR"?
UM... THEY'RE SHOES..
HEY, I'VE SEEN PEOPLE DO SOME PRETTY BAD THINGS WITH HAIR EXTENSIONS, SO...
NO

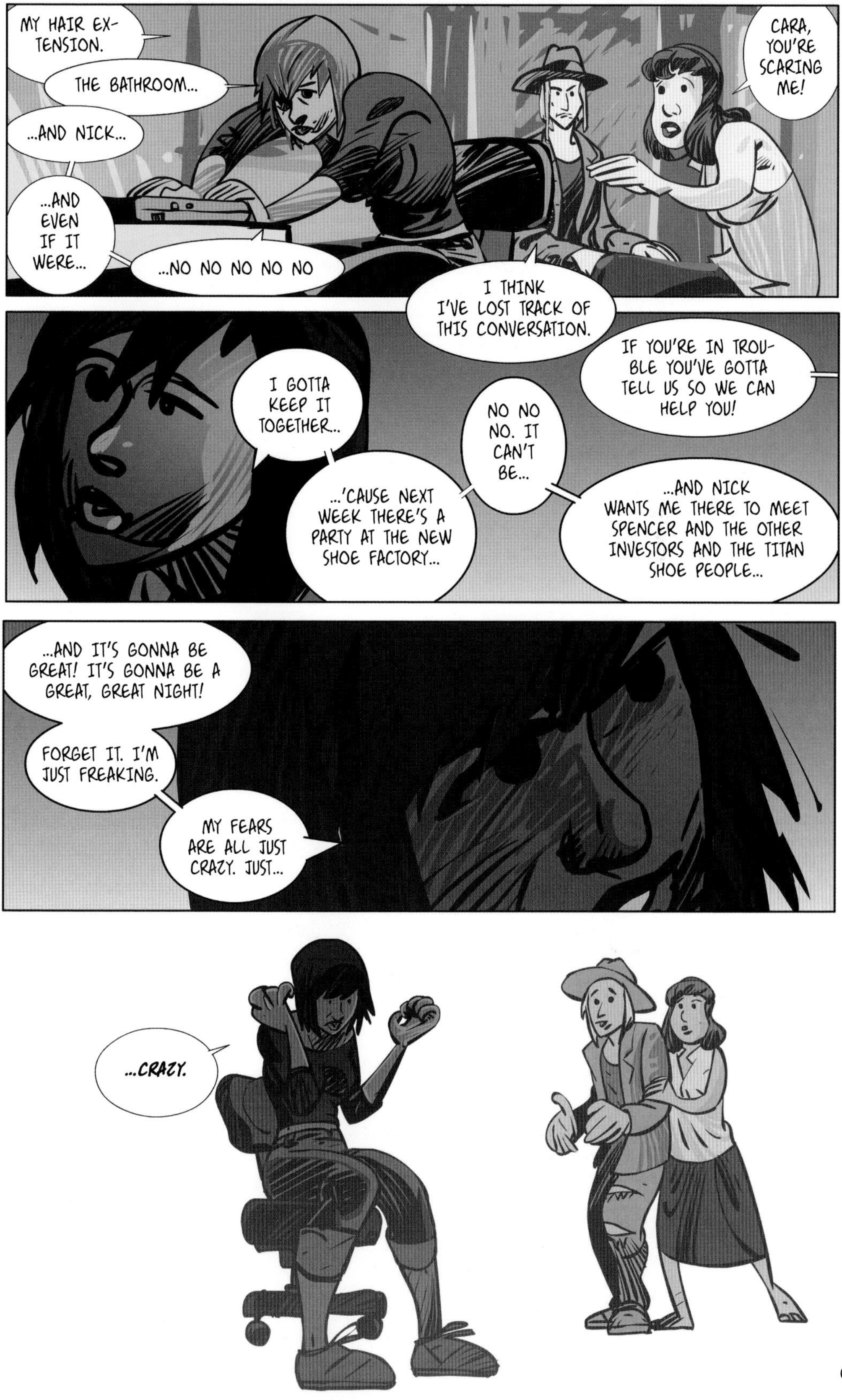
MY HAIR EXTENSION.
THE BATHROOM...
...AND NICK...
...AND EVEN IF IT WERE...
...NO NO NO NO NO
CARA, YOU'RE SCARING ME!
I THINK I'VE LOST TRACK OF THIS CONVERSATION.
IF YOU'RE IN TROUBLE YOU'VE GOTTA TELL US SO WE CAN HELP YOU!
I GOTTA KEEP IT TOGETHER...
...'CAUSE NEXT WEEK THERE'S A PARTY AT THE NEW SHOE FACTORY...
NO NO NO. IT CAN'T BE...
...AND NICK WANTS ME THERE TO MEET SPENCER AND THE OTHER INVESTORS AND THE TITAN SHOE PEOPLE...
...AND IT'S GONNA BE GREAT! IT'S GONNA BE A GREAT, GREAT NIGHT!
FORGET IT. I'M JUST FREAKING.
MY FEARS ARE ALL JUST CRAZY. JUST...
...CRAZY.

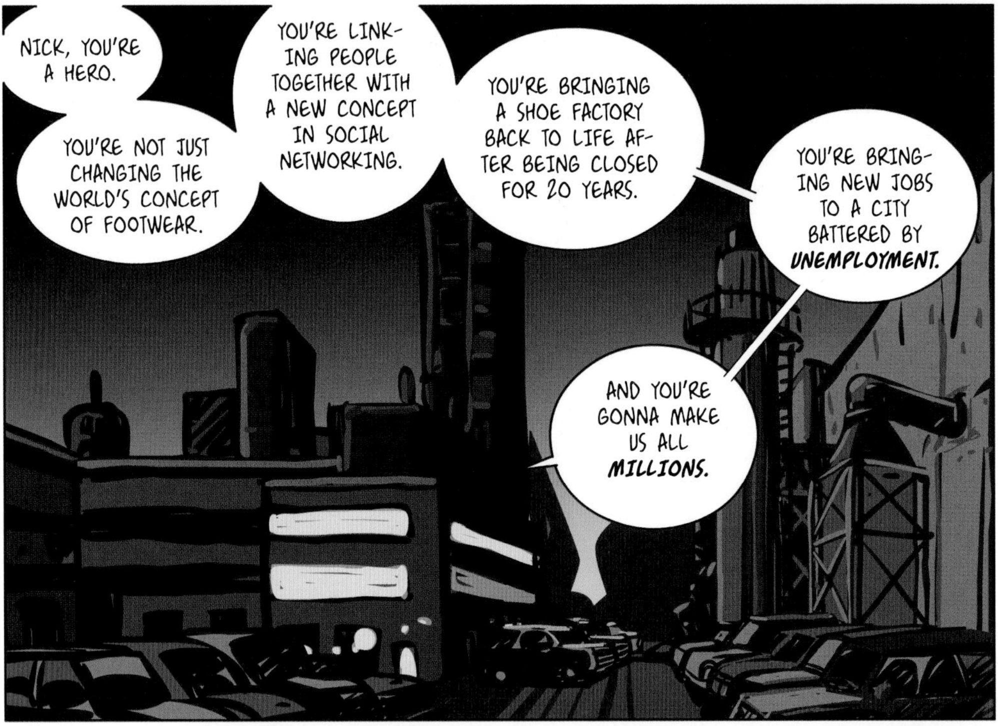
NICK, YOU'RE A HERO.
YOU'RE NOT JUST CHANGING THE WORLD'S CONCEPT OF FOOTWEAR.
YOU'RE LINKING PEOPLE TOGETHER WITH A NEW CONCEPT IN SOCIAL NETWORKING.
YOU'RE BRINGING A SHOE FACTORY BACK TO LIFE AFTER BEING CLOSED FOR 20 YEARS.
YOU'RE BRINGING NEW JOBS TO A CITY BATTERED BY ***UNEMPLOYMENT.***
AND YOU'RE GONNA MAKE US ALL ***MILLIONS.***

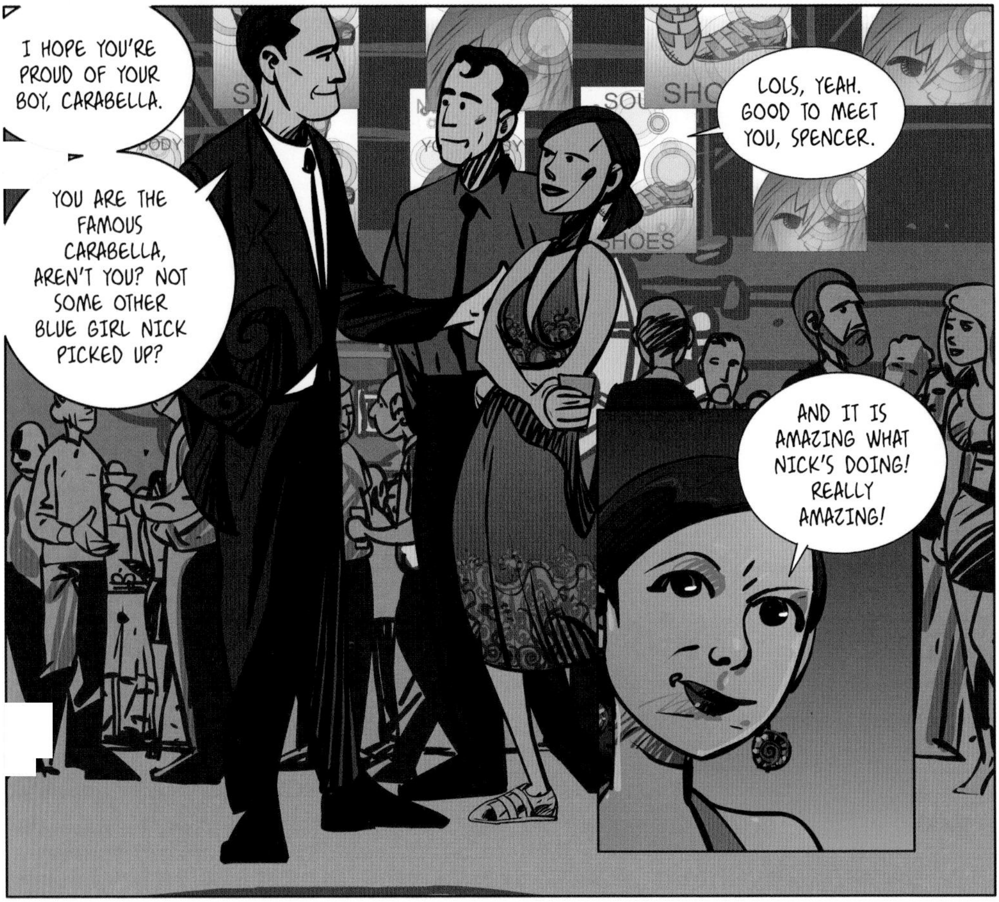
I HOPE YOU'RE PROUD OF YOUR BOY, CARABELLA.
YOU ARE THE FAMOUS CARABELLA, AREN'T YOU? NOT SOME OTHER BLUE GIRL NICK PICKED UP?
LOLS, YEAH. GOOD TO MEET YOU, SPENCER.
AND IT IS AMAZING WHAT NICK'S DOING! REALLY AMAZING!

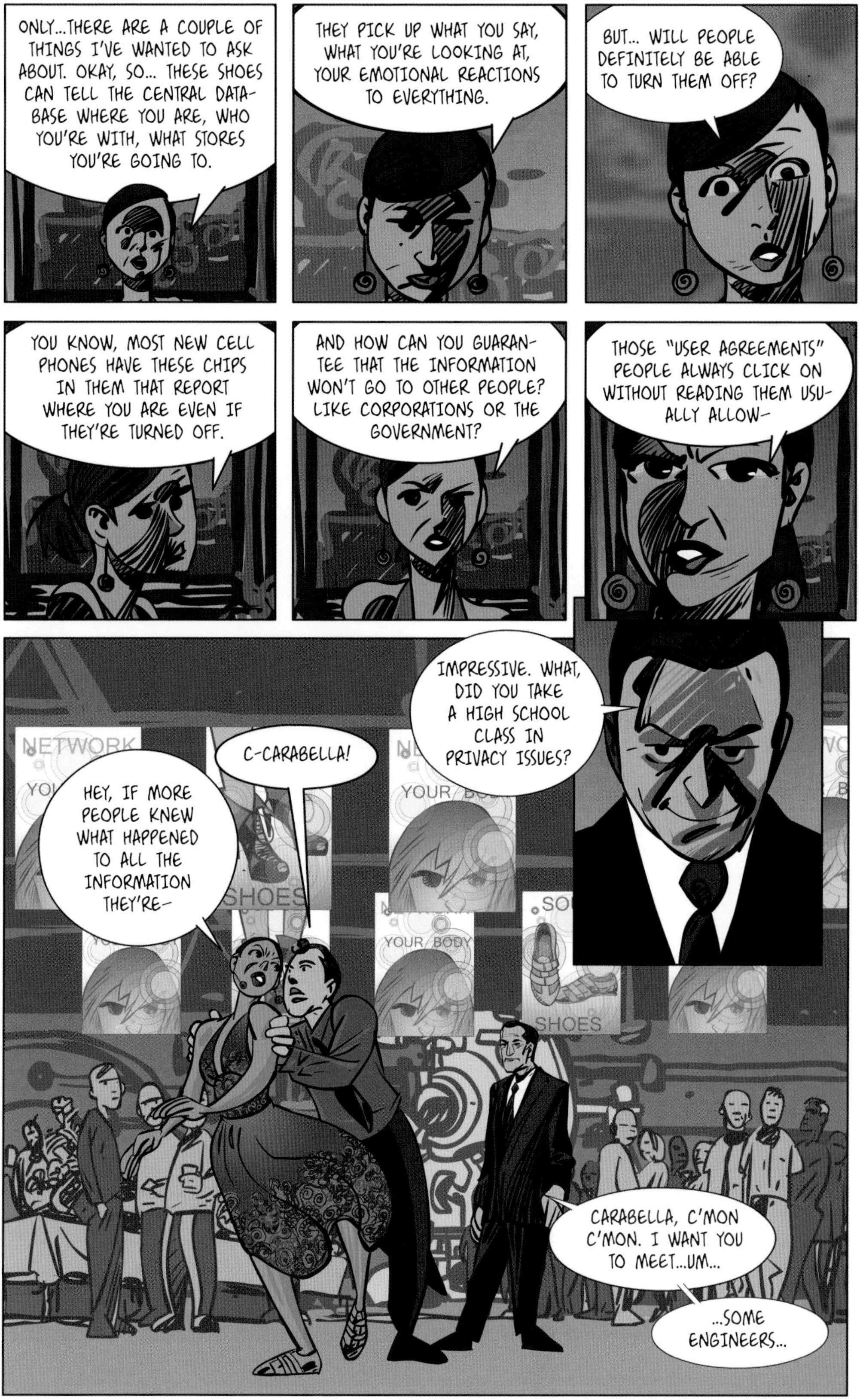
ONLY...THERE ARE A COUPLE OF THINGS I'VE WANTED TO ASK ABOUT. OKAY, SO... THESE SHOES CAN TELL THE CENTRAL DATA-BASE WHERE YOU ARE, WHO YOU'RE WITH, WHAT STORES YOU'RE GOING TO.
THEY PICK UP WHAT YOU SAY, WHAT YOU'RE LOOKING AT, YOUR EMOTIONAL REACTIONS TO EVERYTHING.
BUT... WILL PEOPLE DEFINITELY BE ABLE TO TURN THEM OFF?
YOU KNOW, MOST NEW CELL PHONES HAVE THESE CHIPS IN THEM THAT REPORT WHERE YOU ARE EVEN IF THEY'RE TURNED OFF.
AND HOW CAN YOU GUARAN-TEE THAT THE INFORMATION WON'T GO TO OTHER PEOPLE? LIKE CORPORATIONS OR THE GOVERNMENT?
THOSE "USER AGREEMENTS" PEOPLE ALWAYS CLICK ON WITHOUT READING THEM USU-ALLY ALLOW–
IMPRESSIVE. WHAT, DID YOU TAKE A HIGH SCHOOL CLASS IN PRIVACY ISSUES?
HEY, IF MORE PEOPLE KNEW WHAT HAPPENED TO ALL THE INFORMATION THEY'RE–
C-CARABELLA!
NETWORK
YOUR BODY
SHOES
CARABELLA, C'MON C'MON. I WANT YOU TO MEET...UM...
...SOME ENGINEERS...

I'M SORRY, NICK. BUT THIS IS ALL HAPPENING SO FAST...

YOU SAID YOU WANTED WHATEVER YOU DO TO BE FOR PEOPLE'S GOOD, RIGHT?

OH, C'MON! YOU KNOW I DO!

BUT YOU CAN'T DO GOOD UNLESS YOU DO SOMETHING, RIGHT?

YOU KNOW HOW TRENDS AND TECH CHANGE. THIS COULD BE THE ONLY MOMENT WE HAVE TO MAKE THIS HAPPEN!

LOOK AT THIS! THE MOST SOPHISTICATED MANUFACTURING CENTER IN HISTORY! I DON'T KNOW WHERE THEY EVEN GOT MOST OF THIS TECHNOLOGY!

IN JUST TWO WEEKS THEY'LL BE SENDING 10,000 SHOES TO RETAILERS EVERYWHERE— AND THEY'LL ALL LINK BACK TO THIS ROOM!

SPENCER SAYS WE HAVE TO JUMP ON THIS NOW. WE'LL HAVE TIME FOR PROBLEM SOLVING LATER. CAN'T YOU TRUST ME, CARA?

CAN YOU TRUST ME ON THIS?

I TRUST YOU, NICK. I JUST...

OH, NEVER MIND. I'M JUST BEING WEIRD.

NOW SHOW ME WHERE THE BATHROOM IS AND I PROMISE I'LL JUST HAVE FUN FOR THE REST OF THE PARTY.

OH... ACTUALLY...I DON'T KNOW WHERE...

'SOKAY! I'LL FIND IT.

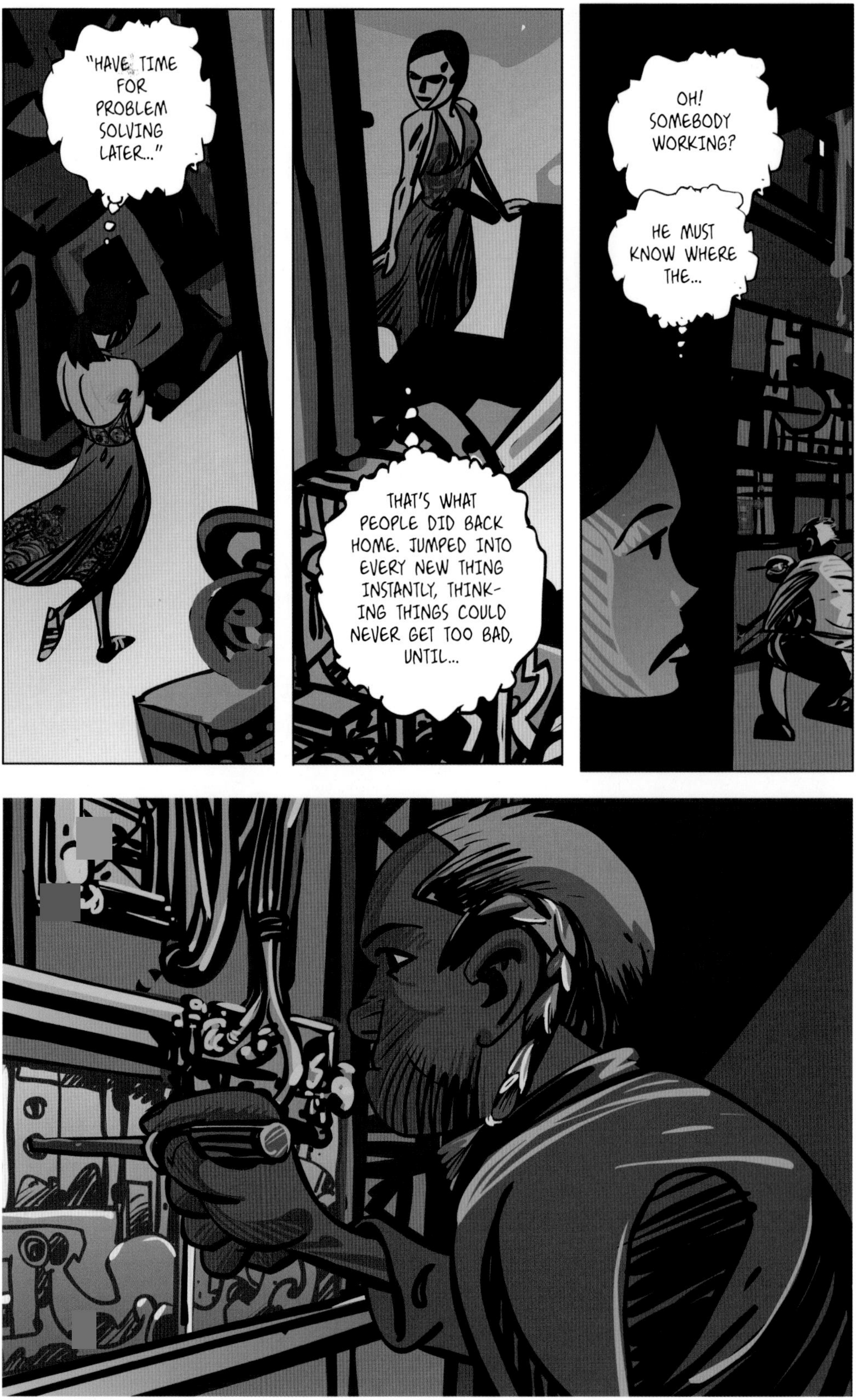
"HAVE TIME FOR PROBLEM SOLVING LATER..."
THAT'S WHAT PEOPLE DID BACK HOME. JUMPED INTO EVERY NEW THING INSTANTLY, THINK-ING THINGS COULD NEVER GET TOO BAD, UNTIL...
OH! SOMEBODY WORKING?
HE MUST KNOW WHERE THE...

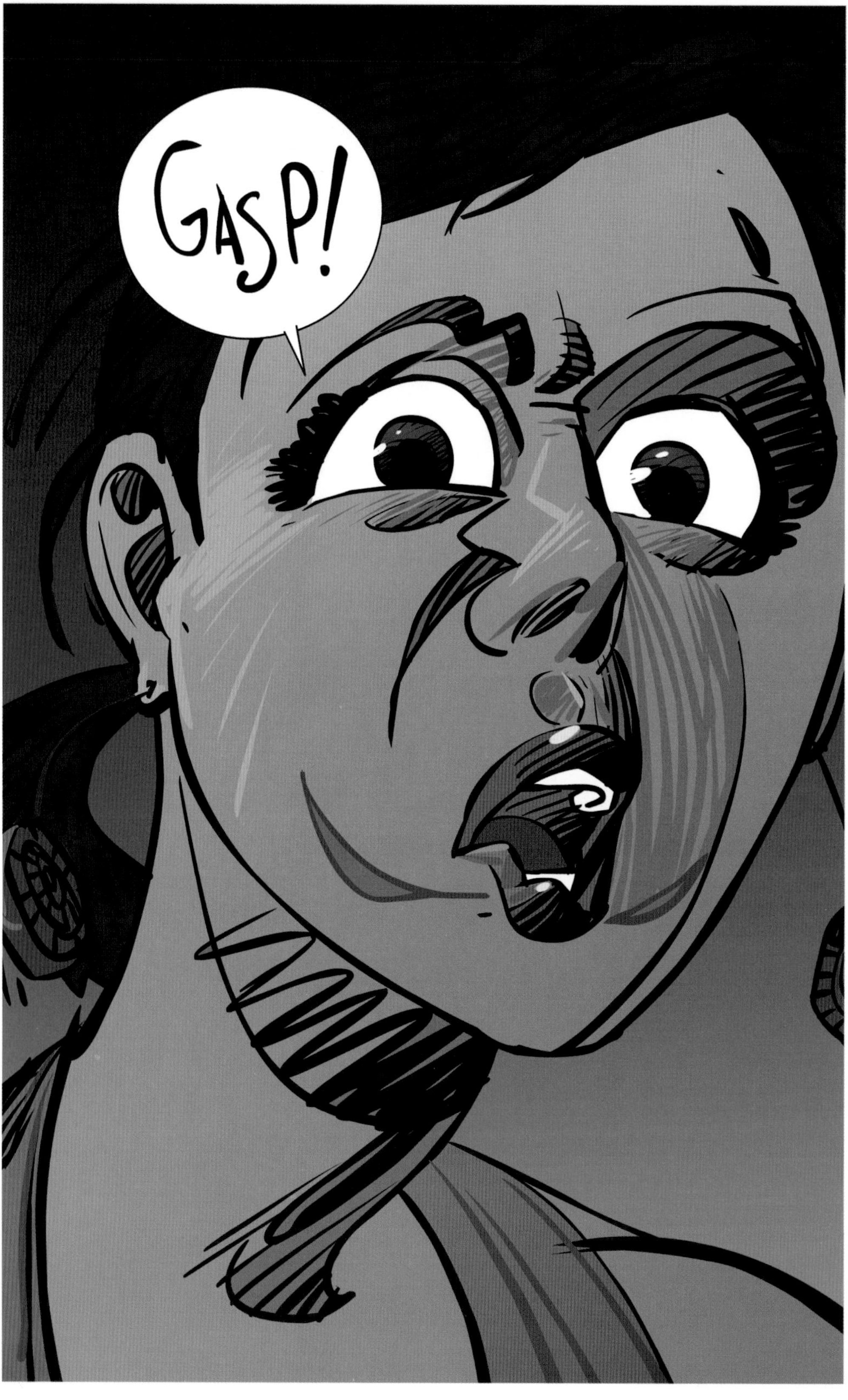
GASP!

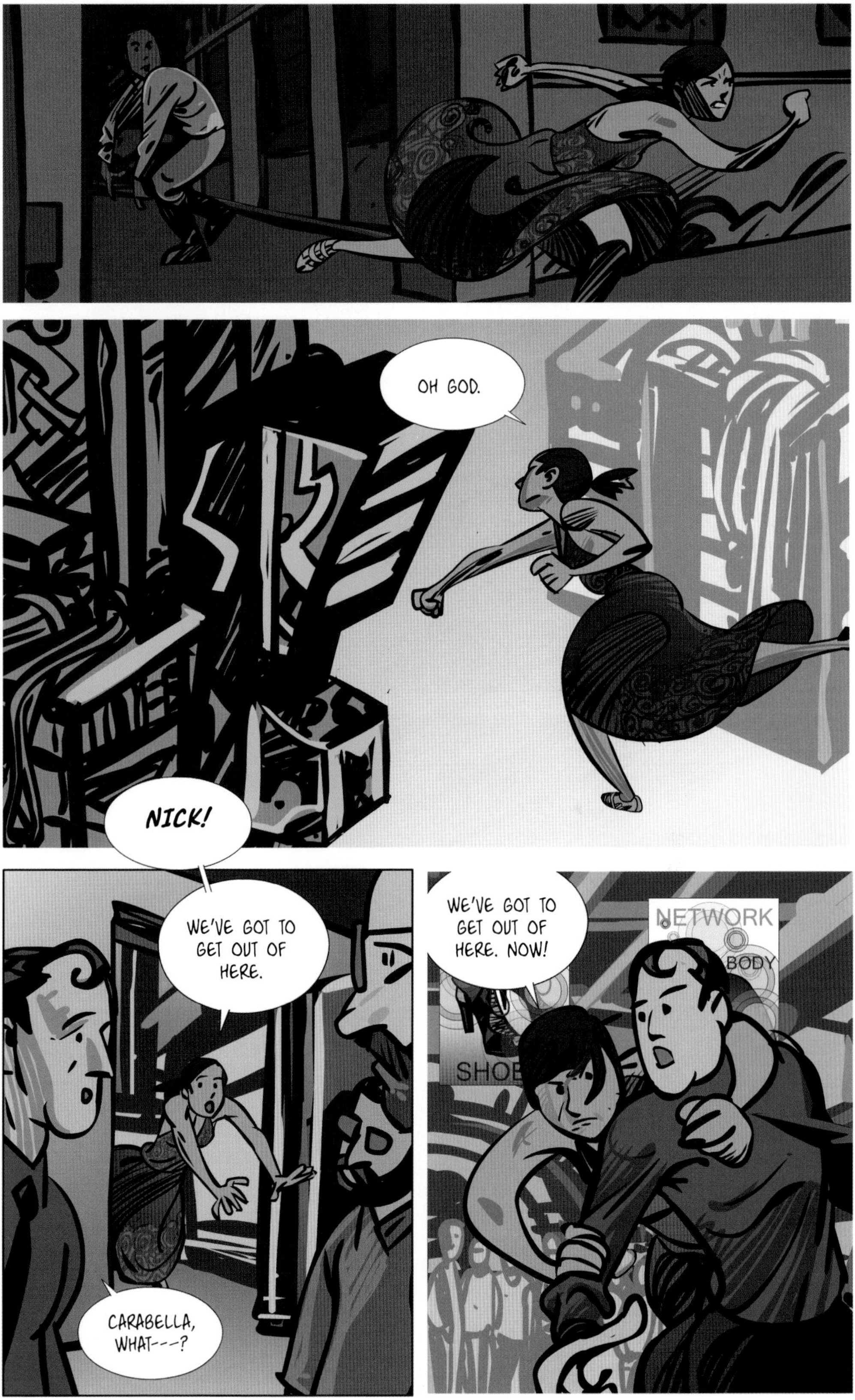
OH GOD.
NICK!
WE'VE GOT TO GET OUT OF HERE.
CARABELLA, WHAT---?
WE'VE GOT TO GET OUT OF HERE. NOW!
NETWORK
BODY

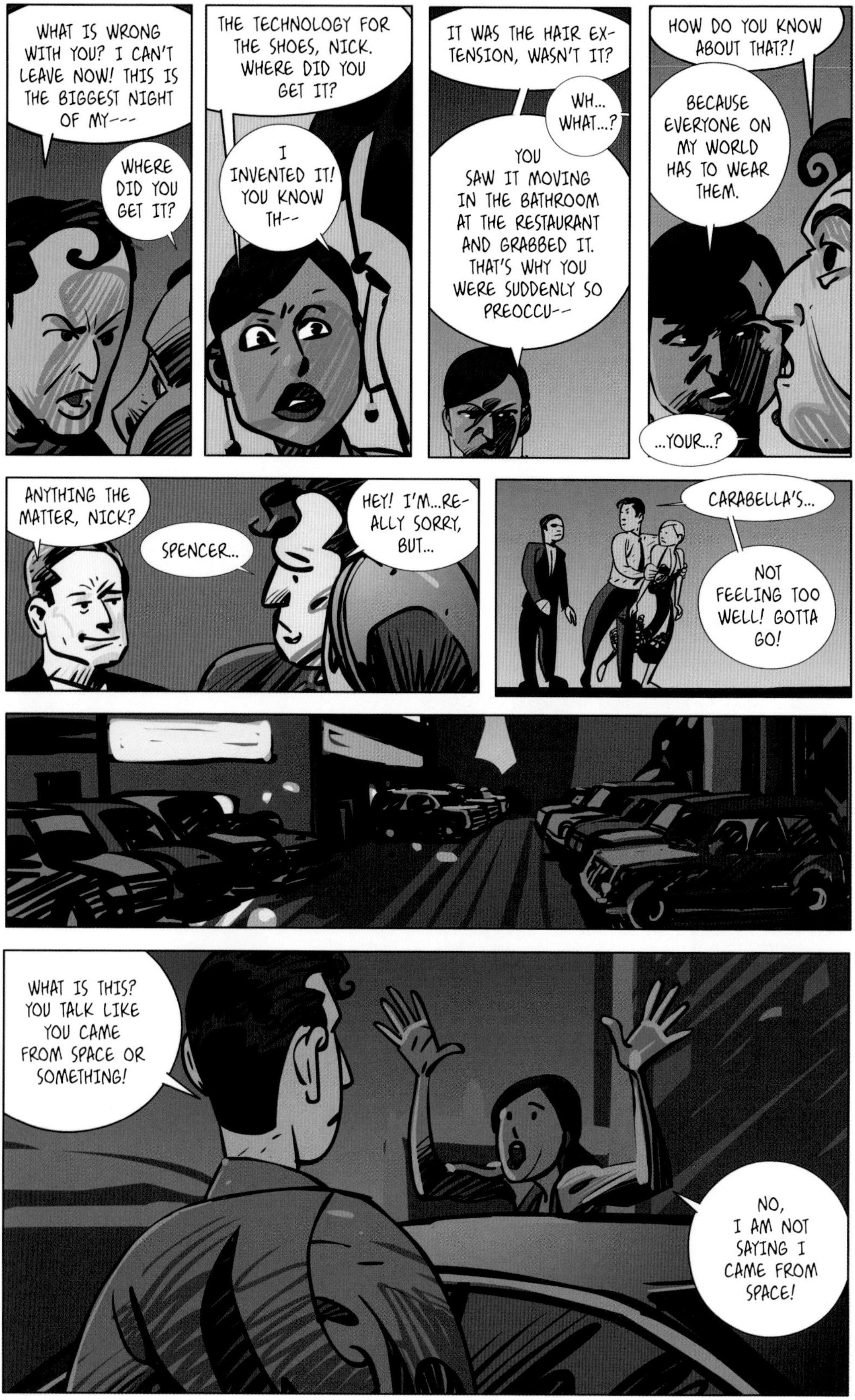
WHAT IS WRONG WITH YOU? I CAN'T LEAVE NOW! THIS IS THE BIGGEST NIGHT OF MY---
WHERE DID YOU GET IT?
THE TECHNOLOGY FOR THE SHOES, NICK. WHERE DID YOU GET IT?
I INVENTED IT! YOU KNOW TH--
IT WAS THE HAIR EX-TENSION, WASN'T IT?
WH... WHAT...?
YOU SAW IT MOVING IN THE BATHROOM AT THE RESTAURANT AND GRABBED IT. THAT'S WHY YOU WERE SUDDENLY SO PREOCCU--
HOW DO YOU KNOW ABOUT THAT?!
BECAUSE EVERYONE ON MY WORLD HAS TO WEAR THEM.
...YOUR...?
ANYTHING THE MATTER, NICK?
SPENCER...
HEY! I'M...RE-ALLY SORRY, BUT...
CARABELLA'S...
NOT FEELING TOO WELL! GOTTA GO!
WHAT IS THIS? YOU TALK LIKE YOU CAME FROM SPACE OR SOMETHING!
NO, I AM NOT SAYING I CAME FROM SPACE!

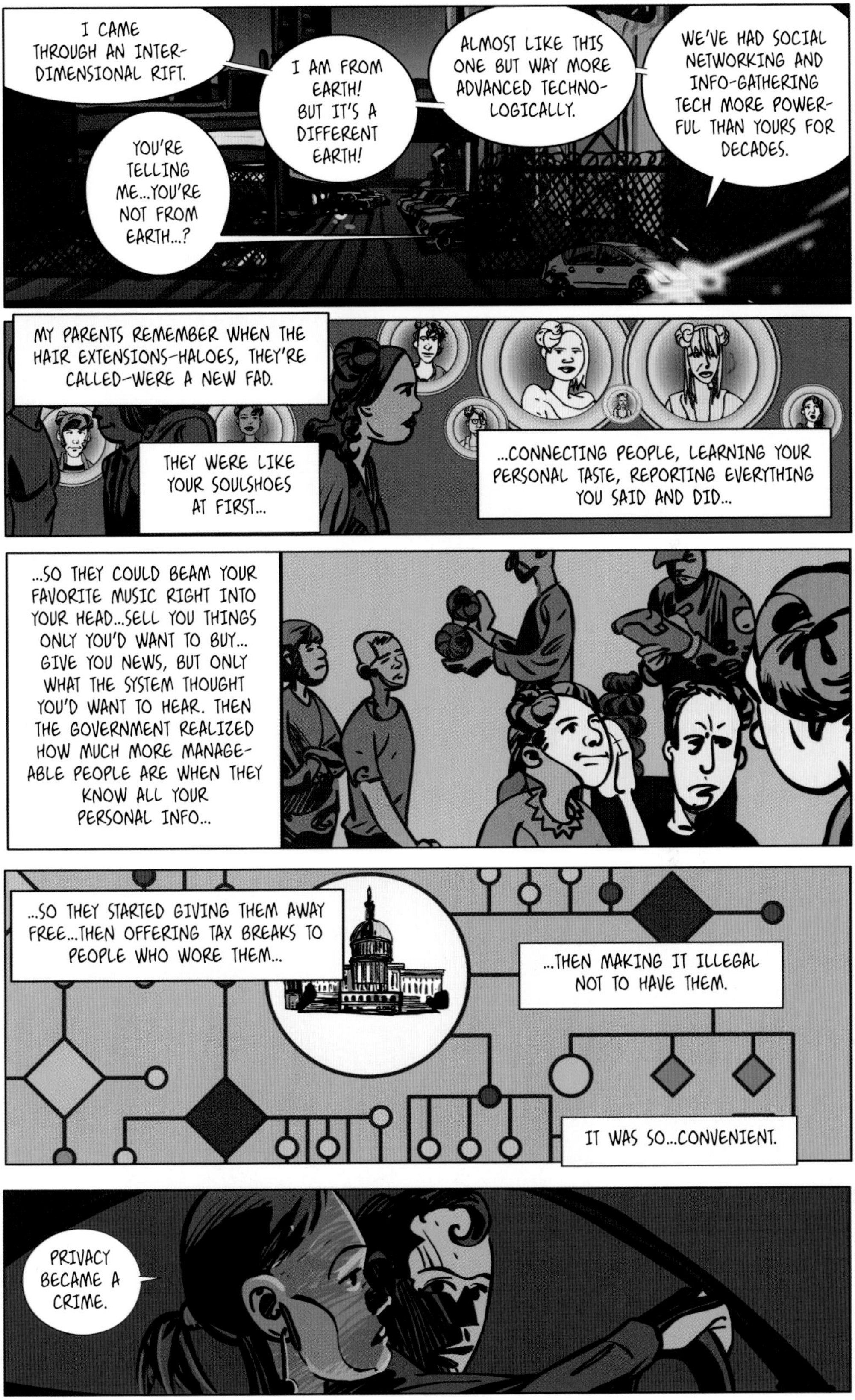
I CAME THROUGH AN INTER-DIMENSIONAL RIFT.
YOU'RE TELLING ME...YOU'RE NOT FROM EARTH...?
I AM FROM EARTH! BUT IT'S A DIFFERENT EARTH!
ALMOST LIKE THIS ONE BUT WAY MORE ADVANCED TECHNO-LOGICALLY.
WE'VE HAD SOCIAL NETWORKING AND INFO-GATHERING TECH MORE POWER-FUL THAN YOURS FOR DECADES.
MY PARENTS REMEMBER WHEN THE HAIR EXTENSIONS—HALOES, THEY'RE CALLED—WERE A NEW FAD.
THEY WERE LIKE YOUR SOULSHOES AT FIRST...
...CONNECTING PEOPLE, LEARNING YOUR PERSONAL TASTE, REPORTING EVERYTHING YOU SAID AND DID...
...SO THEY COULD BEAM YOUR FAVORITE MUSIC RIGHT INTO YOUR HEAD...SELL YOU THINGS ONLY YOU'D WANT TO BUY... GIVE YOU NEWS, BUT ONLY WHAT THE SYSTEM THOUGHT YOU'D WANT TO HEAR. THEN THE GOVERNMENT REALIZED HOW MUCH MORE MANAGE-ABLE PEOPLE ARE WHEN THEY KNOW ALL YOUR PERSONAL INFO...
...SO THEY STARTED GIVING THEM AWAY FREE...THEN OFFERING TAX BREAKS TO PEOPLE WHO WORE THEM...
...THEN MAKING IT ILLEGAL NOT TO HAVE THEM.
IT WAS SO...CONVENIENT.
PRIVACY BECAME A CRIME.

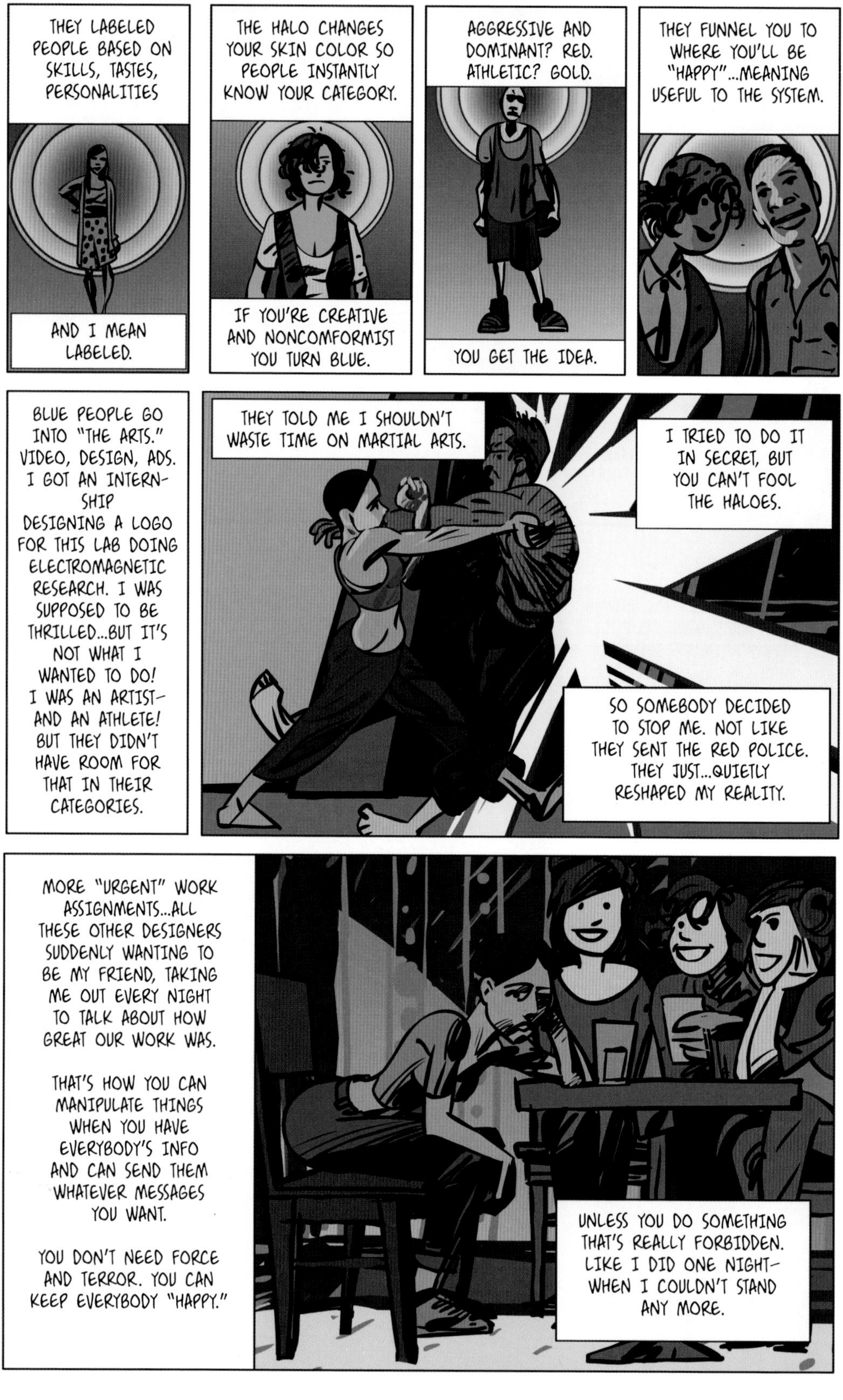
THEY LABELED PEOPLE BASED ON SKILLS, TASTES, PERSONALITIES
AND I MEAN LABELED.
THE HALO CHANGES YOUR SKIN COLOR SO PEOPLE INSTANTLY KNOW YOUR CATEGORY.
IF YOU'RE CREATIVE AND NONCOMFORMIST YOU TURN BLUE.
AGGRESSIVE AND DOMINANT? RED. ATHLETIC? GOLD.
YOU GET THE IDEA.
THEY FUNNEL YOU TO WHERE YOU'LL BE "HAPPY"...MEANING USEFUL TO THE SYSTEM.
BLUE PEOPLE GO INTO "THE ARTS." VIDEO, DESIGN, ADS. I GOT AN INTERN-SHIP DESIGNING A LOGO FOR THIS LAB DOING ELECTROMAGNETIC RESEARCH. I WAS SUPPOSED TO BE THRILLED...BUT IT'S NOT WHAT I WANTED TO DO! I WAS AN ARTIST–AND AN ATHLETE! BUT THEY DIDN'T HAVE ROOM FOR THAT IN THEIR CATEGORIES.
THEY TOLD ME I SHOULDN'T WASTE TIME ON MARTIAL ARTS.
I TRIED TO DO IT IN SECRET, BUT YOU CAN'T FOOL THE HALOES.
SO SOMEBODY DECIDED TO STOP ME. NOT LIKE THEY SENT THE RED POLICE. THEY JUST...QUIETLY RESHAPED MY REALITY.
MORE "URGENT" WORK ASSIGNMENTS...ALL THESE OTHER DESIGNERS SUDDENLY WANTING TO BE MY FRIEND, TAKING ME OUT EVERY NIGHT TO TALK ABOUT HOW GREAT OUR WORK WAS.
THAT'S HOW YOU CAN MANIPULATE THINGS WHEN YOU HAVE EVERYBODY'S INFO AND CAN SEND THEM WHATEVER MESSAGES YOU WANT.
YOU DON'T NEED FORCE AND TERROR. YOU CAN KEEP EVERYBODY "HAPPY."
UNLESS YOU DO SOMETHING THAT'S REALLY FORBIDDEN. LIKE I DID ONE NIGHT–WHEN I COULDN'T STAND ANY MORE.

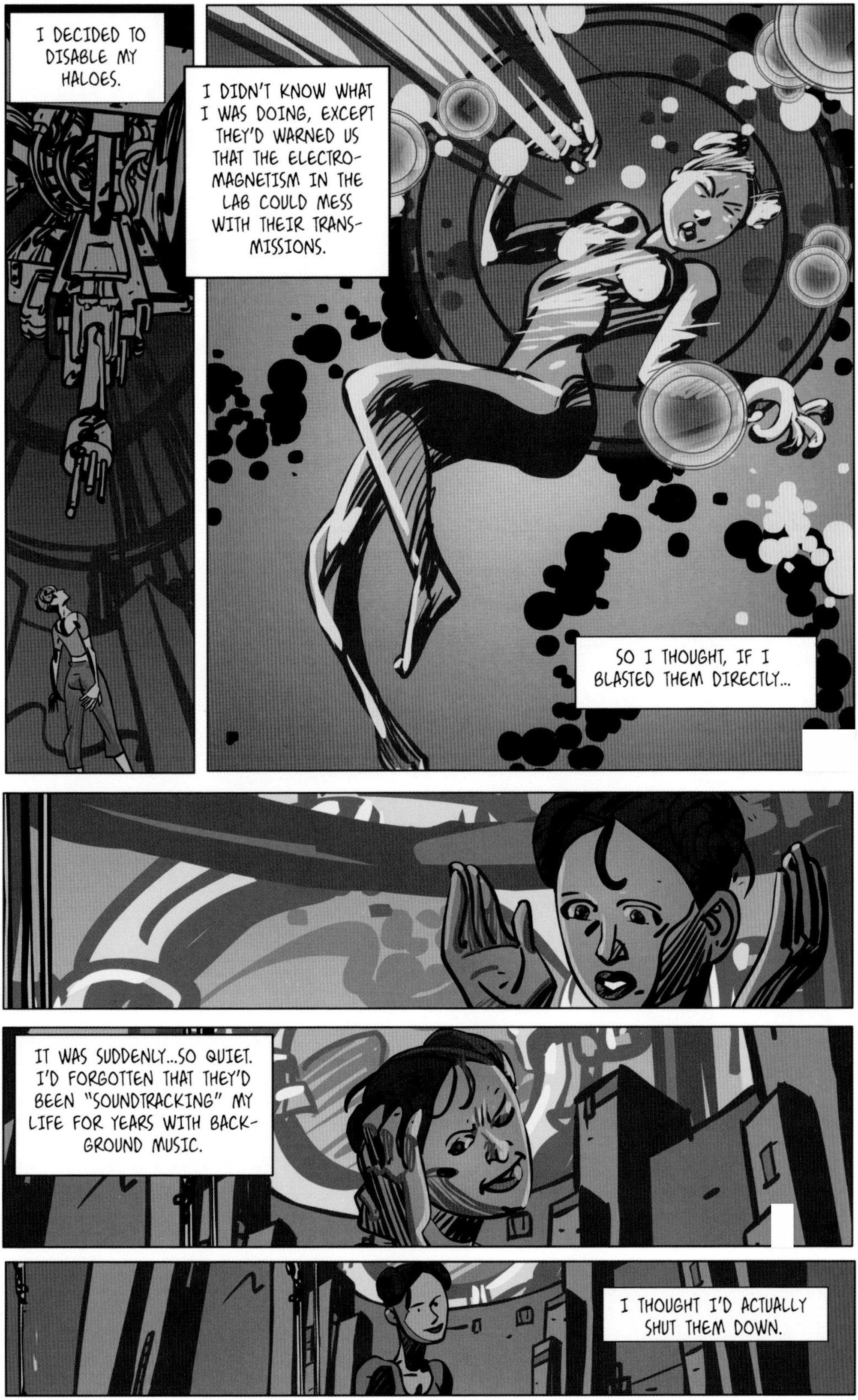
I DECIDED TO DISABLE MY HALOES.
I DIDN'T KNOW WHAT I WAS DOING, EXCEPT THEY'D WARNED US THAT THE ELECTRO-MAGNETISM IN THE LAB COULD MESS WITH THEIR TRANS-MISSIONS.
SO I THOUGHT, IF I BLASTED THEM DIRECTLY...
IT WAS SUDDENLY...SO QUIET. I'D FORGOTTEN THAT THEY'D BEEN "SOUNDTRACKING" MY LIFE FOR YEARS WITH BACK-GROUND MUSIC.
I THOUGHT I'D ACTUALLY SHUT THEM DOWN.

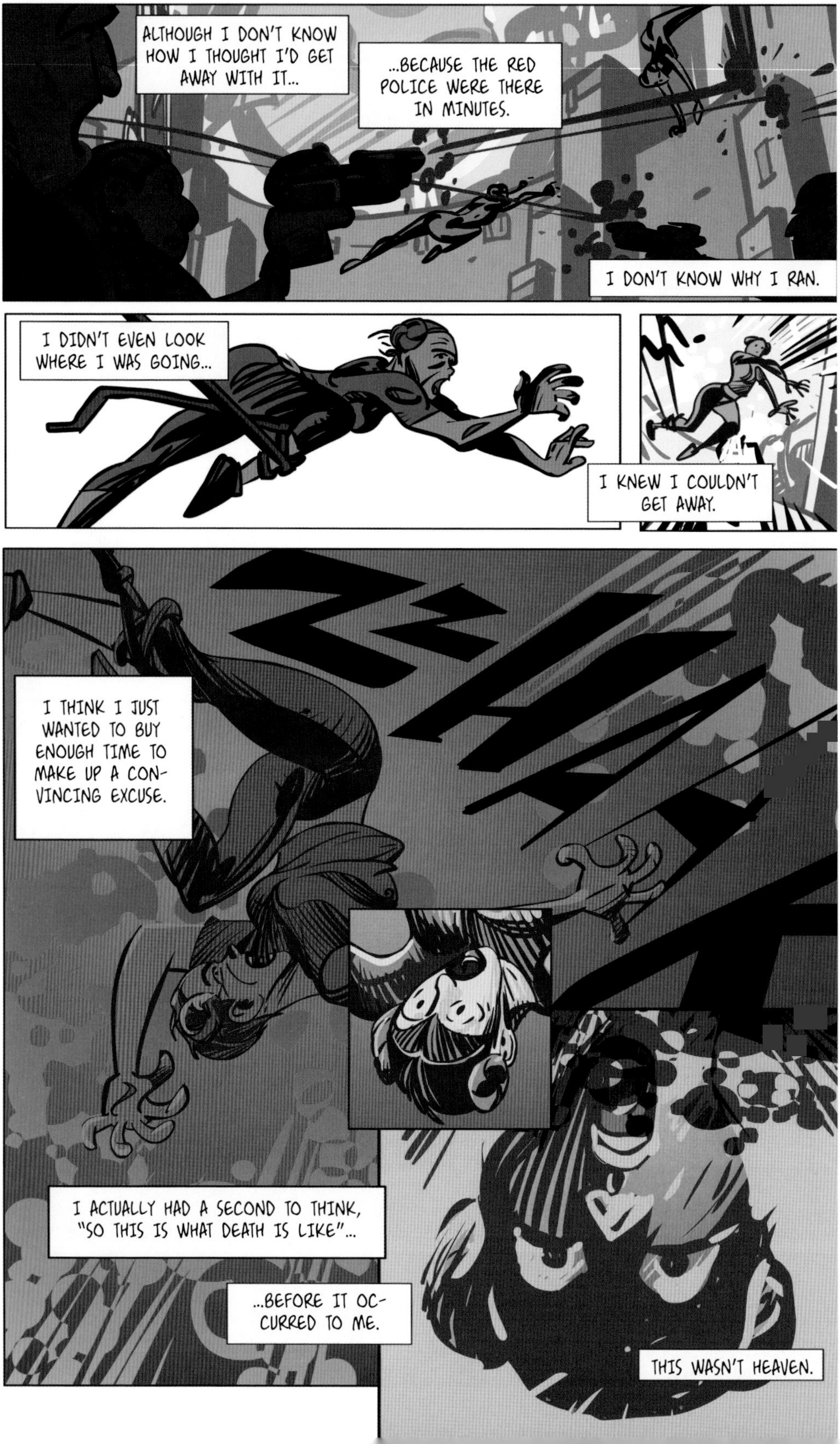

ALTHOUGH I DON'T KNOW HOW I THOUGHT I'D GET AWAY WITH IT...
...BECAUSE THE RED POLICE WERE THERE IN MINUTES.
I DON'T KNOW WHY I RAN.
I DIDN'T EVEN LOOK WHERE I WAS GOING...
I KNEW I COULDN'T GET AWAY.
I THINK I JUST WANTED TO BUY ENOUGH TIME TO MAKE UP A CON-VINCING EXCUSE.
I ACTUALLY HAD A SECOND TO THINK, "SO THIS IS WHAT DEATH IS LIKE"...
...BEFORE IT OC-CURRED TO ME.
THIS WASN'T HEAVEN.

AND IT WASN'T EARTH, EITHER. NOT MY EARTH.

IT'S A LONG STORY HOW I LEARNED TO BLUFF MY WAY THROUGH LIFE HERE, INTO COLLEGE, ALL THAT.

IT DIDN'T TAKE ME TOO LONG TO FIGURE IT OUT. I MEAN, I'VE SEEN ENOUGH SCI-FI SHOWS TO KNOW ABOUT PARALLEL EARTHS.

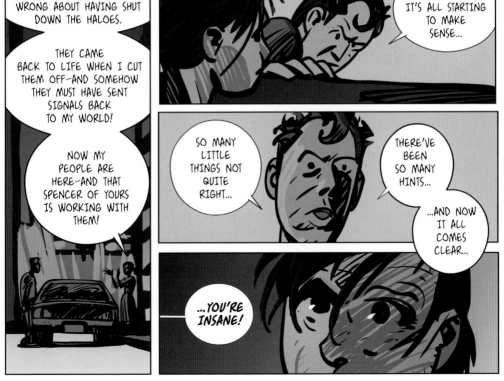

WHAT MATTERS IS—I WAS WRONG ABOUT HAVING SHUT DOWN THE HALOES.

THEY CAME BACK TO LIFE WHEN I CUT THEM OFF—AND SOMEHOW THEY MUST HAVE SENT SIGNALS BACK TO MY WORLD!

NOW MY PEOPLE ARE HERE—AND THAT SPENCER OF YOURS IS WORKING WITH THEM!

SUDDENLY... IT'S ALL STARTING TO MAKE SENSE...

SO MANY LITTLE THINGS NOT QUITE RIGHT...

THERE'VE BEEN SO MANY HINTS...

...AND NOW IT ALL COMES CLEAR..

...YOU'RE INSANE!

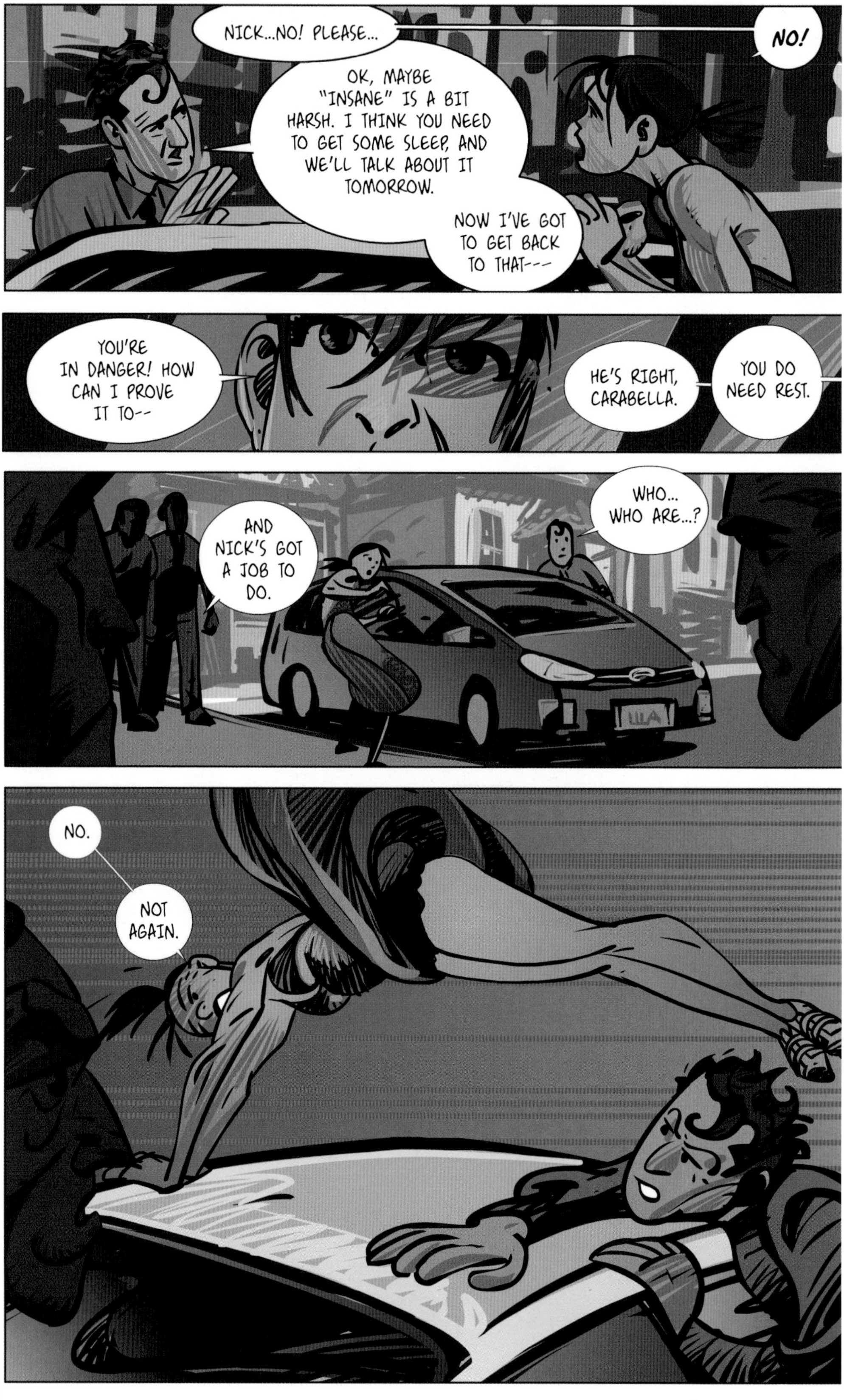
NICK...NO! PLEASE...
NO!
OK, MAYBE "INSANE" IS A BIT HARSH. I THINK YOU NEED TO GET SOME SLEEP, AND WE'LL TALK ABOUT IT TOMORROW.
NOW I'VE GOT TO GET BACK TO THAT---
YOU'RE IN DANGER! HOW CAN I PROVE IT TO--
HE'S RIGHT, CARABELLA.
YOU DO NEED REST.
AND NICK'S GOT A JOB TO DO.
WHO... WHO ARE...?
NO.
NOT AGAIN.

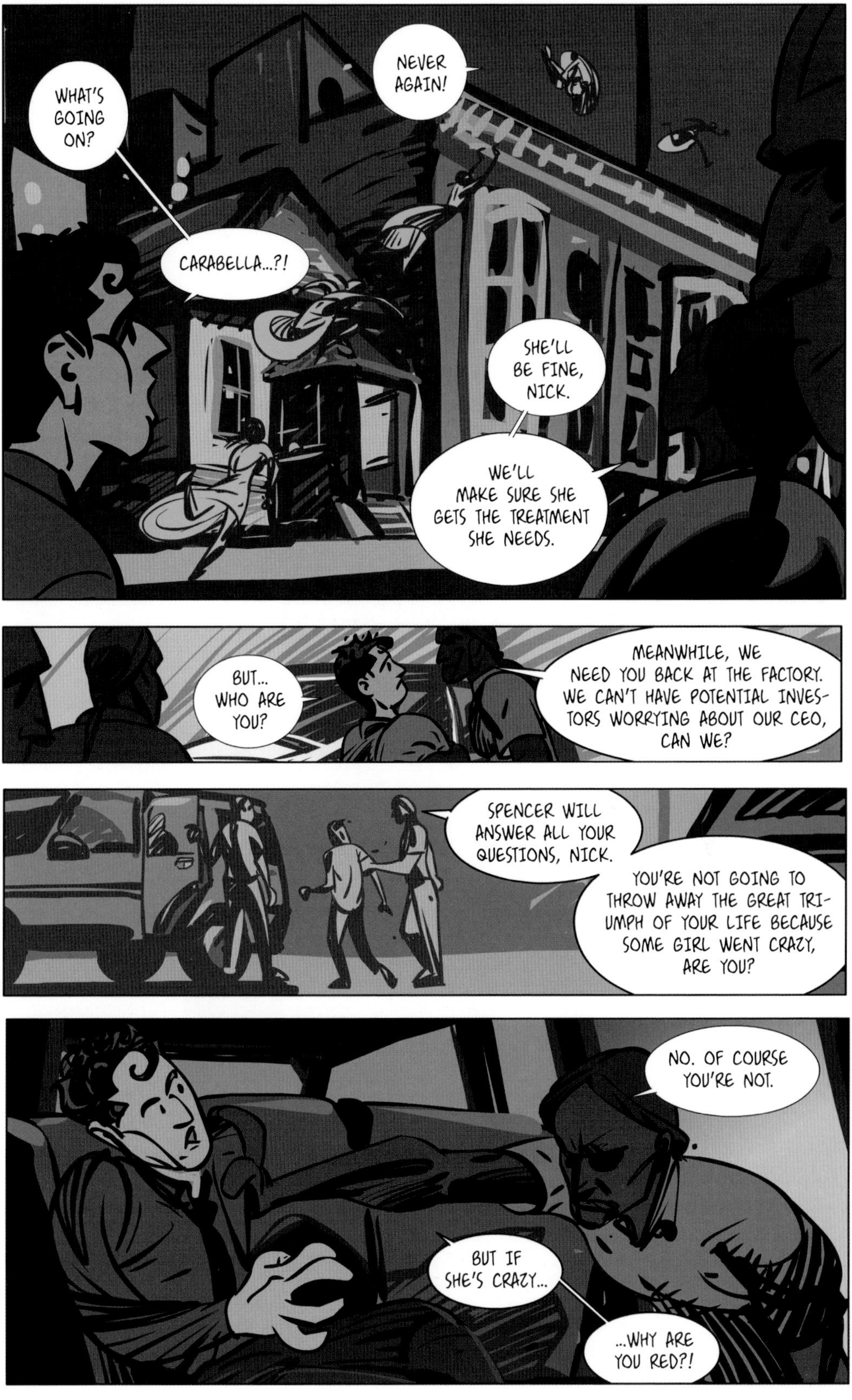
WHAT'S GOING ON?
CARABELLA...?!
NEVER AGAIN!
SHE'LL BE FINE, NICK.
WE'LL MAKE SURE SHE GETS THE TREATMENT SHE NEEDS.
BUT... WHO ARE YOU?
MEANWHILE, WE NEED YOU BACK AT THE FACTORY. WE CAN'T HAVE POTENTIAL INVESTORS WORRYING ABOUT OUR CEO, CAN WE?
SPENCER WILL ANSWER ALL YOUR QUESTIONS, NICK.
YOU'RE NOT GOING TO THROW AWAY THE GREAT TRIUMPH OF YOUR LIFE BECAUSE SOME GIRL WENT CRAZY, ARE YOU?
NO. OF COURSE YOU'RE NOT.
BUT IF SHE'S CRAZY...
...WHY ARE YOU RED?!

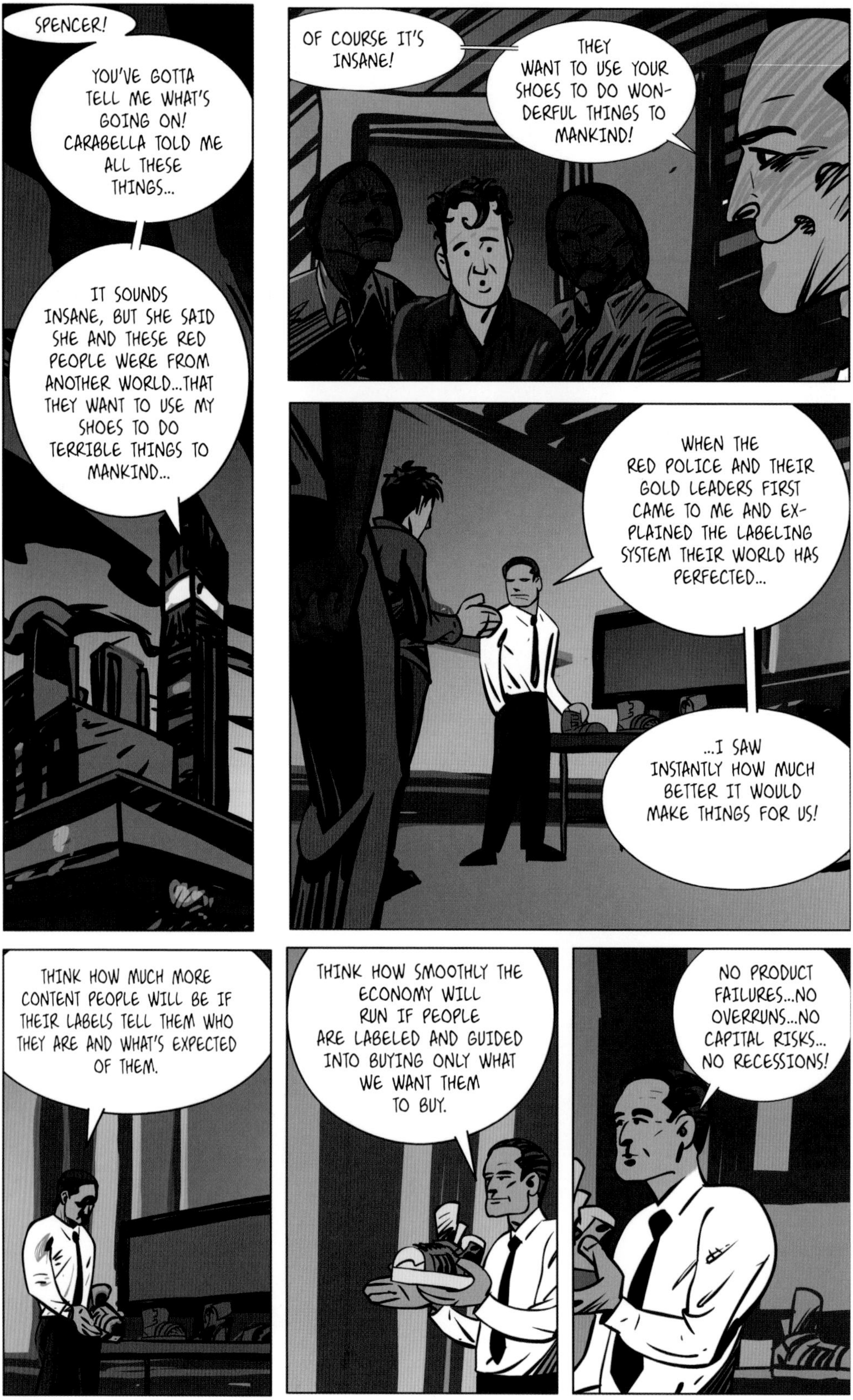
SPENCER!
YOU'VE GOTTA TELL ME WHAT'S GOING ON! CARABELLA TOLD ME ALL THESE THINGS...
IT SOUNDS INSANE, BUT SHE SAID SHE AND THESE RED PEOPLE WERE FROM ANOTHER WORLD...THAT THEY WANT TO USE MY SHOES TO DO TERRIBLE THINGS TO MANKIND...
OF COURSE IT'S INSANE!
THEY WANT TO USE YOUR SHOES TO DO WONDERFUL THINGS TO MANKIND!
WHEN THE RED POLICE AND THEIR GOLD LEADERS FIRST CAME TO ME AND EXPLAINED THE LABELING SYSTEM THEIR WORLD HAS PERFECTED...
...I SAW INSTANTLY HOW MUCH BETTER IT WOULD MAKE THINGS FOR US!
THINK HOW MUCH MORE CONTENT PEOPLE WILL BE IF THEIR LABELS TELL THEM WHO THEY ARE AND WHAT'S EXPECTED OF THEM.
THINK HOW SMOOTHLY THE ECONOMY WILL RUN IF PEOPLE ARE LABELED AND GUIDED INTO BUYING ONLY WHAT WE WANT THEM TO BUY.
NO PRODUCT FAILURES...NO OVERRUNS...NO CAPITAL RISKS... NO RECESSIONS!

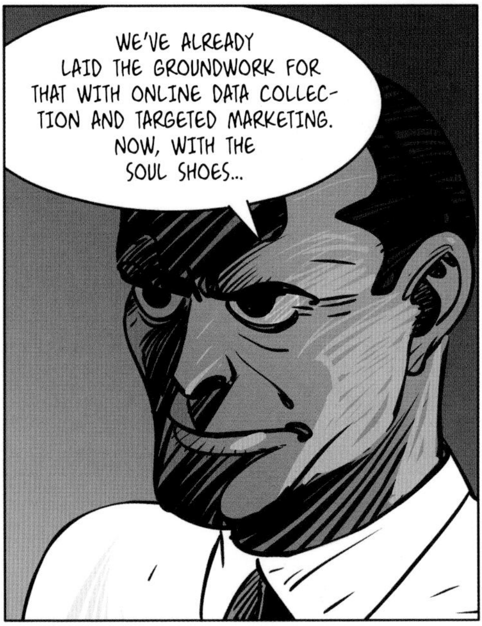
WE'VE ALREADY LAID THE GROUNDWORK FOR THAT WITH ONLINE DATA COLLECTION AND TARGETED MARKETING. NOW, WITH THE SOUL SHOES...

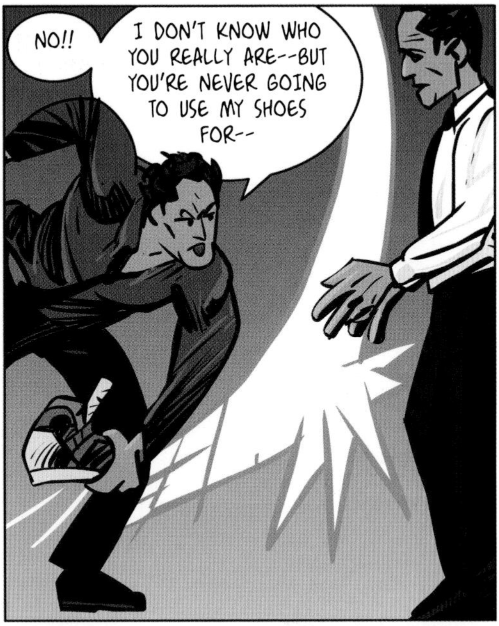
NO!!
I DON'T KNOW WHO YOU REALLY ARE--BUT YOU'RE NEVER GOING TO USE MY SHOES FOR--

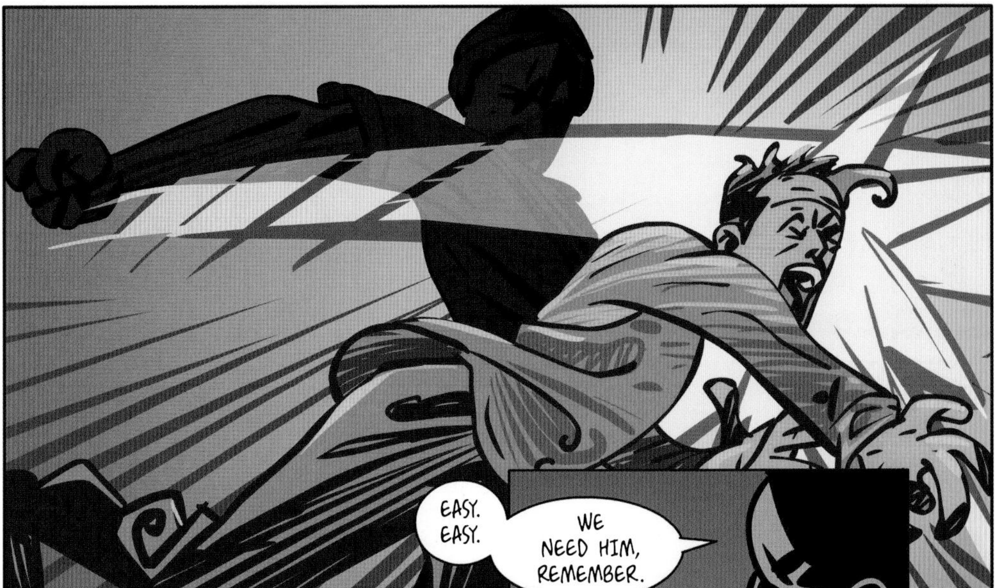

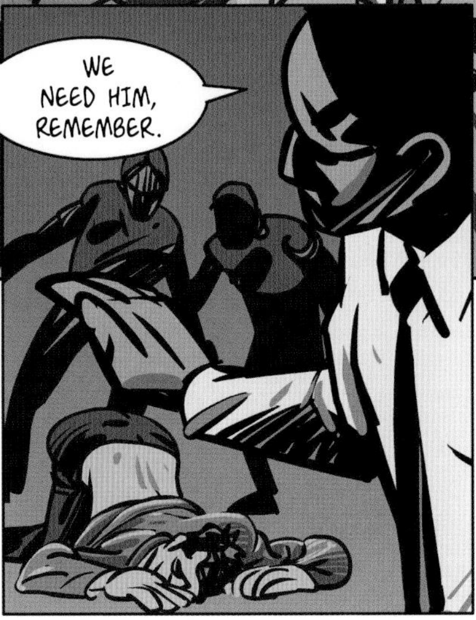
EASY. EASY.
WE NEED HIM, REMEMBER.

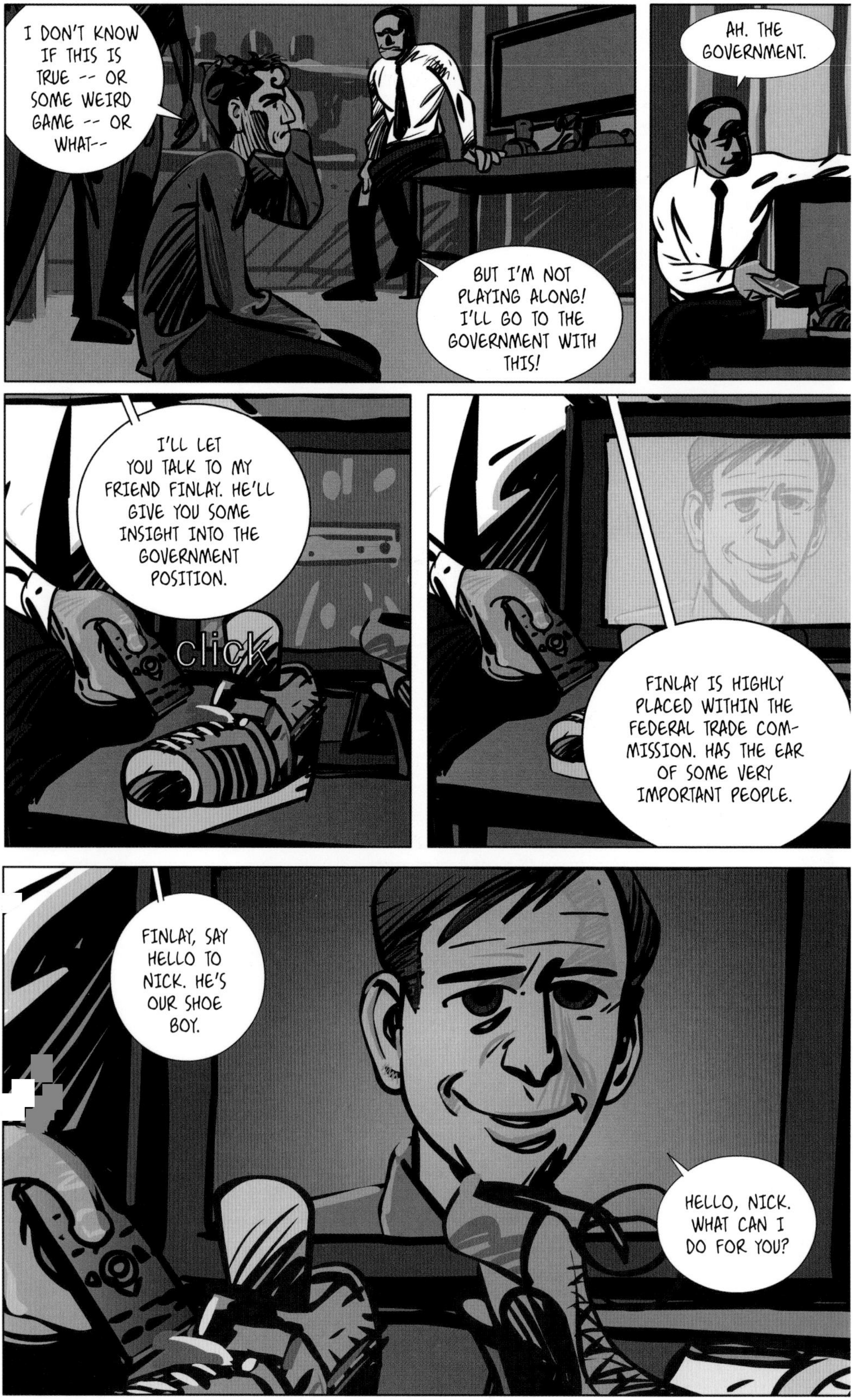
I DON'T KNOW IF THIS IS TRUE -- OR SOME WEIRD GAME -- OR WHAT--
BUT I'M NOT PLAYING ALONG! I'LL GO TO THE GOVERNMENT WITH THIS!
AH. THE GOVERNMENT.
I'LL LET YOU TALK TO MY FRIEND FINLAY. HE'LL GIVE YOU SOME INSIGHT INTO THE GOVERNMENT POSITION.
click
FINLAY IS HIGHLY PLACED WITHIN THE FEDERAL TRADE COM-MISSION. HAS THE EAR OF SOME VERY IMPORTANT PEOPLE.
FINLAY, SAY HELLO TO NICK. HE'S OUR SHOE BOY.
HELLO, NICK. WHAT CAN I DO FOR YOU?

THESE... THESE STORIES...

THE OTHER DIMENSION... THE LABELING...

INCREDIBLE, ISN'T IT? FOR GENERATIONS WE IN THE GOVERNMENT HAVE BEEN LOOKING FOR BETTER WAYS TO MANAGE PEOPLE.

WE'VE BEEN MAKING HUGE PROGRESS, OF COURSE, WITH ALL THE DATA WE'VE BEEN ABLE TO COLLECT ONLINE, WITH THE HELP OF SOCIAL NETWORKING SITES AND MARKETERS AND WHAT NOT...

...BUT THE ARRIVAL OF THESE--SHALL WE SAY--PEOPLE OF COLOR...WAS A MIRACLE!

AND WE'RE SO GRATEFUL THAT THEY CHOSE TO CONTACT AN INVESTOR OF SPENCER'S GRASP OF THE BIG PICTURE!

THEN THE GOVERNMENT...IS IN ON IT...?

NOW, NOW! LET'S NOT BE IMPATIENT!

SPENCER AND I GO WAY BACK. BUT I HAVE A LOT MORE PEOPLE TO CONVINCE IN WASHINGTON BEFORE THE GOVERNMENT'S REALLY BEHIND US!

THAT'S WHY YOU'VE GOT TO MAKE THIS SHOE PLAN WORK, SON.

YOUR NATION IS COUNTING ON YOU.

THANK YOU, FINLAY.

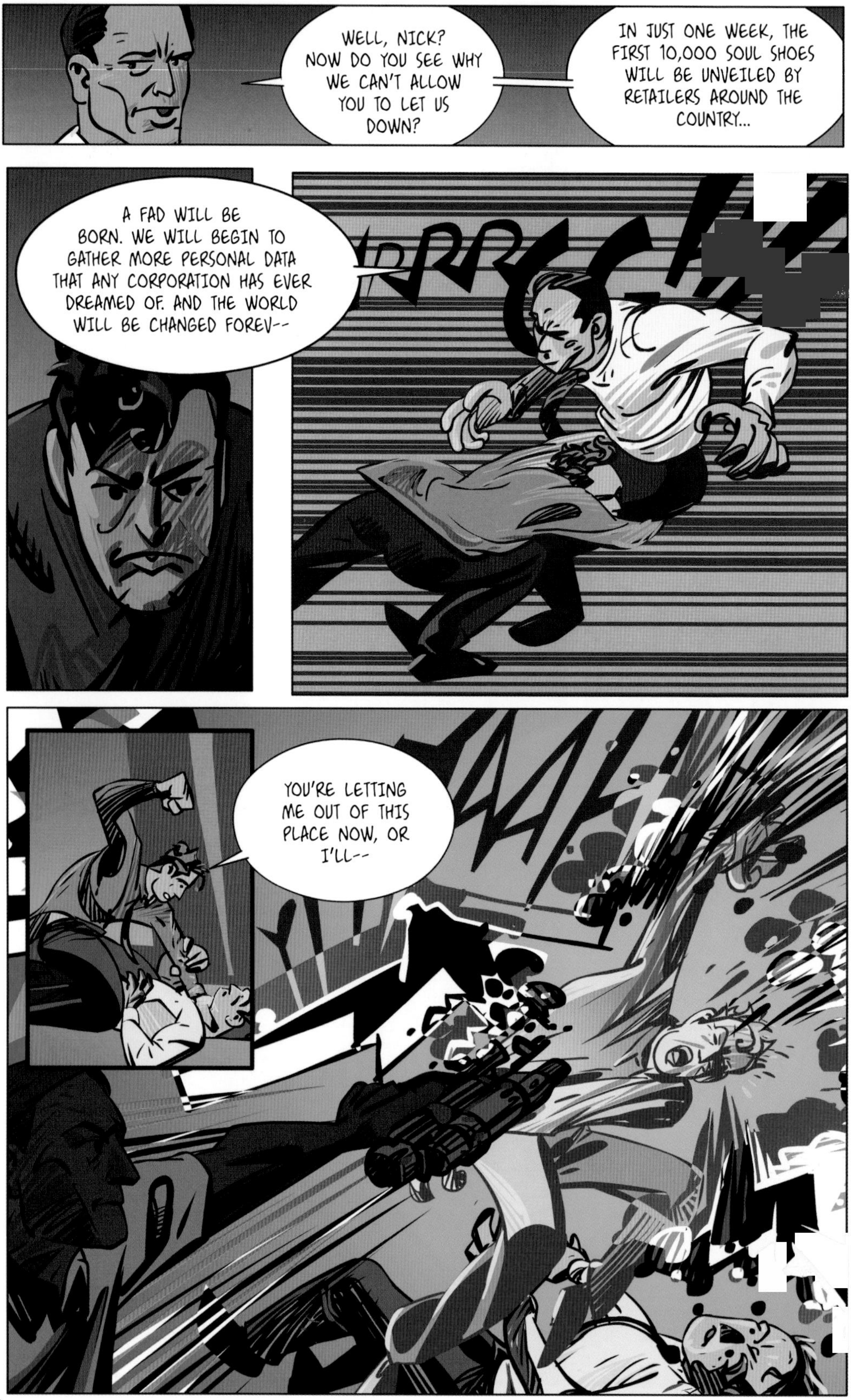
WELL, NICK? NOW DO YOU SEE WHY WE CAN'T ALLOW YOU TO LET US DOWN?
IN JUST ONE WEEK, THE FIRST 10,000 SOUL SHOES WILL BE UNVEILED BY RETAILERS AROUND THE COUNTRY...
A FAD WILL BE BORN. WE WILL BEGIN TO GATHER MORE PERSONAL DATA THAT ANY CORPORATION HAS EVER DREAMED OF. AND THE WORLD WILL BE CHANGED FOREV--
YOU'RE LETTING ME OUT OF THIS PLACE NOW, OR I'LL--

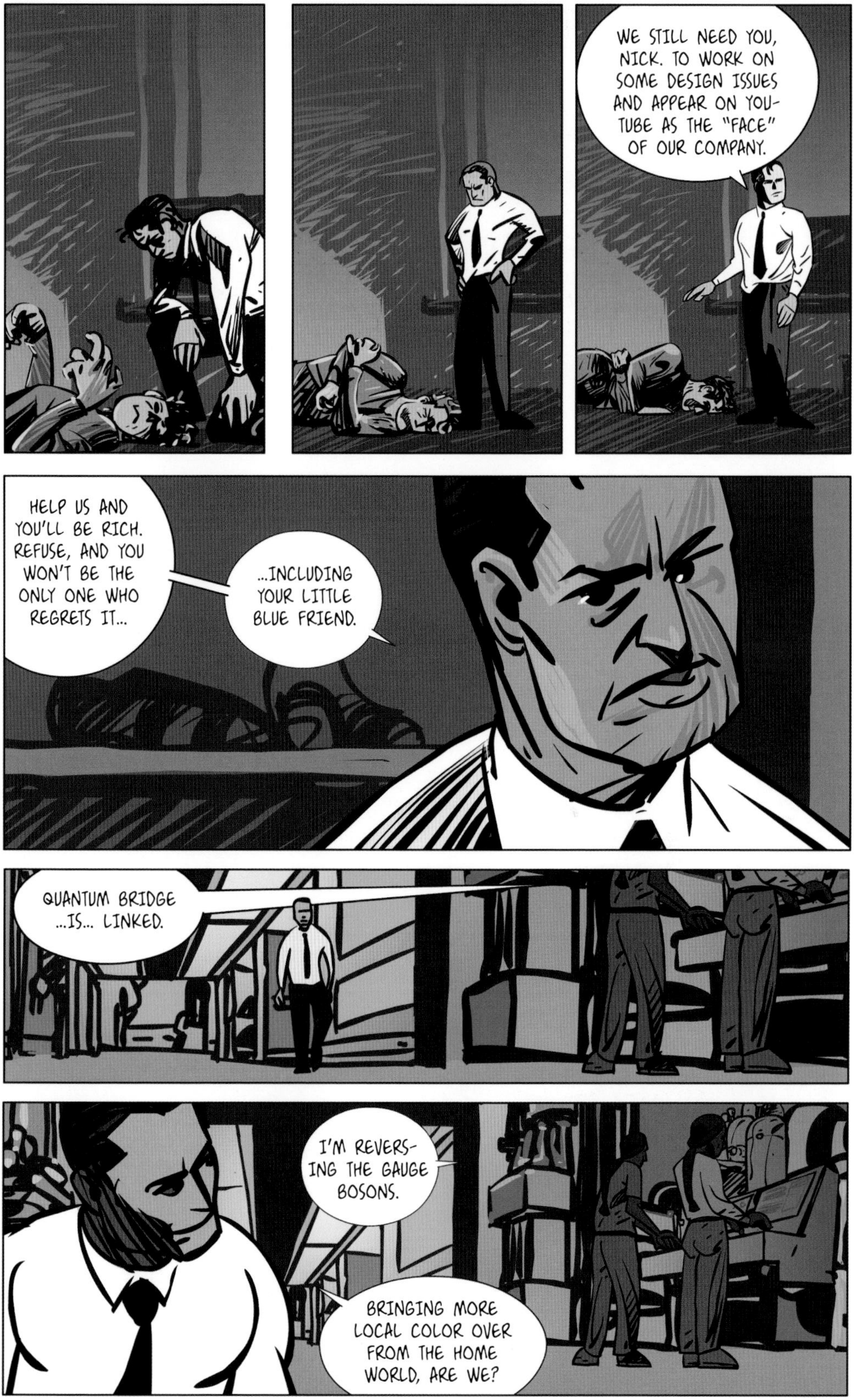
WE STILL NEED YOU, NICK. TO WORK ON SOME DESIGN ISSUES AND APPEAR ON YOU-TUBE AS THE "FACE" OF OUR COMPANY.
HELP US AND YOU'LL BE RICH. REFUSE, AND YOU WON'T BE THE ONLY ONE WHO REGRETS IT...
...INCLUDING YOUR LITTLE BLUE FRIEND.
QUANTUM BRIDGE ...IS... LINKED.
I'M REVERS-ING THE GAUGE BOSONS.
BRINGING MORE LOCAL COLOR OVER FROM THE HOME WORLD, ARE WE?

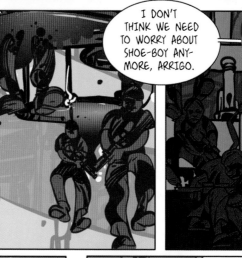

I DON'T THINK WE NEED TO WORRY ABOUT SHOE-BOY ANYMORE, ARRIGO.

FOUND YOUR BLUE HOME GIRL YET?

FORTUNATELY SHE'S WEARING A PAIR OF HIS SHOES...

...AND THEY'RE TELLING US EXACTLY WHERE SHE IS.

AND HOW, TONIGHT OF ALL NIGHTS, COULD SHE NOT?

WE'LL HAVE OUR LAST LOOSE END TIED UP IN MINUTES.

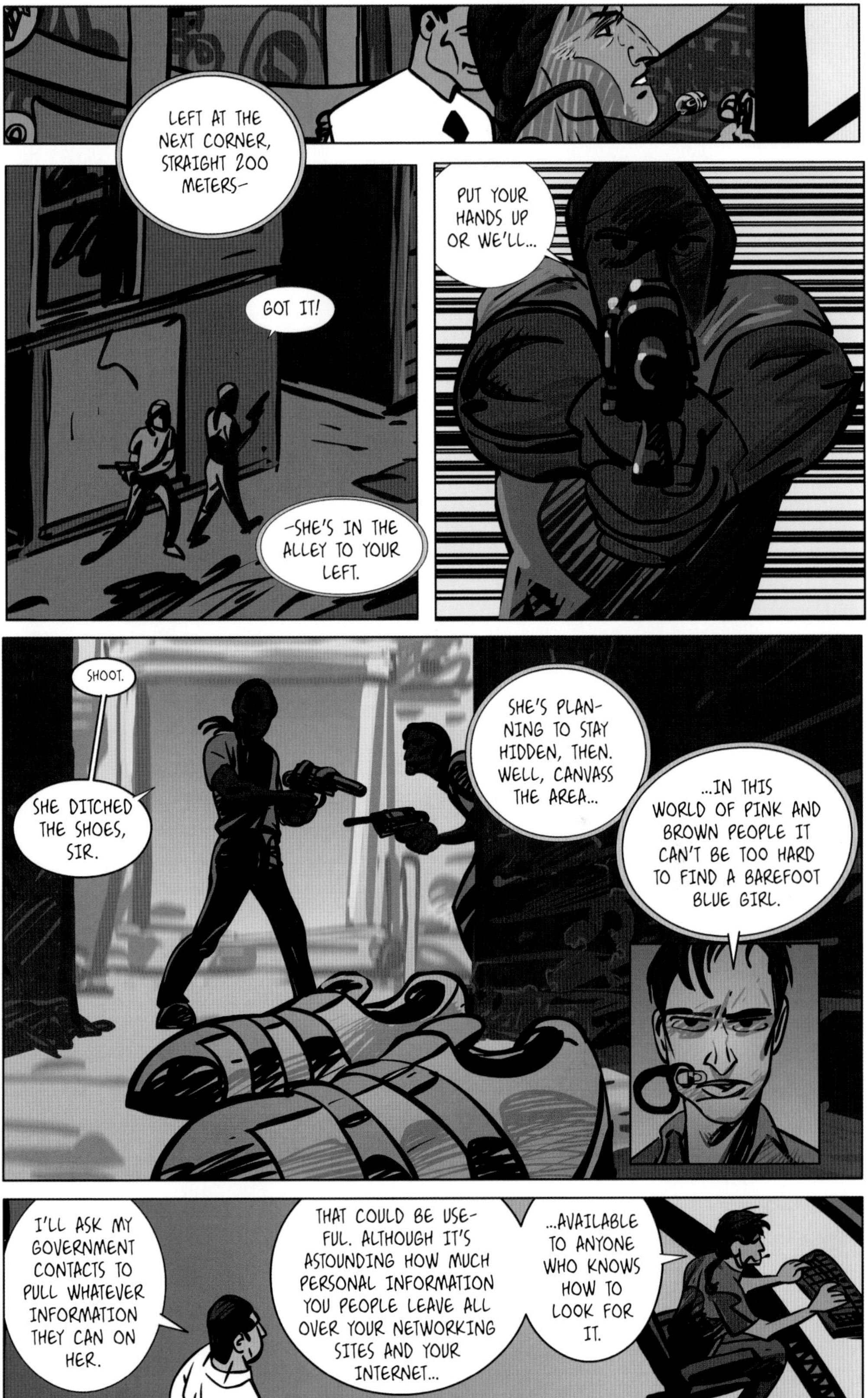
LEFT AT THE NEXT CORNER, STRAIGHT 200 METERS–
GOT IT!
–SHE'S IN THE ALLEY TO YOUR LEFT.
PUT YOUR HANDS UP OR WE'LL...
SHOOT.
SHE DITCHED THE SHOES, SIR.
SHE'S PLAN-NING TO STAY HIDDEN, THEN. WELL, CANVASS THE AREA...
...IN THIS WORLD OF PINK AND BROWN PEOPLE IT CAN'T BE TOO HARD TO FIND A BAREFOOT BLUE GIRL.
I'LL ASK MY GOVERNMENT CONTACTS TO PULL WHATEVER INFORMATION THEY CAN ON HER.
THAT COULD BE USE-FUL. ALTHOUGH IT'S ASTOUNDING HOW MUCH PERSONAL INFORMATION YOU PEOPLE LEAVE ALL OVER YOUR NETWORKING SITES AND YOUR INTERNET...
...AVAILABLE TO ANYONE WHO KNOWS HOW TO LOOK FOR IT.

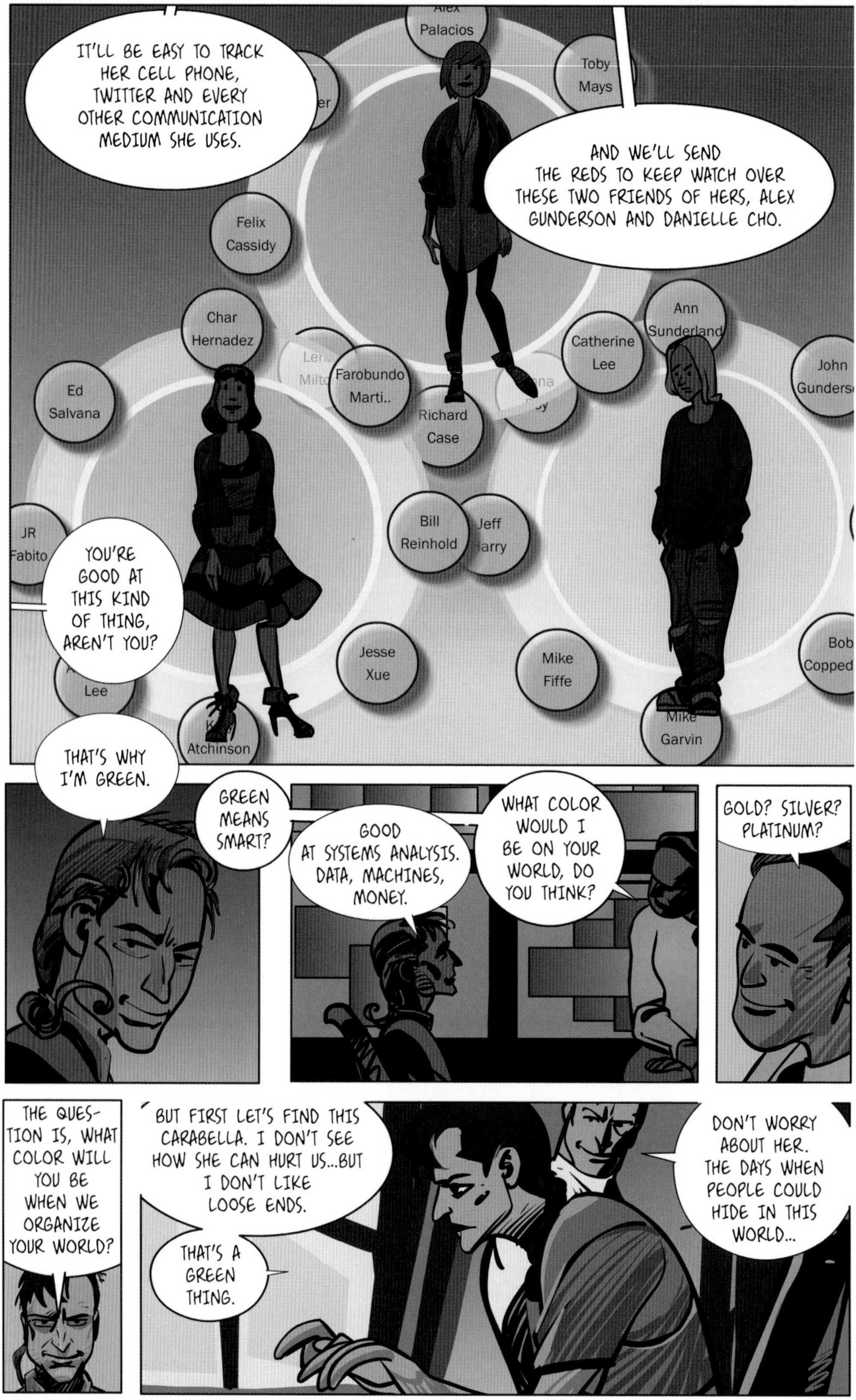
IT'LL BE EASY TO TRACK HER CELL PHONE, TWITTER AND EVERY OTHER COMMUNICATION MEDIUM SHE USES.
AND WE'LL SEND THE REDS TO KEEP WATCH OVER THESE TWO FRIENDS OF HERS, ALEX GUNDERSON AND DANIELLE CHO.
Palacios
Toby Mays
Felix Cassidy
Char Hernadez
Farobundo Marti..
Richard Case
Catherine Lee
Ann Sunderland
Ed Salvana
Bill Reinhold
JR Fabito
Jesse Xue
Mike Fiffe
Lee
Atchinson
Garvin
YOU'RE GOOD AT THIS KIND OF THING, AREN'T YOU?
THAT'S WHY I'M GREEN.
GREEN MEANS SMART?
GOOD AT SYSTEMS ANALYSIS. DATA, MACHINES, MONEY.
WHAT COLOR WOULD I BE ON YOUR WORLD, DO YOU THINK?
GOLD? SILVER? PLATINUM?
THE QUES-TION IS, WHAT COLOR WILL YOU BE WHEN WE ORGANIZE YOUR WORLD?
BUT FIRST LET'S FIND THIS CARABELLA. I DON'T SEE HOW SHE CAN HURT US...BUT I DON'T LIKE LOOSE ENDS.
THAT'S A GREEN THING.
DON'T WORRY ABOUT HER. THE DAYS WHEN PEOPLE COULD HIDE IN THIS WORLD...

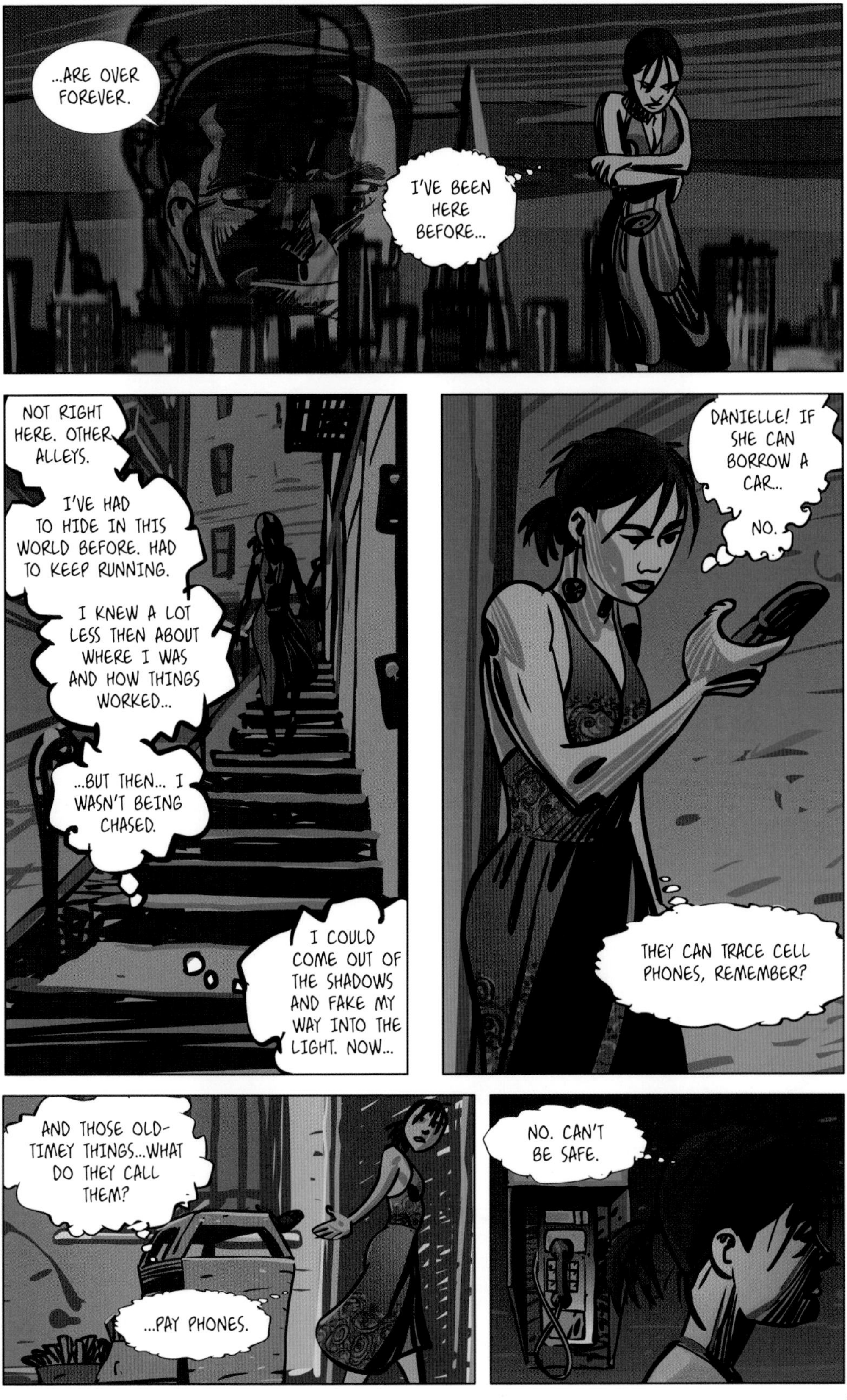

...ARE OVER FOREVER.
I'VE BEEN HERE BEFORE...
NOT RIGHT HERE. OTHER ALLEYS.
I'VE HAD TO HIDE IN THIS WORLD BEFORE. HAD TO KEEP RUNNING.
I KNEW A LOT LESS THEN ABOUT WHERE I WAS AND HOW THINGS WORKED...
...BUT THEN... I WASN'T BEING CHASED.
I COULD COME OUT OF THE SHADOWS AND FAKE MY WAY INTO THE LIGHT. NOW...
DANIELLE! IF SHE CAN BORROW A CAR...
NO.
THEY CAN TRACE CELL PHONES, REMEMBER?
AND THOSE OLD-TIMEY THINGS...WHAT DO THEY CALL THEM?
...PAY PHONES.
NO. CAN'T BE SAFE.

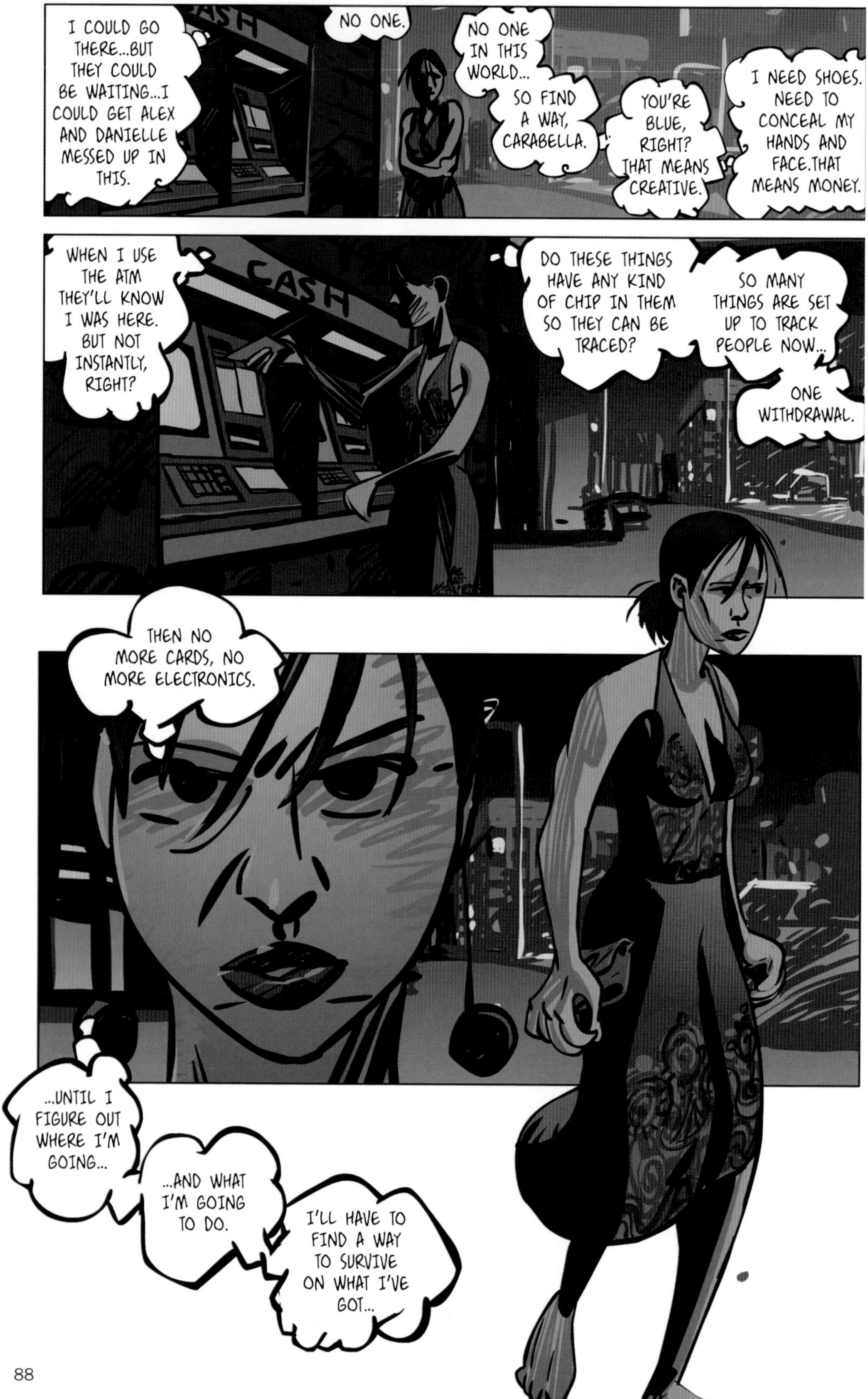
I COULD GO THERE...BUT THEY COULD BE WAITING...I COULD GET ALEX AND DANIELLE MESSED UP IN THIS.
NO ONE.
NO ONE IN THIS WORLD...
SO FIND A WAY, CARABELLA.
YOU'RE BLUE, RIGHT? THAT MEANS CREATIVE.
I NEED SHOES. NEED TO CONCEAL MY HANDS AND FACE.THAT MEANS MONEY.
CASH
WHEN I USE THE ATM THEY'LL KNOW I WAS HERE. BUT NOT INSTANTLY, RIGHT?
DO THESE THINGS HAVE ANY KIND OF CHIP IN THEM SO THEY CAN BE TRACED?
SO MANY THINGS ARE SET UP TO TRACK PEOPLE NOW...
ONE WITHDRAWAL.
THEN NO MORE CARDS, NO MORE ELECTRONICS.
...UNTIL I FIGURE OUT WHERE I'M GOING...
...AND WHAT I'M GOING TO DO.
I'LL HAVE TO FIND A WAY TO SURVIVE ON WHAT I'VE GOT...

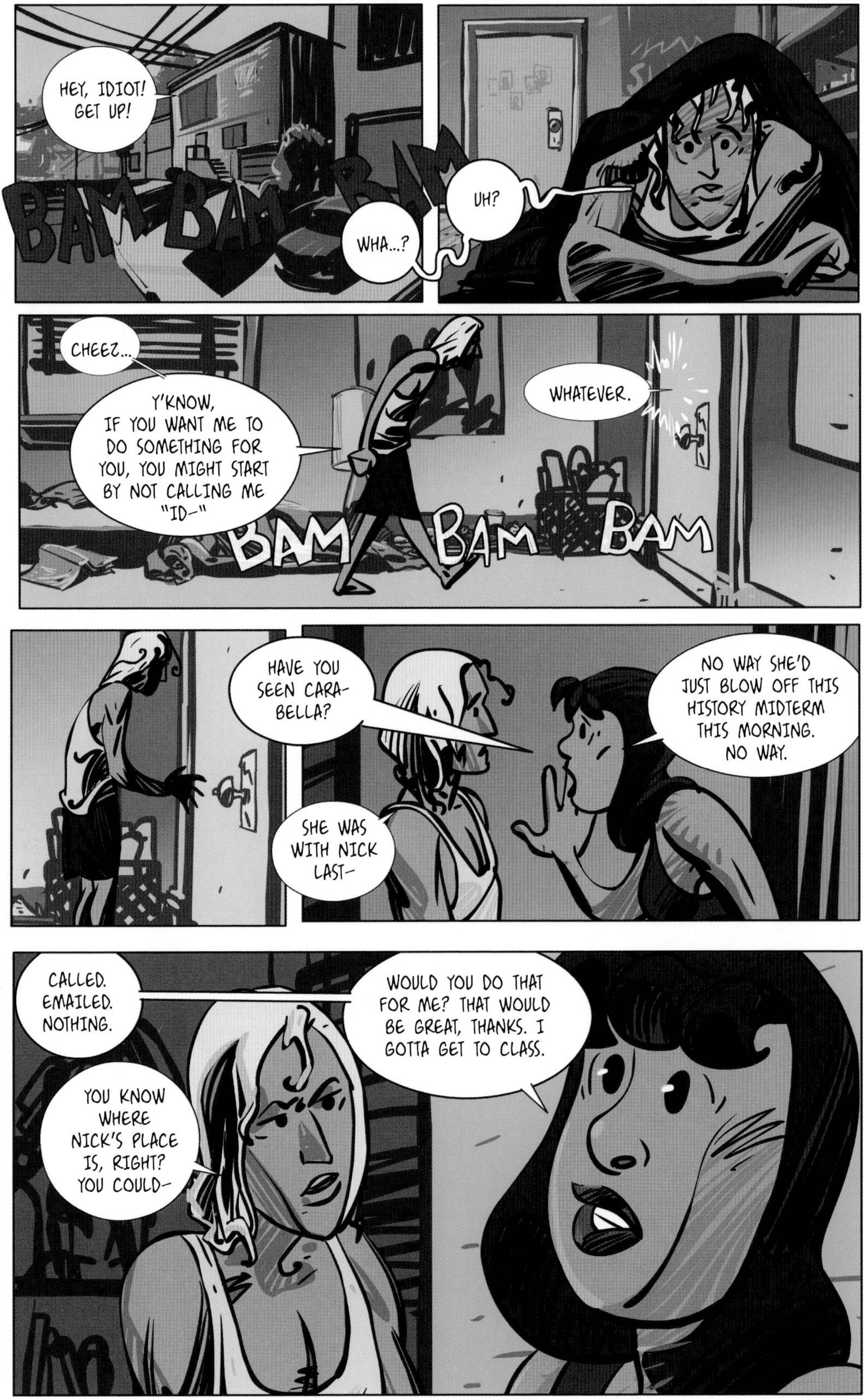
HEY, IDIOT! GET UP!
BAM BAM BAM BAM
UH?
WHA...?
CHEEZ...
Y'KNOW, IF YOU WANT ME TO DO SOMETHING FOR YOU, YOU MIGHT START BY NOT CALLING ME "ID–"
WHATEVER.
BAM BAM BAM
HAVE YOU SEEN CARA-BELLA?
SHE WAS WITH NICK LAST–
NO WAY SHE'D JUST BLOW OFF THIS HISTORY MIDTERM THIS MORNING. NO WAY.
CALLED. EMAILED. NOTHING.
YOU KNOW WHERE NICK'S PLACE IS, RIGHT? YOU COULD–
WOULD YOU DO THAT FOR ME? THAT WOULD BE GREAT, THANKS. I GOTTA GET TO CLASS.

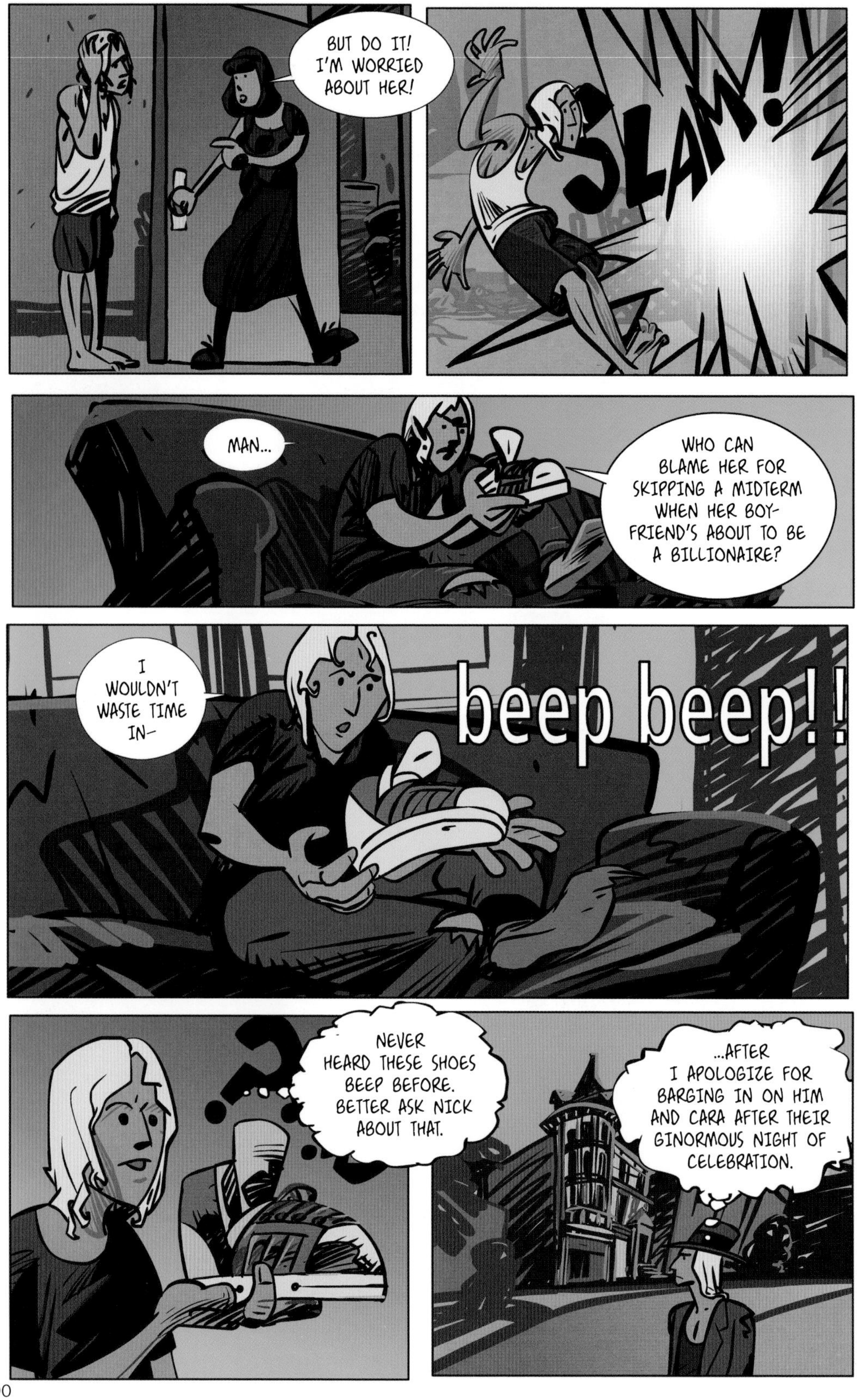
BUT DO IT! I'M WORRIED ABOUT HER!
SLAM!
MAN...
WHO CAN BLAME HER FOR SKIPPING A MIDTERM WHEN HER BOY-FRIEND'S ABOUT TO BE A BILLIONAIRE?
I WOULDN'T WASTE TIME IN-
beep beep!!
NEVER HEARD THESE SHOES BEEP BEFORE. BETTER ASK NICK ABOUT THAT.
...AFTER I APOLOGIZE FOR BARGING IN ON HIM AND CARA AFTER THEIR GINORMOUS NIGHT OF CELEBRATION.

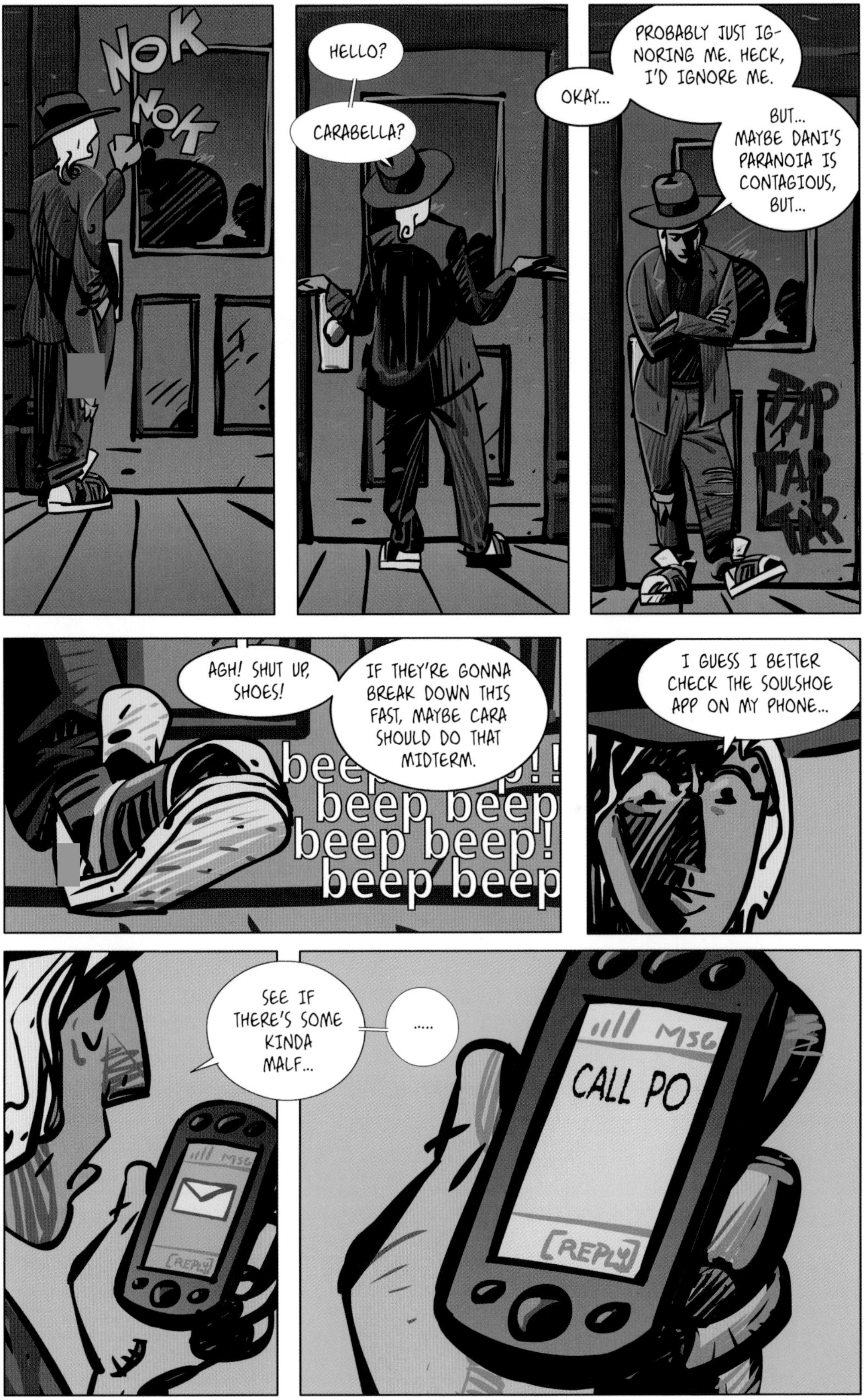
NOK
NOK
HELLO?
CARABELLA?
OKAY...
PROBABLY JUST IG-NORING ME. HECK, I'D IGNORE ME.
BUT... MAYBE DANI'S PARANOIA IS CONTAGIOUS, BUT...
TAP TAP TAP
AGH! SHUT UP, SHOES!
IF THEY'RE GONNA BREAK DOWN THIS FAST, MAYBE CARA SHOULD DO THAT MIDTERM.
beep beep
beep beep!
beep beep
I GUESS I BETTER CHECK THE SOULSHOE APP ON MY PHONE...
SEE IF THERE'S SOME KINDA MALF...
.....
MSG
REPLY
MSG
CALL PO
REPLY

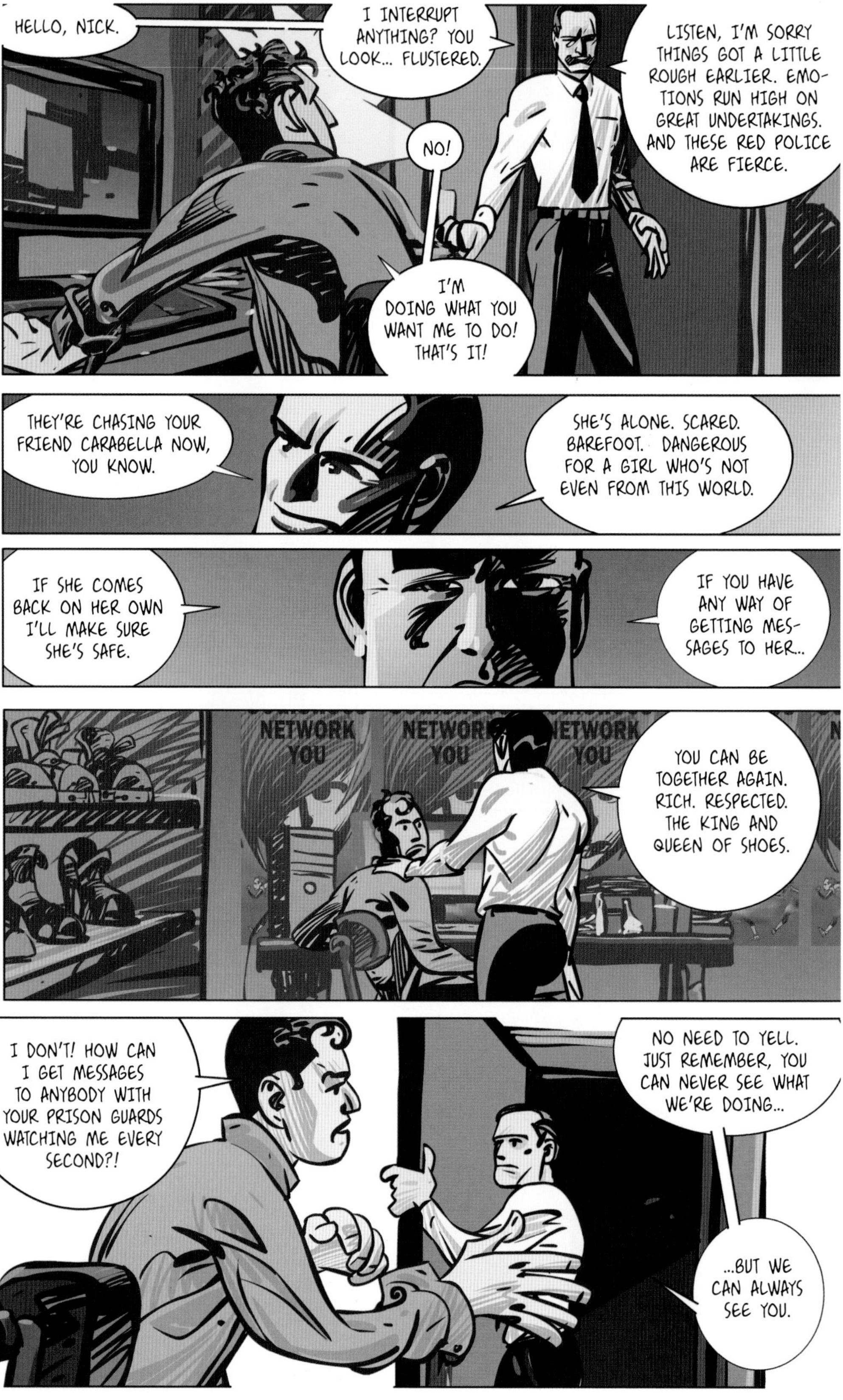
HELLO, NICK.
I INTERRUPT ANYTHING? YOU LOOK... FLUSTERED.
LISTEN, I'M SORRY THINGS GOT A LITTLE ROUGH EARLIER. EMOTIONS RUN HIGH ON GREAT UNDERTAKINGS. AND THESE RED POLICE ARE FIERCE.
NO!
I'M DOING WHAT YOU WANT ME TO DO! THAT'S IT!
THEY'RE CHASING YOUR FRIEND CARABELLA NOW, YOU KNOW.
SHE'S ALONE. SCARED. BAREFOOT. DANGEROUS FOR A GIRL WHO'S NOT EVEN FROM THIS WORLD.
IF SHE COMES BACK ON HER OWN I'LL MAKE SURE SHE'S SAFE.
IF YOU HAVE ANY WAY OF GETTING MESSAGES TO HER...
NETWORK YOU
NETWORK YOU
NETWORK YOU
YOU CAN BE TOGETHER AGAIN. RICH. RESPECTED. THE KING AND QUEEN OF SHOES.
I DON'T! HOW CAN I GET MESSAGES TO ANYBODY WITH YOUR PRISON GUARDS WATCHING ME EVERY SECOND?!
NO NEED TO YELL. JUST REMEMBER, YOU CAN NEVER SEE WHAT WE'RE DOING...
...BUT WE CAN ALWAYS SEE YOU.

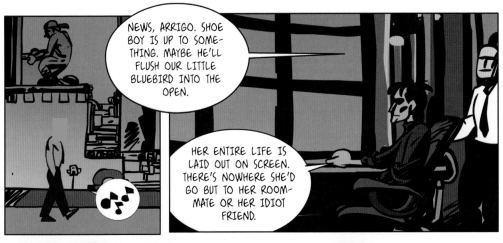

NEWS, ARRIGO. SHOE BOY IS UP TO SOMETHING. MAYBE HE'LL FLUSH OUR LITTLE BLUEBIRD INTO THE OPEN.

HER ENTIRE LIFE IS LAID OUT ON SCREEN. THERE'S NOWHERE SHE'D GO BUT TO HER ROOMMATE OR HER IDIOT FRIEND.

THEN I WANT YOU TO GET ME INTO NICK'S EMAIL ACCOUNT...

NO. FACESPACE. PEOPLE DON'T QUESTION THOSE MESSAGES THE WAY THEY DO EMAIL.

I THINK IT'S THOSE LITTLE PICTURES THAT GO ALONG WITH THEM.

LET'S HAVE NICK SEND A MESSAGE TO DANIELLE CHO.

HEY DANI. TOTALLY SWAMPED WITH SHOE STUFF..."

BUT WHAT DOES THAT EVEN MEAN, "CALL PO"?

WASN'T HE THE RED ONE WITH THE SCOOTER?

IT COULD MEAN CALL THE POLICE... BUT WHY? ABOUT WHAT?

YOU CAN'T REPORT SOMEBODY MISSING AFTER ONE NIGHT, CAN YOU?

IT'S PROBABLY JUST SOME STUPID BOT OR VIRUS OR...

HEY! MESSAGE FROM NICK!

"HEY DANI. TOTALLY SWAMPED WITH SHOE STUFF. CARA KINDA FLIPPED OUT AND RAN OFF. IF YOU HEAR FROM HER YOU GOTTA GET HER TO YOUR PLACE AND CALL ME. ITS IMPORTANT!!! OK?"

SHE FLIPPED OUT...?

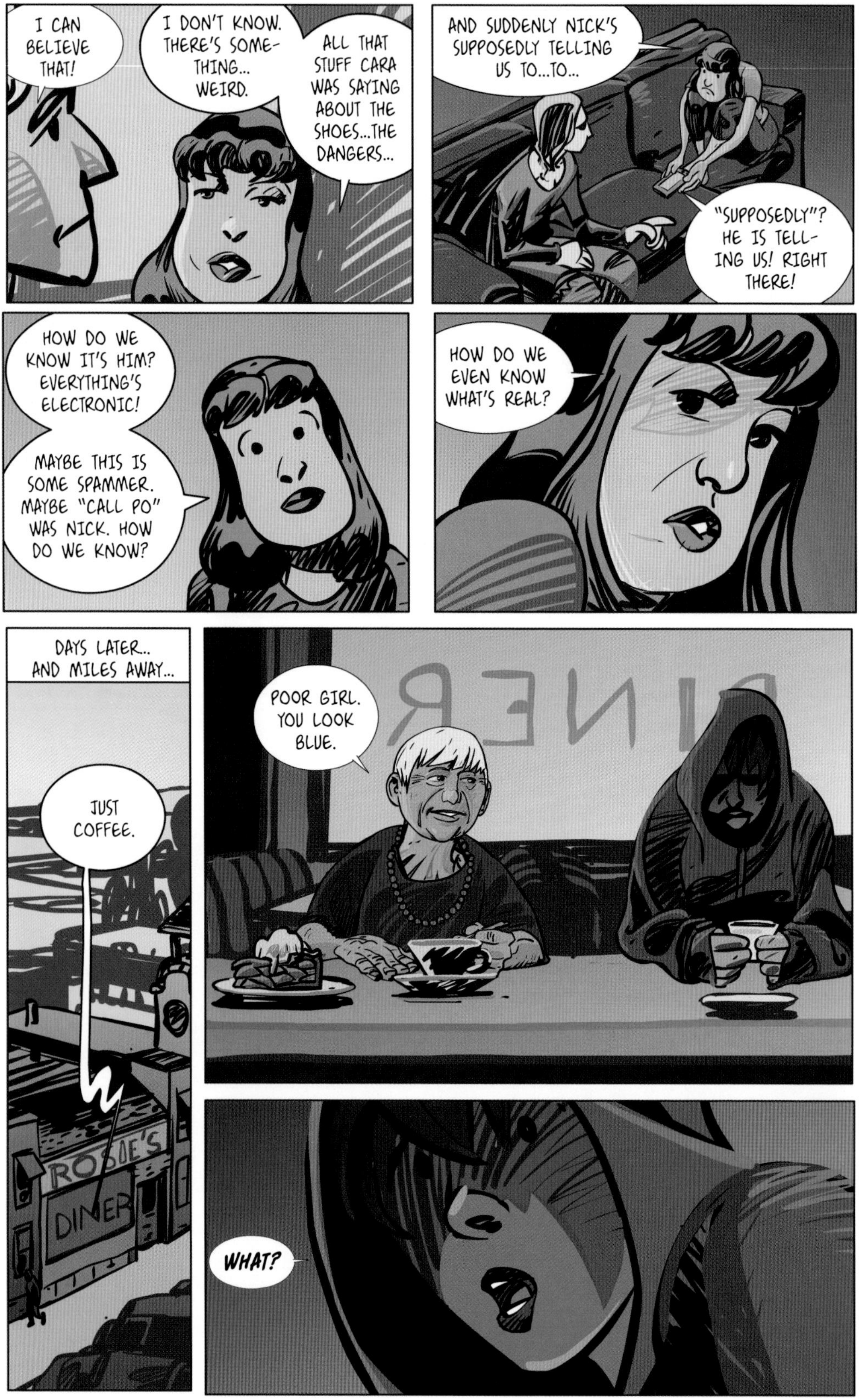
I CAN BELIEVE THAT!
I DON'T KNOW. THERE'S SOME-THING... WEIRD.
ALL THAT STUFF CARA WAS SAYING ABOUT THE SHOES...THE DANGERS...
AND SUDDENLY NICK'S SUPPOSEDLY TELLING US TO...TO...
"SUPPOSEDLY"? HE IS TELL-ING US! RIGHT THERE!
HOW DO WE KNOW IT'S HIM? EVERYTHING'S ELECTRONIC!
MAYBE THIS IS SOME SPAMMER. MAYBE "CALL PO" WAS NICK. HOW DO WE KNOW?
HOW DO WE EVEN KNOW WHAT'S REAL?
DAYS LATER... AND MILES AWAY...
JUST COFFEE.
ROSIE'S
DINER
POOR GIRL. YOU LOOK BLUE.
WHAT?

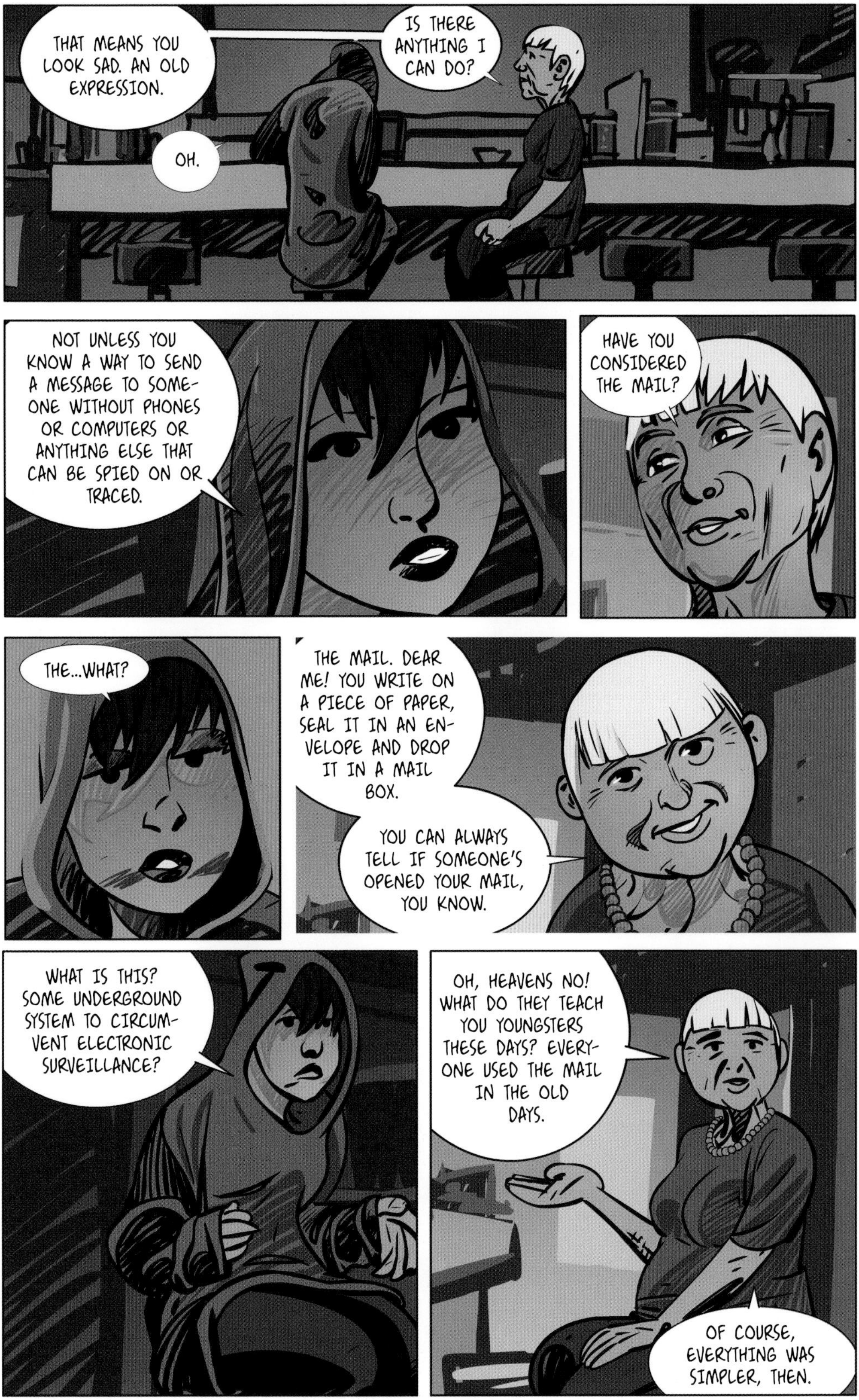
THAT MEANS YOU LOOK SAD. AN OLD EXPRESSION.
IS THERE ANYTHING I CAN DO?
OH.
NOT UNLESS YOU KNOW A WAY TO SEND A MESSAGE TO SOMEONE WITHOUT PHONES OR COMPUTERS OR ANYTHING ELSE THAT CAN BE SPIED ON OR TRACED.
HAVE YOU CONSIDERED THE MAIL?
THE...WHAT?
THE MAIL. DEAR ME! YOU WRITE ON A PIECE OF PAPER, SEAL IT IN AN ENVELOPE AND DROP IT IN A MAIL BOX.
YOU CAN ALWAYS TELL IF SOMEONE'S OPENED YOUR MAIL, YOU KNOW.
WHAT IS THIS? SOME UNDERGROUND SYSTEM TO CIRCUMVENT ELECTRONIC SURVEILLANCE?
OH, HEAVENS NO! WHAT DO THEY TEACH YOU YOUNGSTERS THESE DAYS? EVERYONE USED THE MAIL IN THE OLD DAYS.
OF COURSE, EVERYTHING WAS SIMPLER, THEN.

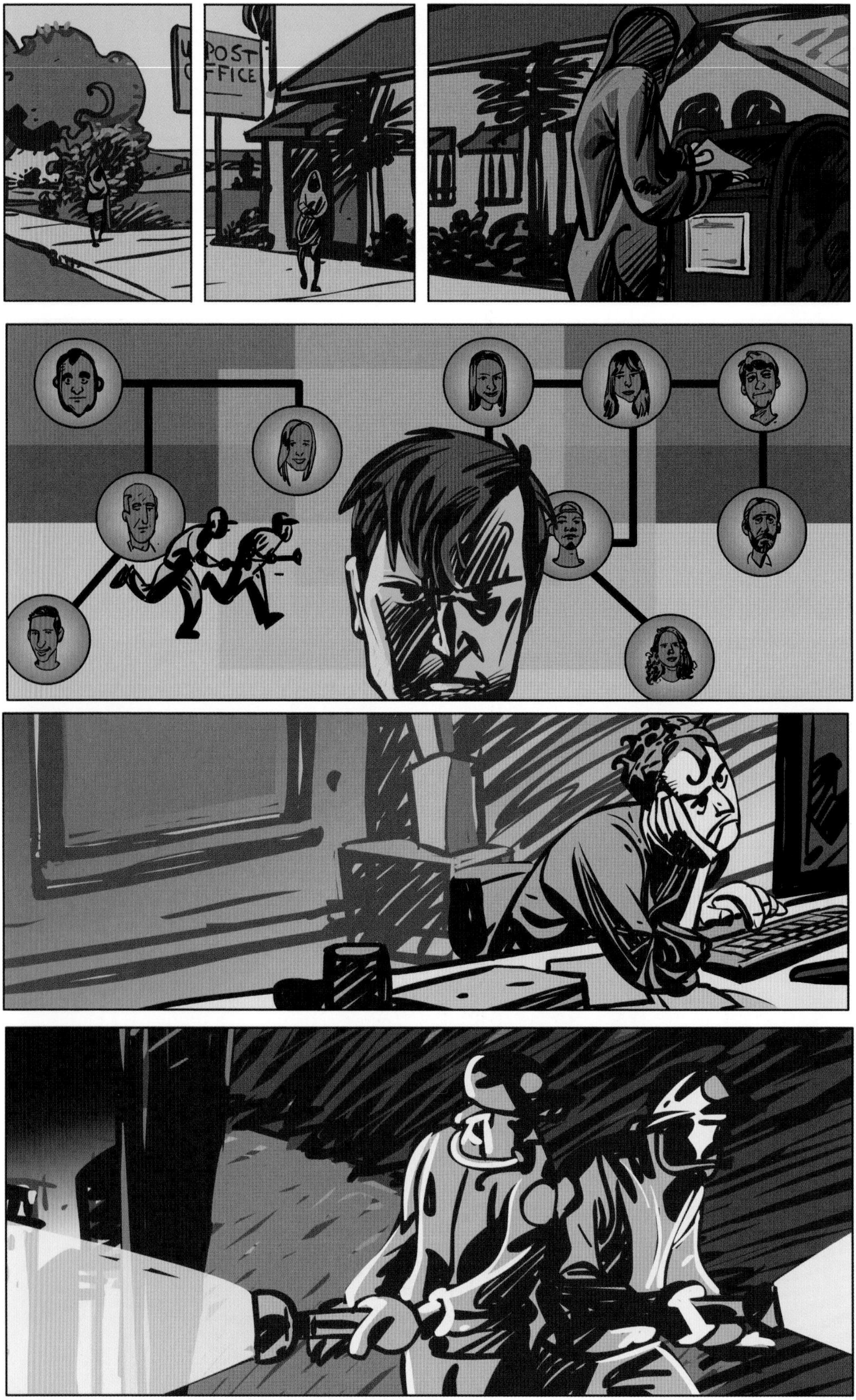
POST OFFICE

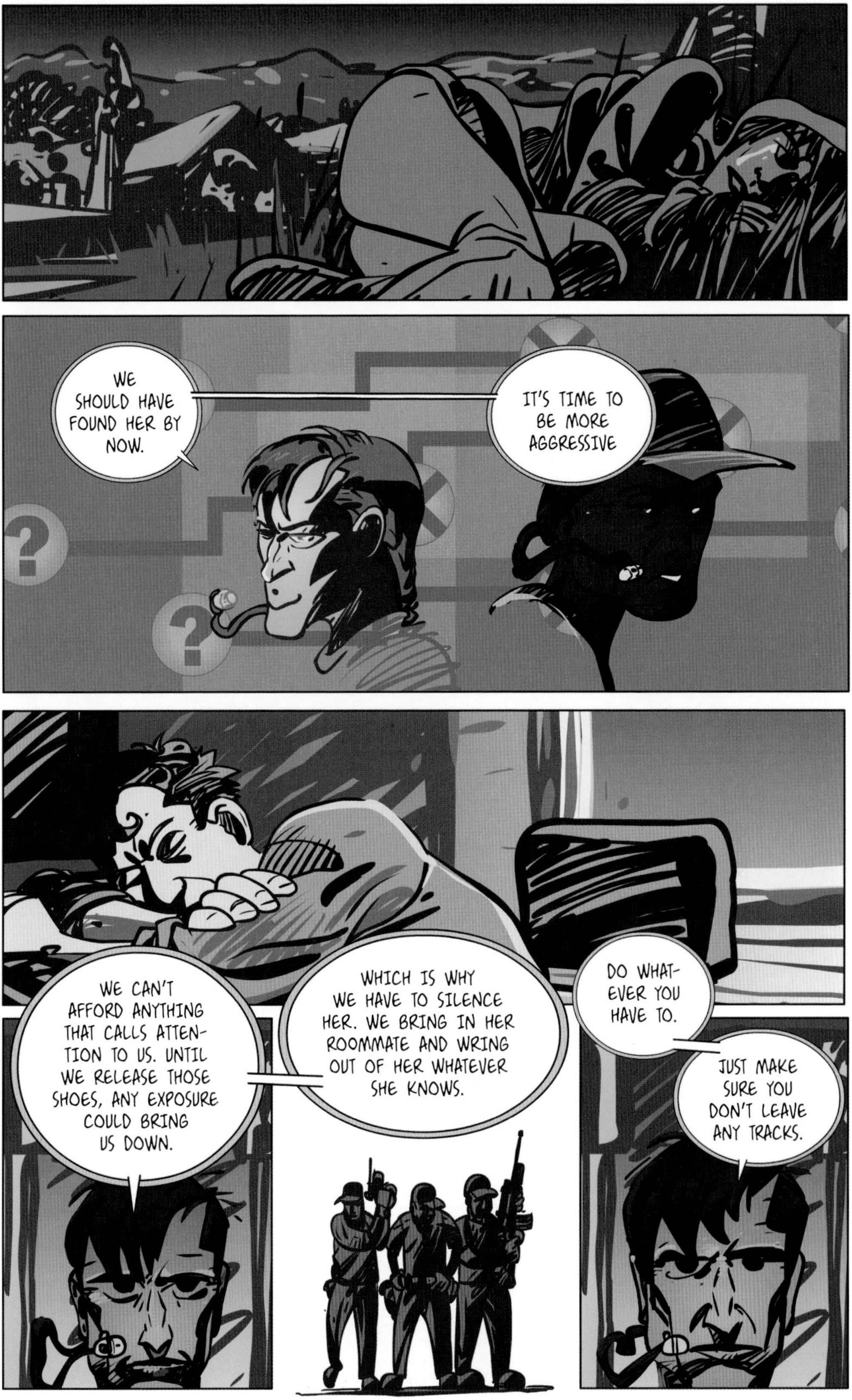
WE SHOULD HAVE FOUND HER BY NOW.
IT'S TIME TO BE MORE AGGRESSIVE
WE CAN'T AFFORD ANYTHING THAT CALLS ATTENTION TO US. UNTIL WE RELEASE THOSE SHOES, ANY EXPOSURE COULD BRING US DOWN.
WHICH IS WHY WE HAVE TO SILENCE HER. WE BRING IN HER ROOMMATE AND WRING OUT OF HER WHATEVER SHE KNOWS.
DO WHATEVER YOU HAVE TO.
JUST MAKE SURE YOU DON'T LEAVE ANY TRACKS.

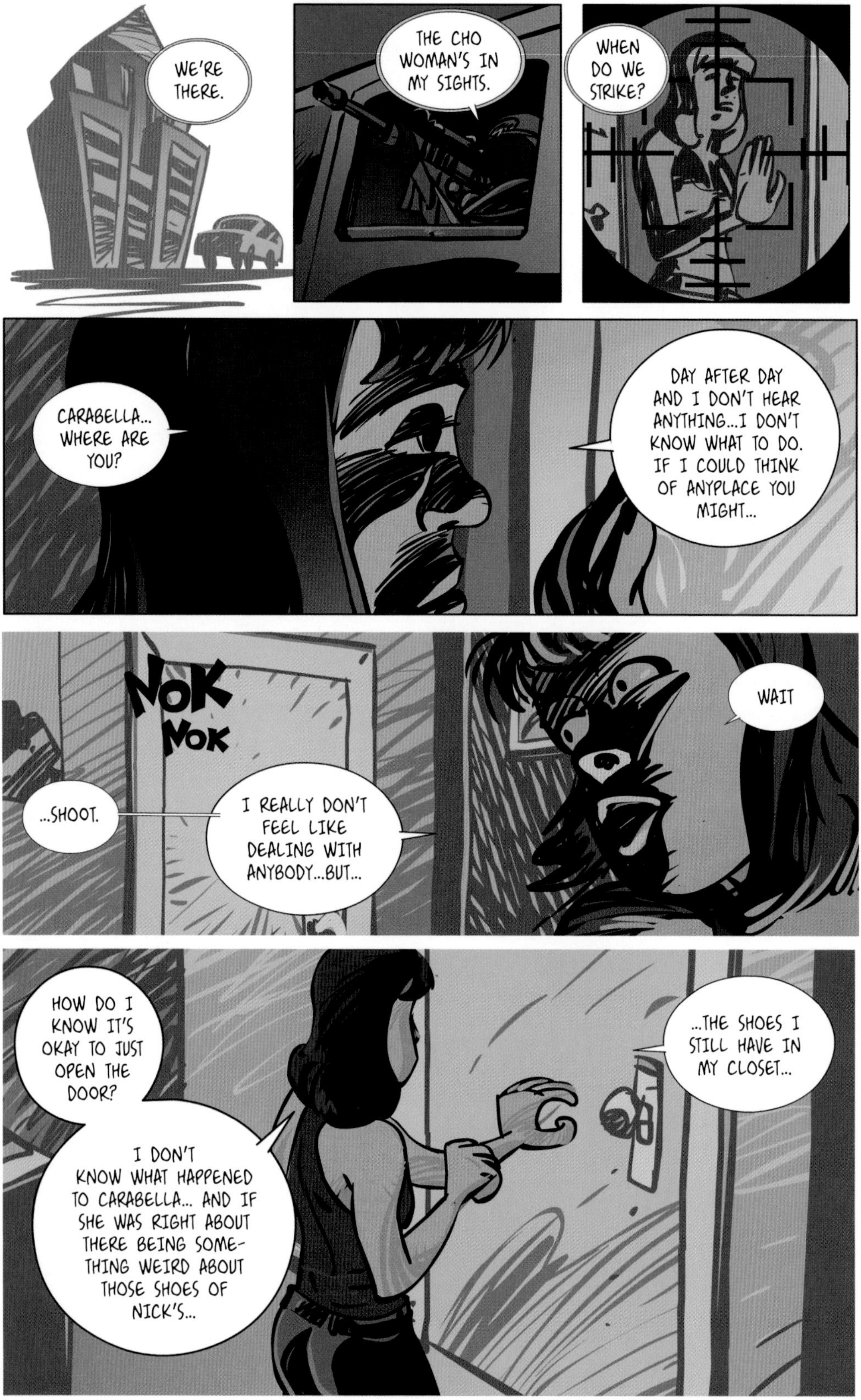
WE'RE THERE.
THE CHO WOMAN'S IN MY SIGHTS.
WHEN DO WE STRIKE?
CARABELLA... WHERE ARE YOU?
DAY AFTER DAY AND I DON'T HEAR ANYTHING...I DON'T KNOW WHAT TO DO. IF I COULD THINK OF ANYPLACE YOU MIGHT...
NOK NOK
WAIT
...SHOOT.
I REALLY DON'T FEEL LIKE DEALING WITH ANYBODY...BUT...
HOW DO I KNOW IT'S OKAY TO JUST OPEN THE DOOR?
I DON'T KNOW WHAT HAPPENED TO CARABELLA... AND IF SHE WAS RIGHT ABOUT THERE BEING SOME-THING WEIRD ABOUT THOSE SHOES OF NICK'S...
...THE SHOES I STILL HAVE IN MY CLOSET...

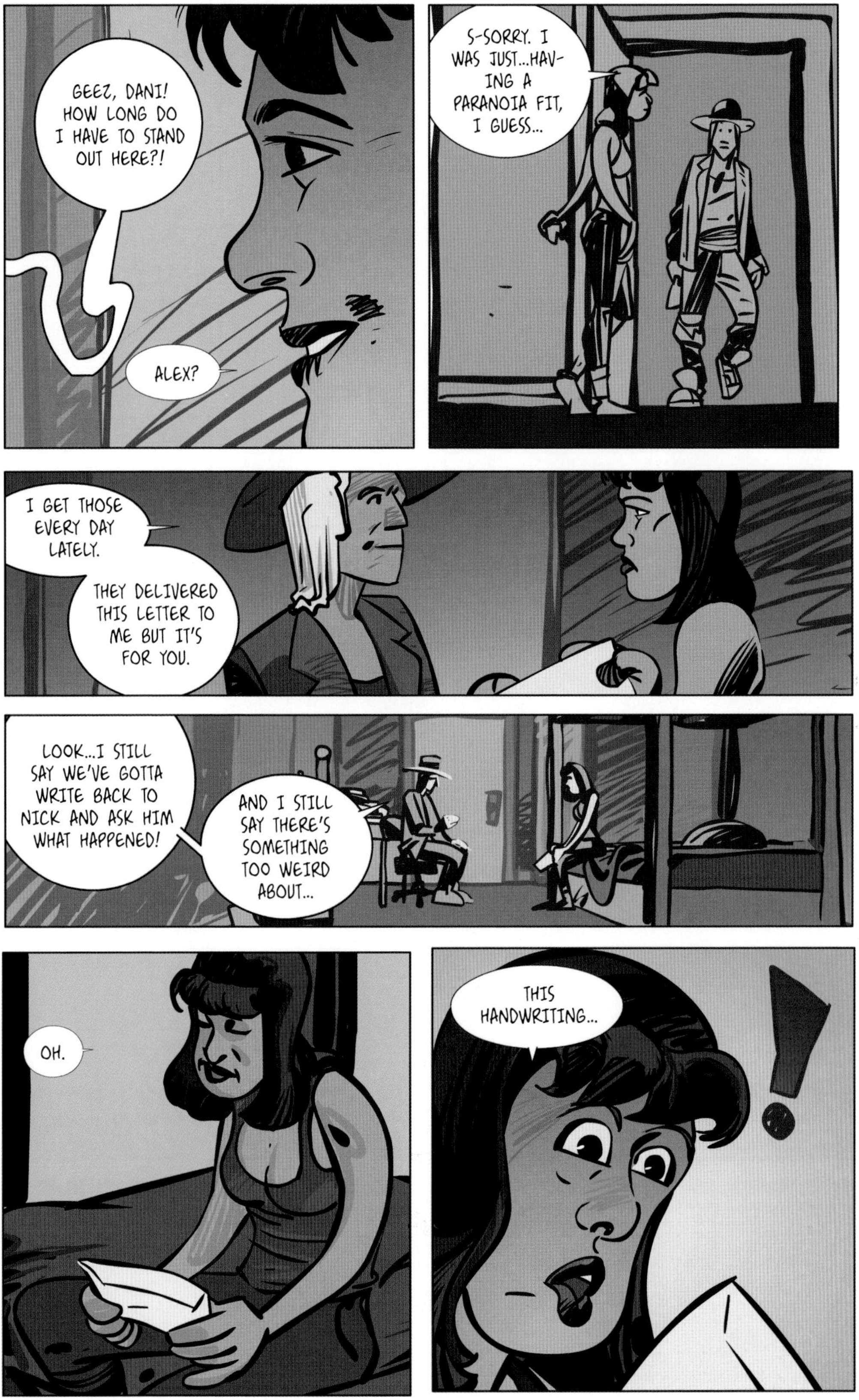
GEEZ, DANI! HOW LONG DO I HAVE TO STAND OUT HERE?!
ALEX?
S-SORRY. I WAS JUST...HAV-ING A PARANOIA FIT, I GUESS...
I GET THOSE EVERY DAY LATELY.
THEY DELIVERED THIS LETTER TO ME BUT IT'S FOR YOU.
LOOK...I STILL SAY WE'VE GOTTA WRITE BACK TO NICK AND ASK HIM WHAT HAPPENED!
AND I STILL SAY THERE'S SOMETHING TOO WEIRD ABOUT...
OH.
THIS HANDWRITING...

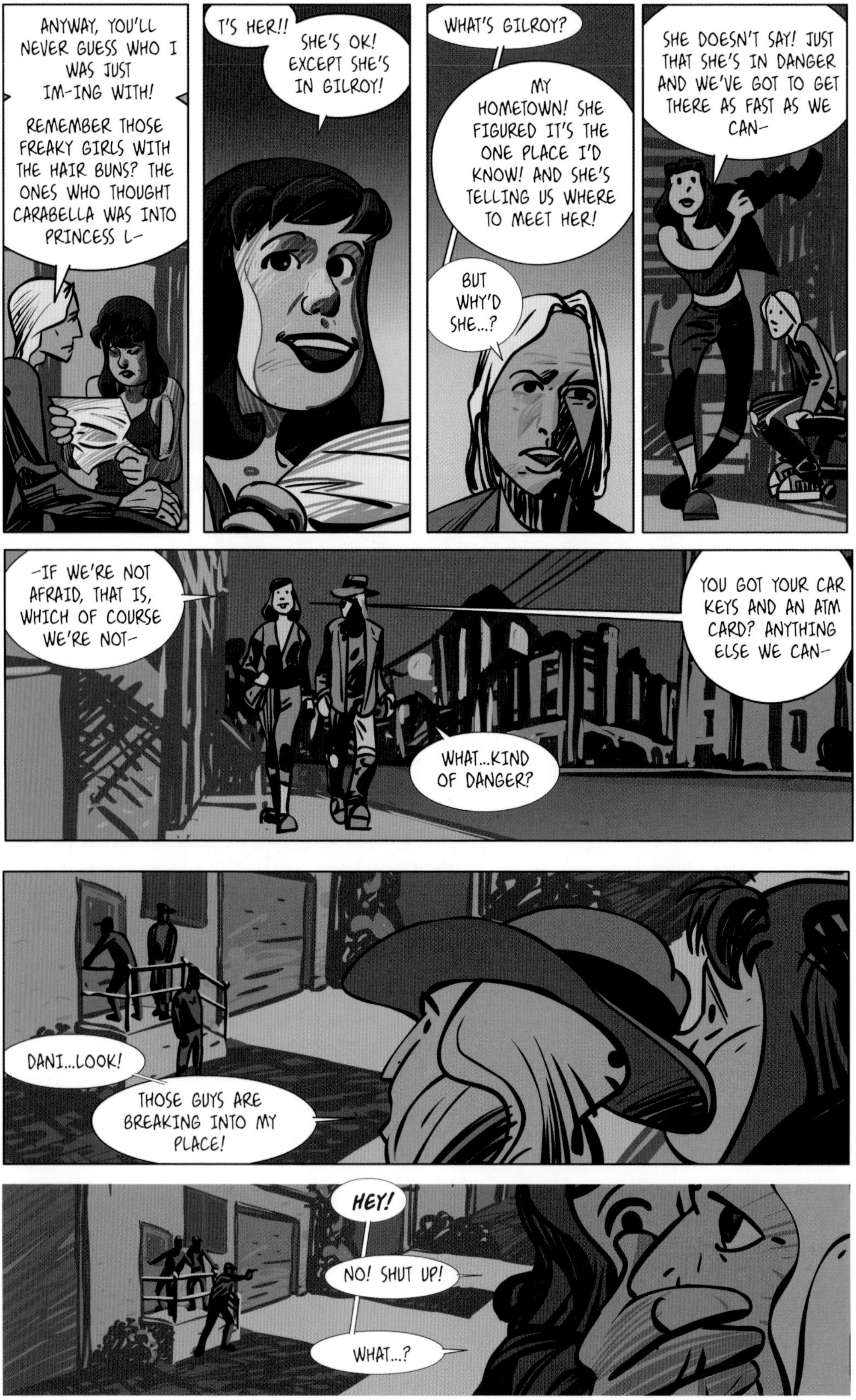
ANYWAY, YOU'LL NEVER GUESS WHO I WAS JUST IM-ING WITH!
REMEMBER THOSE FREAKY GIRLS WITH THE HAIR BUNS? THE ONES WHO THOUGHT CARABELLA WAS INTO PRINCESS L–
T'S HER!!
SHE'S OK! EXCEPT SHE'S IN GILROY!
WHAT'S GILROY?
MY HOMETOWN! SHE FIGURED IT'S THE ONE PLACE I'D KNOW! AND SHE'S TELLING US WHERE TO MEET HER!
BUT WHY'D SHE...?
SHE DOESN'T SAY! JUST THAT SHE'S IN DANGER AND WE'VE GOT TO GET THERE AS FAST AS WE CAN–
–IF WE'RE NOT AFRAID, THAT IS, WHICH OF COURSE WE'RE NOT–
YOU GOT YOUR CAR KEYS AND AN ATM CARD? ANYTHING ELSE WE CAN–
WHAT...KIND OF DANGER?
DANI...LOOK!
THOSE GUYS ARE BREAKING INTO MY PLACE!
HEY!
NO! SHUT UP!
WHAT...?

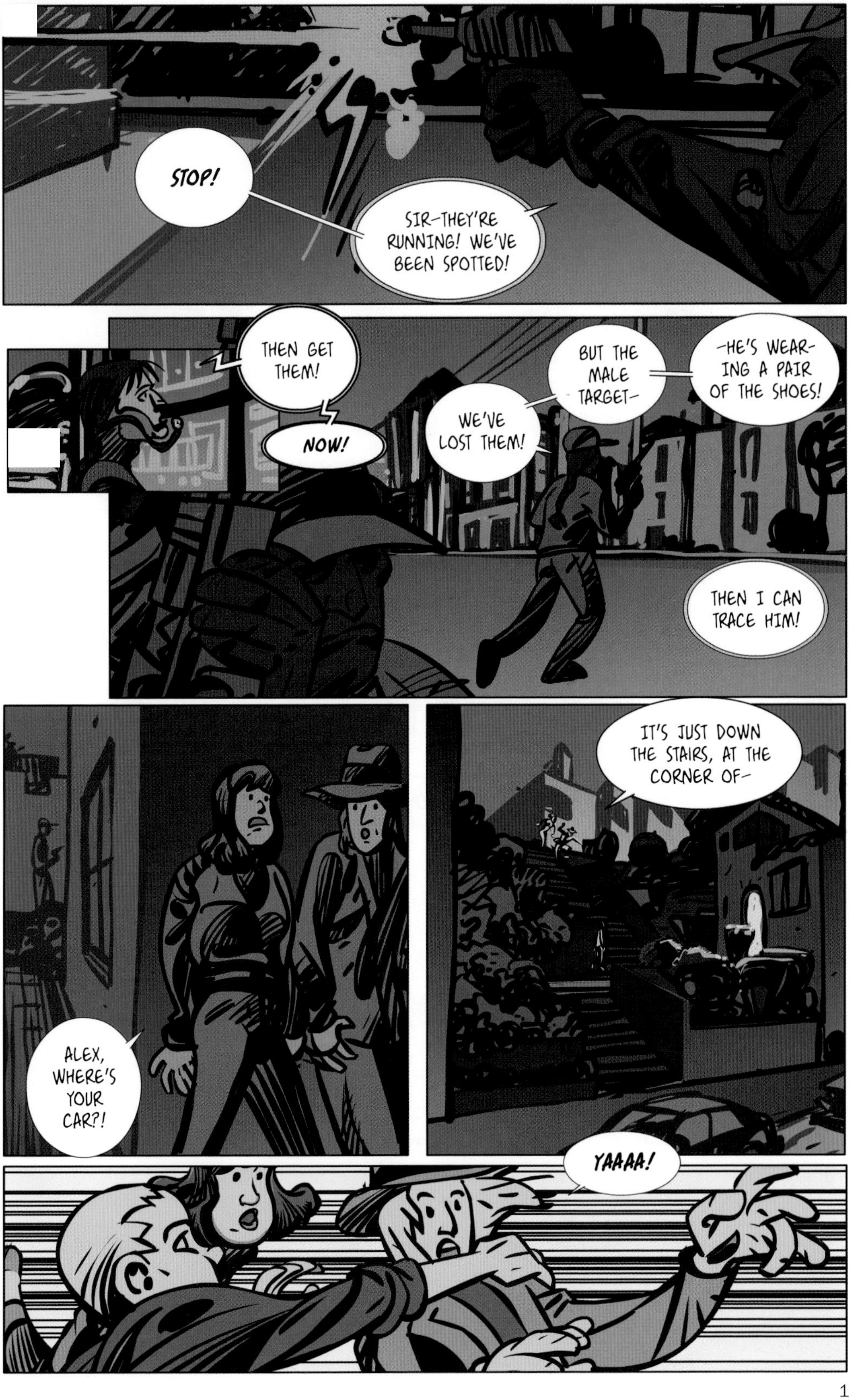
STOP!
SIR—THEY'RE RUNNING! WE'VE BEEN SPOTTED!
THEN GET THEM!
NOW!
WE'VE LOST THEM!
BUT THE MALE TARGET—
—HE'S WEARING A PAIR OF THE SHOES!
THEN I CAN TRACE HIM!
ALEX, WHERE'S YOUR CAR?!
IT'S JUST DOWN THE STAIRS, AT THE CORNER OF—
YAAAA!

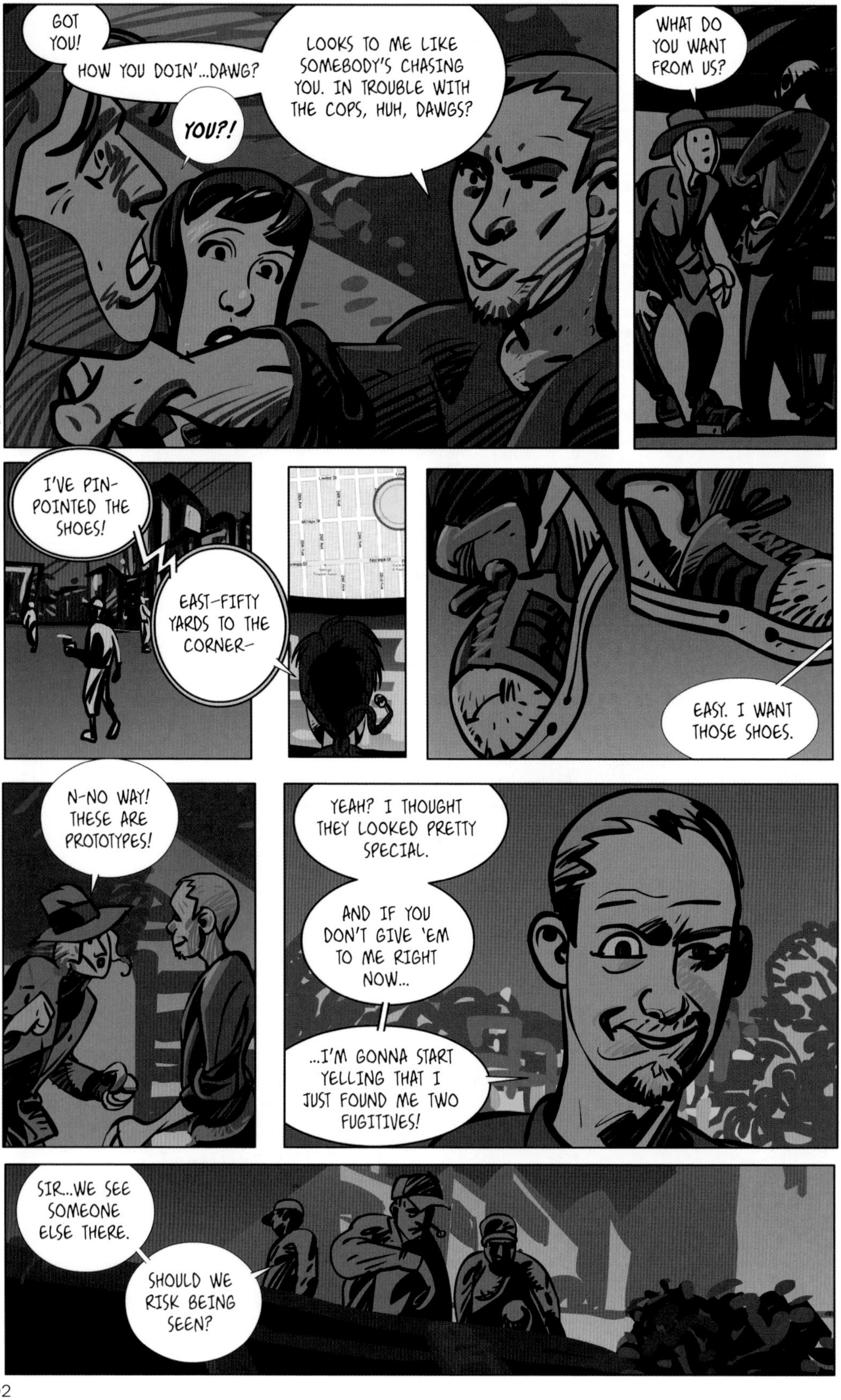
GOT YOU!
HOW YOU DOIN'...DAWG?
YOU?!
LOOKS TO ME LIKE SOMEBODY'S CHASING YOU. IN TROUBLE WITH THE COPS, HUH, DAWGS?
WHAT DO YOU WANT FROM US?
I'VE PIN-POINTED THE SHOES!
EAST-FIFTY YARDS TO THE CORNER-
EASY. I WANT THOSE SHOES.
N-NO WAY! THESE ARE PROTOTYPES!
YEAH? I THOUGHT THEY LOOKED PRETTY SPECIAL.
AND IF YOU DON'T GIVE 'EM TO ME RIGHT NOW...
...I'M GONNA START YELLING THAT I JUST FOUND ME TWO FUGITIVES!
SIR...WE SEE SOMEONE ELSE THERE.
SHOULD WE RISK BEING SEEN?

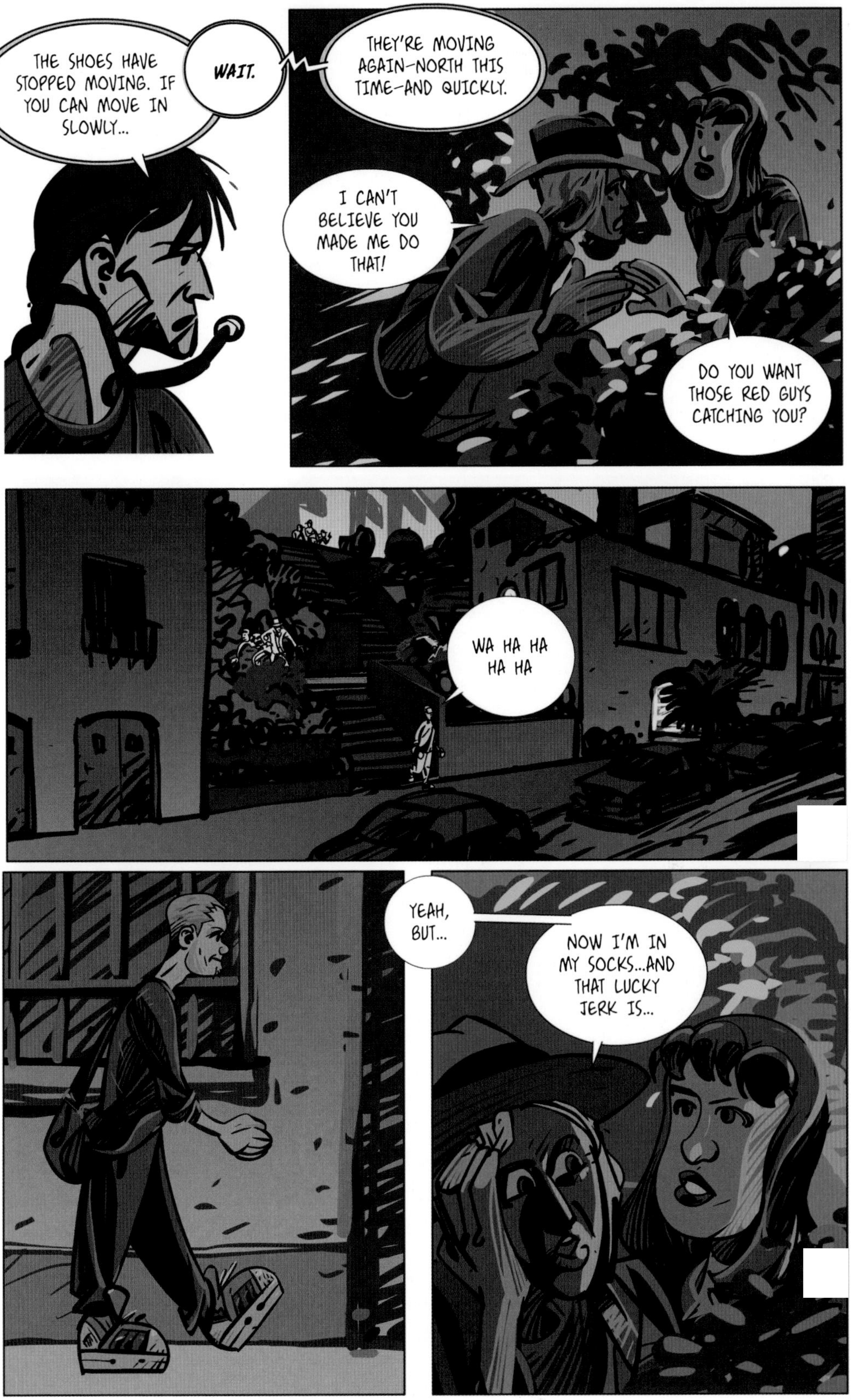
THE SHOES HAVE STOPPED MOVING. IF YOU CAN MOVE IN SLOWLY...
WAIT.
THEY'RE MOVING AGAIN—NORTH THIS TIME—AND QUICKLY.
I CAN'T BELIEVE YOU MADE ME DO THAT!
DO YOU WANT THOSE RED GUYS CATCHING YOU?
WA HA HA HA HA
YEAH, BUT...
NOW I'M IN MY SOCKS...AND THAT LUCKY JERK IS...

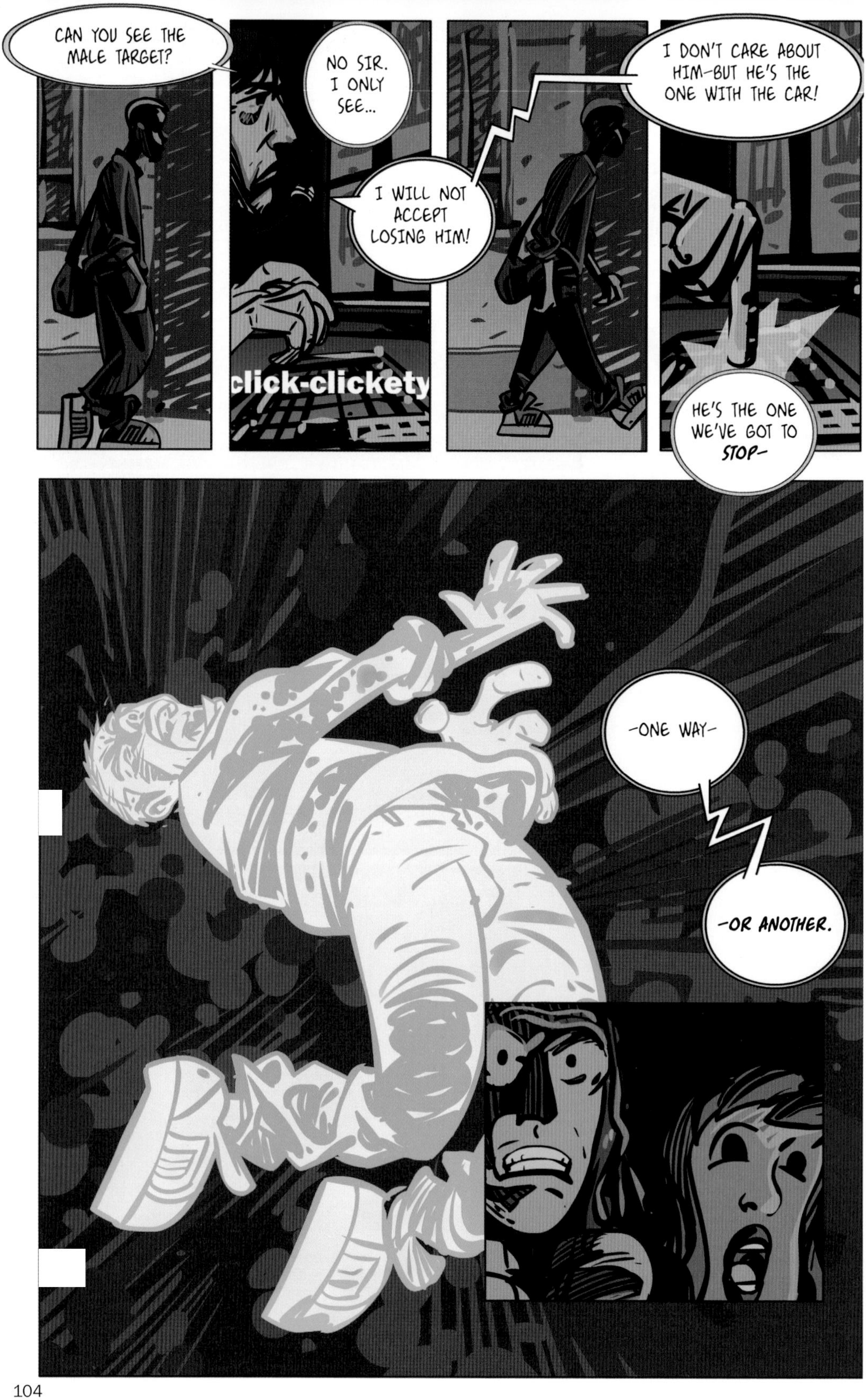

CAN YOU SEE THE MALE TARGET?
NO SIR. I ONLY SEE...
I WILL NOT ACCEPT LOSING HIM!
click-clickety
I DON'T CARE ABOUT HIM—BUT HE'S THE ONE WITH THE CAR!
HE'S THE ONE WE'VE GOT TO STOP—
—ONE WAY—
—OR ANOTHER.

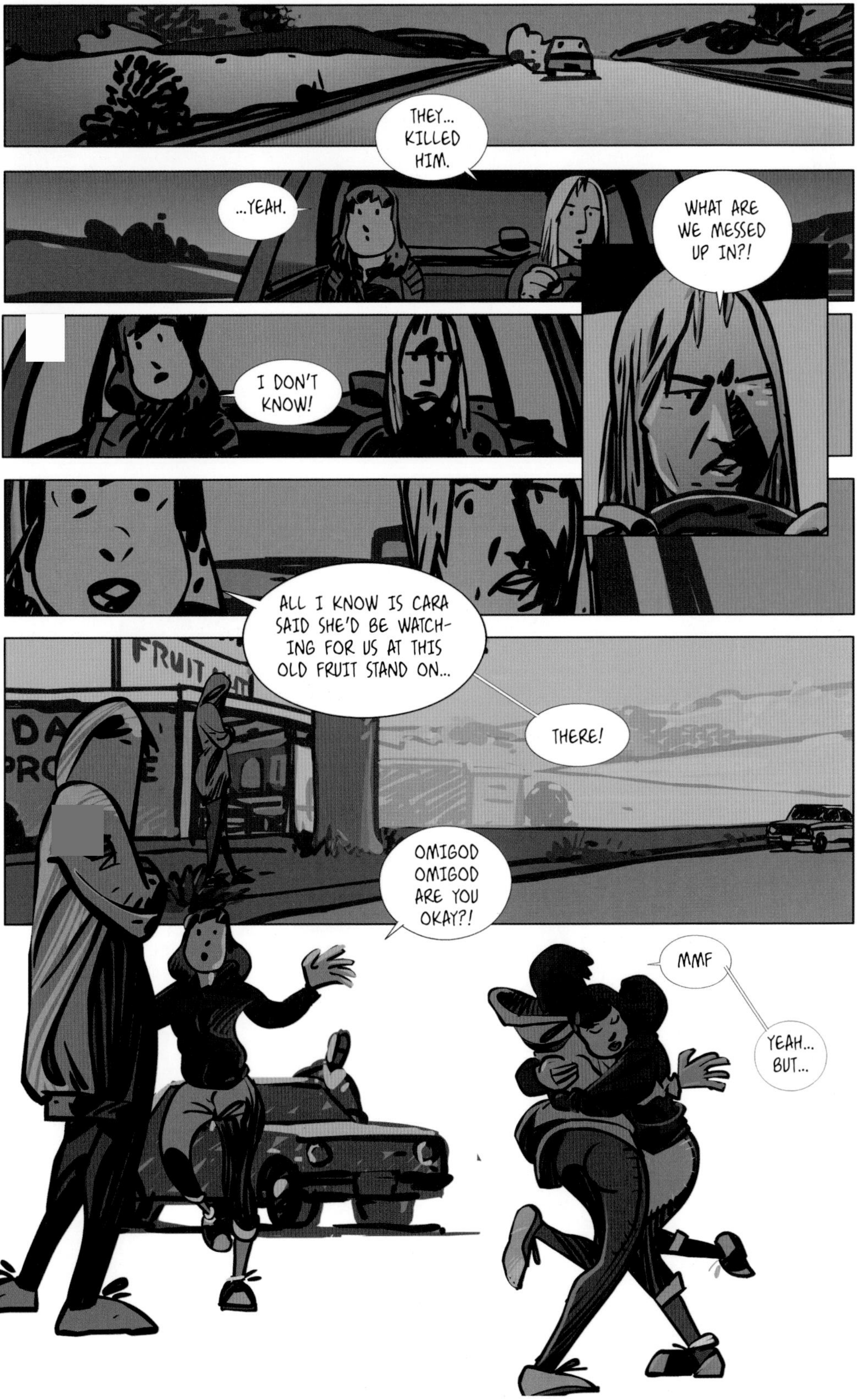
THEY... KILLED HIM.
...YEAH.
WHAT ARE WE MESSED UP IN?!
I DON'T KNOW!
ALL I KNOW IS CARA SAID SHE'D BE WATCH-ING FOR US AT THIS OLD FRUIT STAND ON...
THERE!
OMIGOD OMIGOD ARE YOU OKAY?!
MMF
YEAH... BUT...

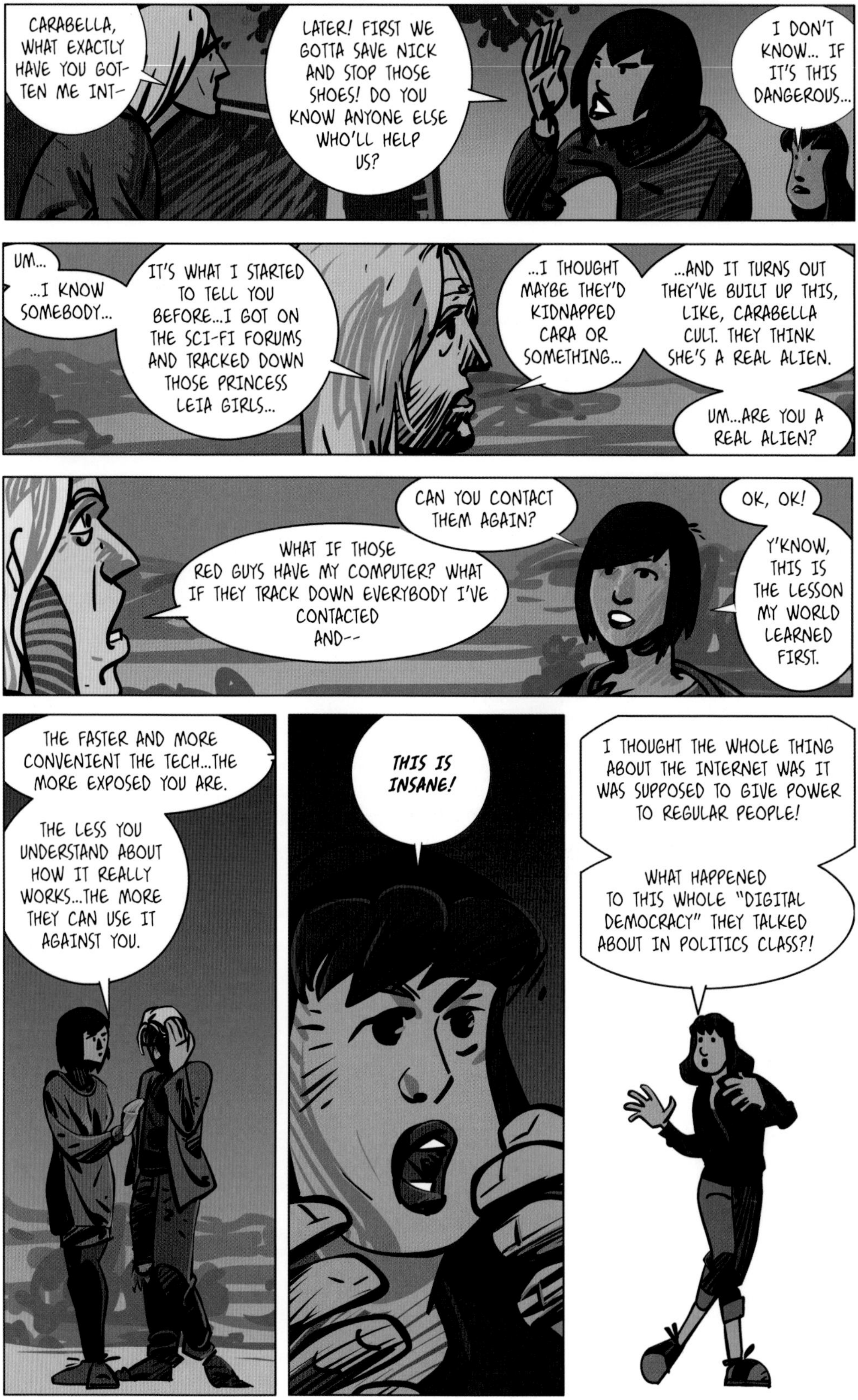
CARABELLA, WHAT EXACTLY HAVE YOU GOTTEN ME INT-
LATER! FIRST WE GOTTA SAVE NICK AND STOP THOSE SHOES! DO YOU KNOW ANYONE ELSE WHO'LL HELP US?
I DON'T KNOW... IF IT'S THIS DANGEROUS...
UM... ...I KNOW SOMEBODY...
IT'S WHAT I STARTED TO TELL YOU BEFORE...I GOT ON THE SCI-FI FORUMS AND TRACKED DOWN THOSE PRINCESS LEIA GIRLS...
...I THOUGHT MAYBE THEY'D KIDNAPPED CARA OR SOMETHING...
...AND IT TURNS OUT THEY'VE BUILT UP THIS, LIKE, CARABELLA CULT. THEY THINK SHE'S A REAL ALIEN.
UM...ARE YOU A REAL ALIEN?
CAN YOU CONTACT THEM AGAIN?
WHAT IF THOSE RED GUYS HAVE MY COMPUTER? WHAT IF THEY TRACK DOWN EVERYBODY I'VE CONTACTED AND--
OK, OK!
Y'KNOW, THIS IS THE LESSON MY WORLD LEARNED FIRST.
THE FASTER AND MORE CONVENIENT THE TECH...THE MORE EXPOSED YOU ARE.
THE LESS YOU UNDERSTAND ABOUT HOW IT REALLY WORKS...THE MORE THEY CAN USE IT AGAINST YOU.
THIS IS INSANE!
I THOUGHT THE WHOLE THING ABOUT THE INTERNET WAS IT WAS SUPPOSED TO GIVE POWER TO REGULAR PEOPLE!
WHAT HAPPENED TO THIS WHOLE "DIGITAL DEMOCRACY" THEY TALKED ABOUT IN POLITICS CLASS?!

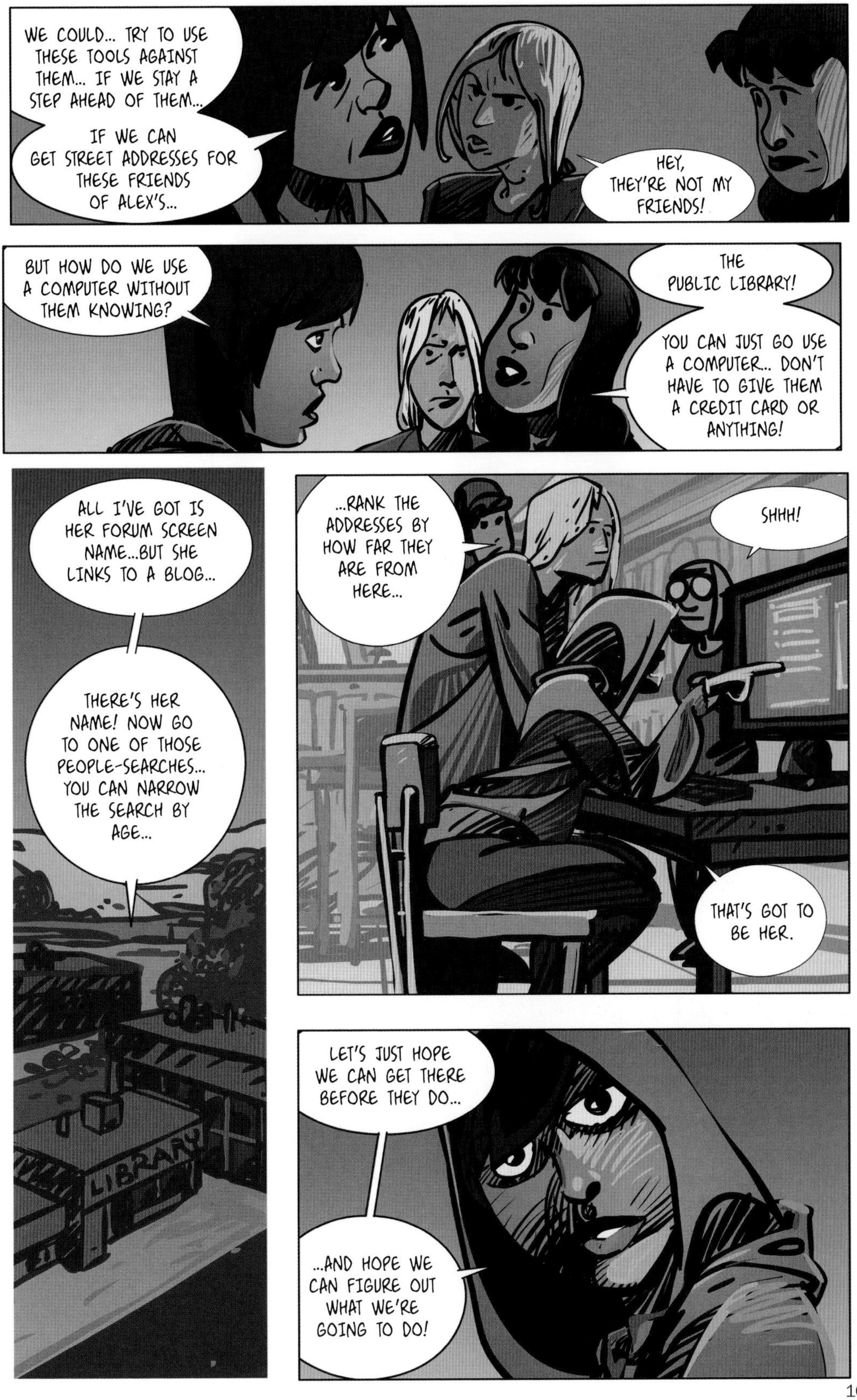

WE COULD... TRY TO USE THESE TOOLS AGAINST THEM... IF WE STAY A STEP AHEAD OF THEM...
IF WE CAN GET STREET ADDRESSES FOR THESE FRIENDS OF ALEX'S...
HEY, THEY'RE NOT MY FRIENDS!
BUT HOW DO WE USE A COMPUTER WITHOUT THEM KNOWING?
THE PUBLIC LIBRARY!
YOU CAN JUST GO USE A COMPUTER... DON'T HAVE TO GIVE THEM A CREDIT CARD OR ANYTHING!
ALL I'VE GOT IS HER FORUM SCREEN NAME...BUT SHE LINKS TO A BLOG...
THERE'S HER NAME! NOW GO TO ONE OF THOSE PEOPLE-SEARCHES... YOU CAN NARROW THE SEARCH BY AGE...
LIBRARY
...RANK THE ADDRESSES BY HOW FAR THEY ARE FROM HERE...
SHHH!
THAT'S GOT TO BE HER.
LET'S JUST HOPE WE CAN GET THERE BEFORE THEY DO...
...AND HOPE WE CAN FIGURE OUT WHAT WE'RE GOING TO DO!

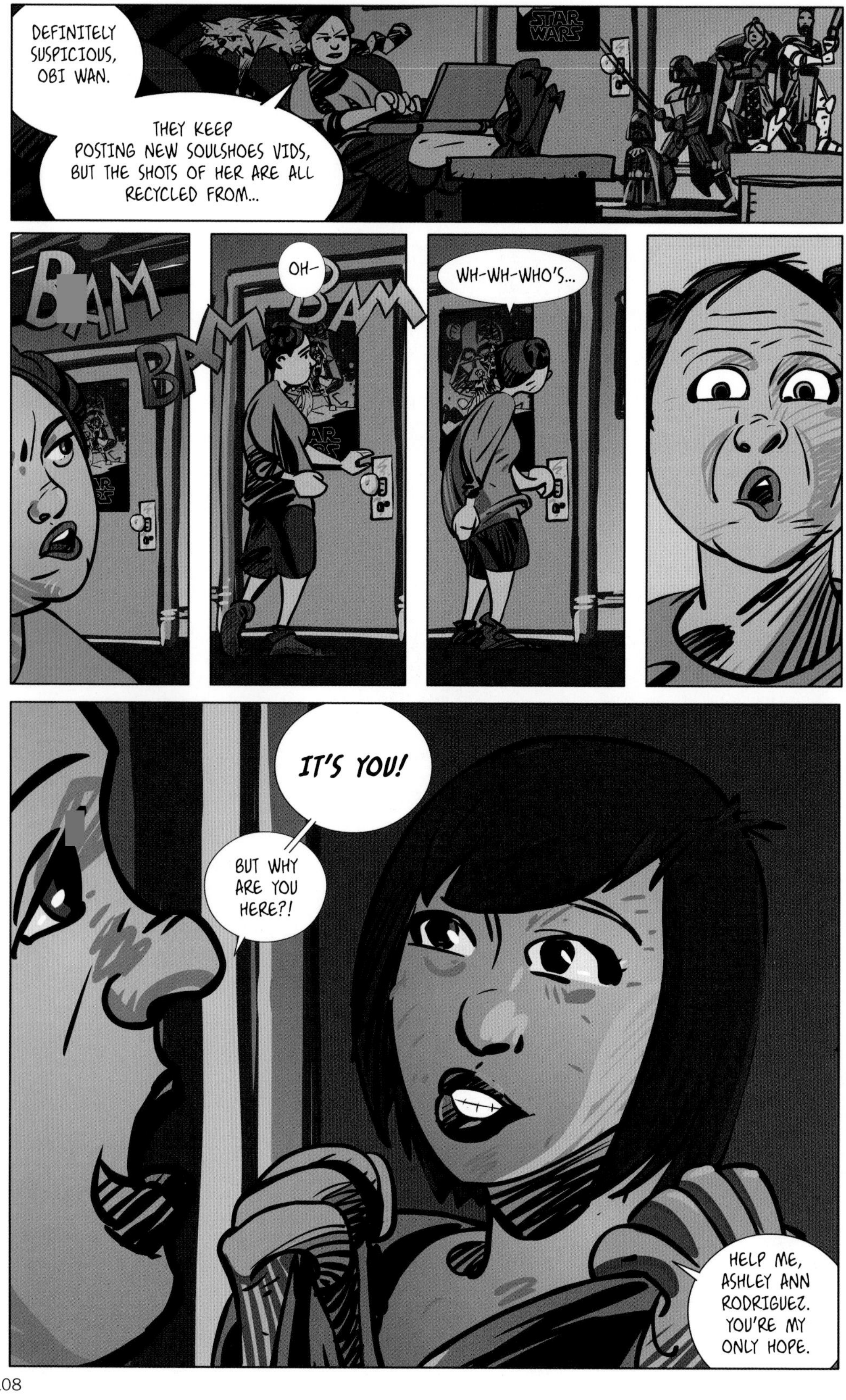
DEFINITELY SUSPICIOUS, OBI WAN.
THEY KEEP POSTING NEW SOULSHOES VIDS, BUT THE SHOTS OF HER ARE ALL RECYCLED FROM...
STAR WARS
BAM
OH–
BAM
BAM
WH-WH-WHO'S...
IT'S YOU!
BUT WHY ARE YOU HERE?!
HELP ME, ASHLEY ANN RODRIGUEZ. YOU'RE MY ONLY HOPE.

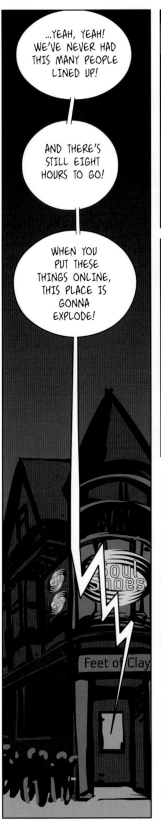

...YEAH, YEAH! WE'VE NEVER HAD THIS MANY PEOPLE LINED UP!

AND THERE'S STILL EIGHT HOURS TO GO!

WHEN YOU PUT THESE THINGS ONLINE, THIS PLACE IS GONNA EXPLODE!

Feet of Clay

LET YOUR CUSTOMERS KNOW THERE'LL BE A SPECIAL TREAT RIGHT BEFORE MID-NIGHT...

MIDNITE

YOU ROCK!

...A LIVE TUTORIAL FROM NICK SCHUMER, THE INVENTOR OF THE SOULSHOES HIMSELF!

IF YOU THINK YOU CAN MAKE ME—

OH, DON'T BE A BUZZ-KILL, NICK. YOU DON'T HAVE TO DO ANYTHING.

NOW YOU'RE LIKE ANY OTHER PIECE OF REDUNDANT HARD-WARE— THE LANDFILL OF TOMORROW.

THIS PAST WEEK WE'VE BEEN RECORDING AND DIGI-TIZING EVERYTHING YOU DO AND SAY. WE CAN GENERATE VIDEO OF YOU SAYING ANYTHING WE WANT.

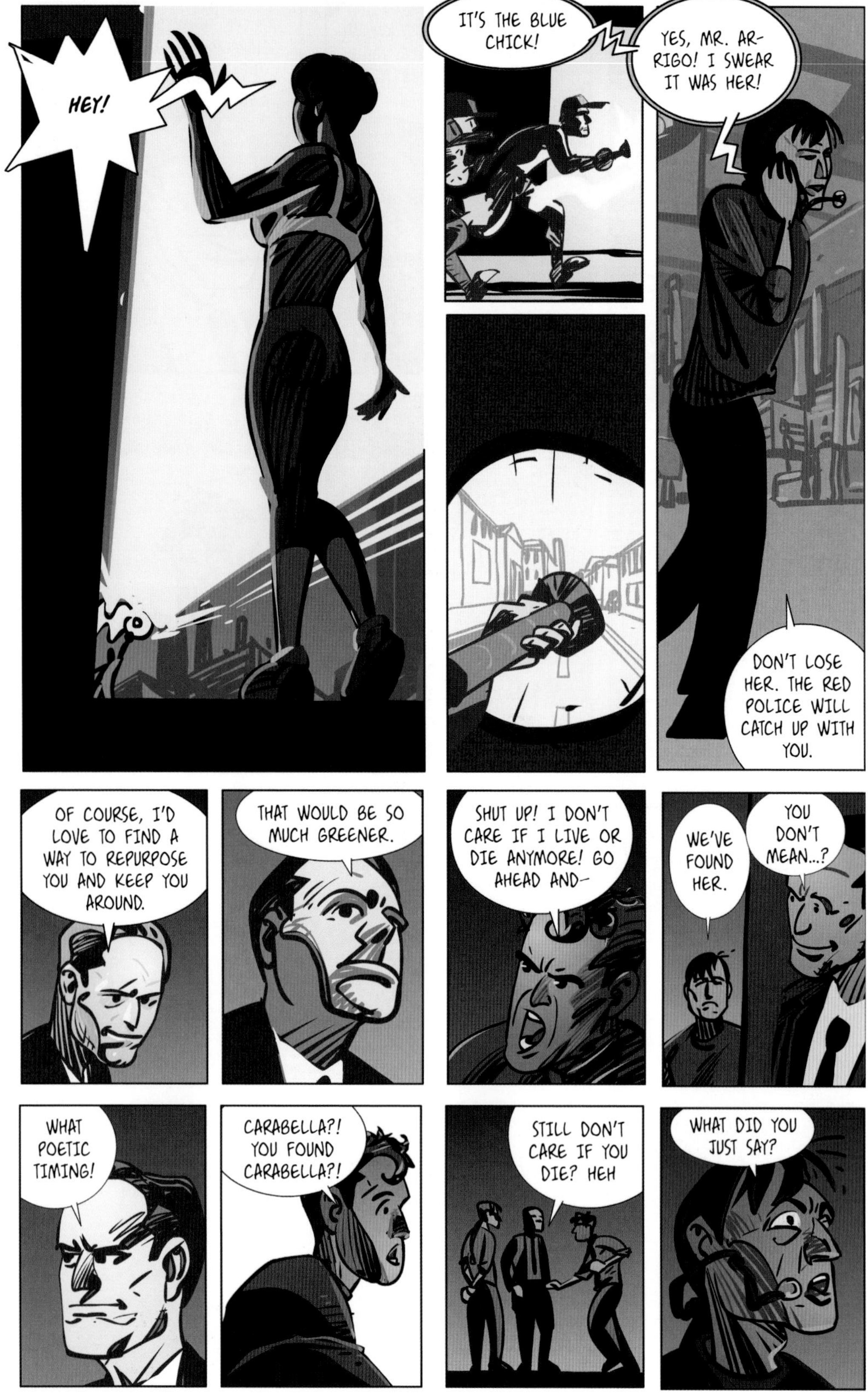
HEY!
IT'S THE BLUE CHICK!
YES, MR. ARRIGO! I SWEAR IT WAS HER!
DON'T LOSE HER. THE RED POLICE WILL CATCH UP WITH YOU.
OF COURSE, I'D LOVE TO FIND A WAY TO REPURPOSE YOU AND KEEP YOU AROUND.
THAT WOULD BE SO MUCH GREENER.
SHUT UP! I DON'T CARE IF I LIVE OR DIE ANYMORE! GO AHEAD AND—
WE'VE FOUND HER.
YOU DON'T MEAN...?
WHAT POETIC TIMING!
CARABELLA?! YOU FOUND CARABELLA?!
STILL DON'T CARE IF YOU DIE? HEH
WHAT DID YOU JUST SAY?

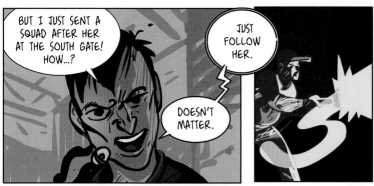

BUT I JUST SENT A SQUAD AFTER HER AT THE SOUTH GATE! HOW...?

JUST FOLLOW HER.

DOESN'T MATTER.

THE BLUE GIRL! JUST PAST THE NORTH GATE!

YOU! NORTH GATE!

WE'RE GOING TO BRING HER IN NO MATTER WHAT IT TAKES!

YES SIR!

HURRY! SHE CUT LEFT UP THERE!

WE'LL CUT HERE AND HEAD HER—

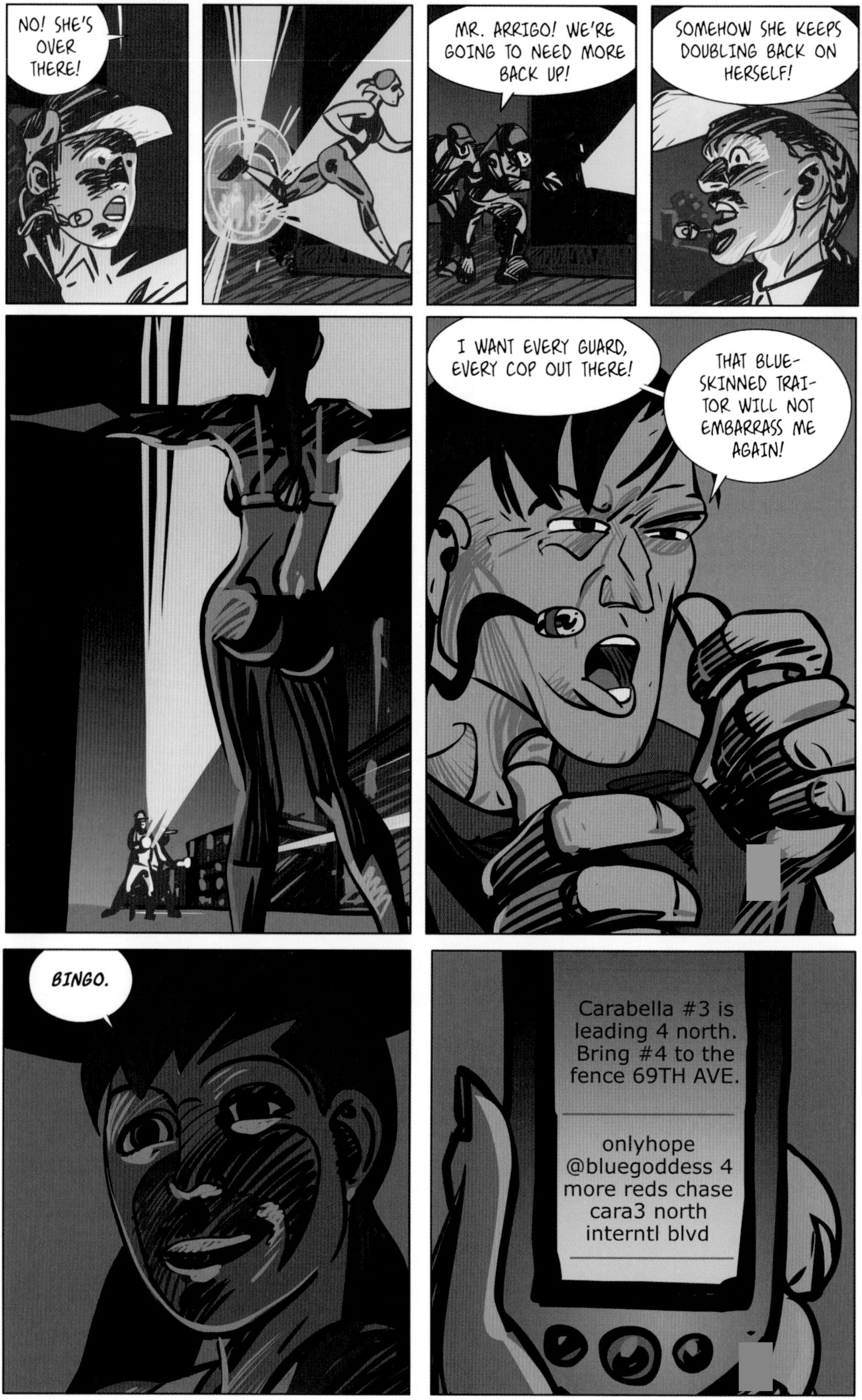
NO! SHE'S OVER THERE!
MR. ARRIGO! WE'RE GOING TO NEED MORE BACK UP!
SOMEHOW SHE KEEPS DOUBLING BACK ON HERSELF!
I WANT EVERY GUARD, EVERY COP OUT THERE!
THAT BLUE-SKINNED TRAITOR WILL NOT EMBARRASS ME AGAIN!
BINGO.
Carabella #3 is leading 4 north. Bring #4 to the fence 69TH AVE.
onlyhope @bluegoddess 4 more reds chase cara3 north interntl blvd

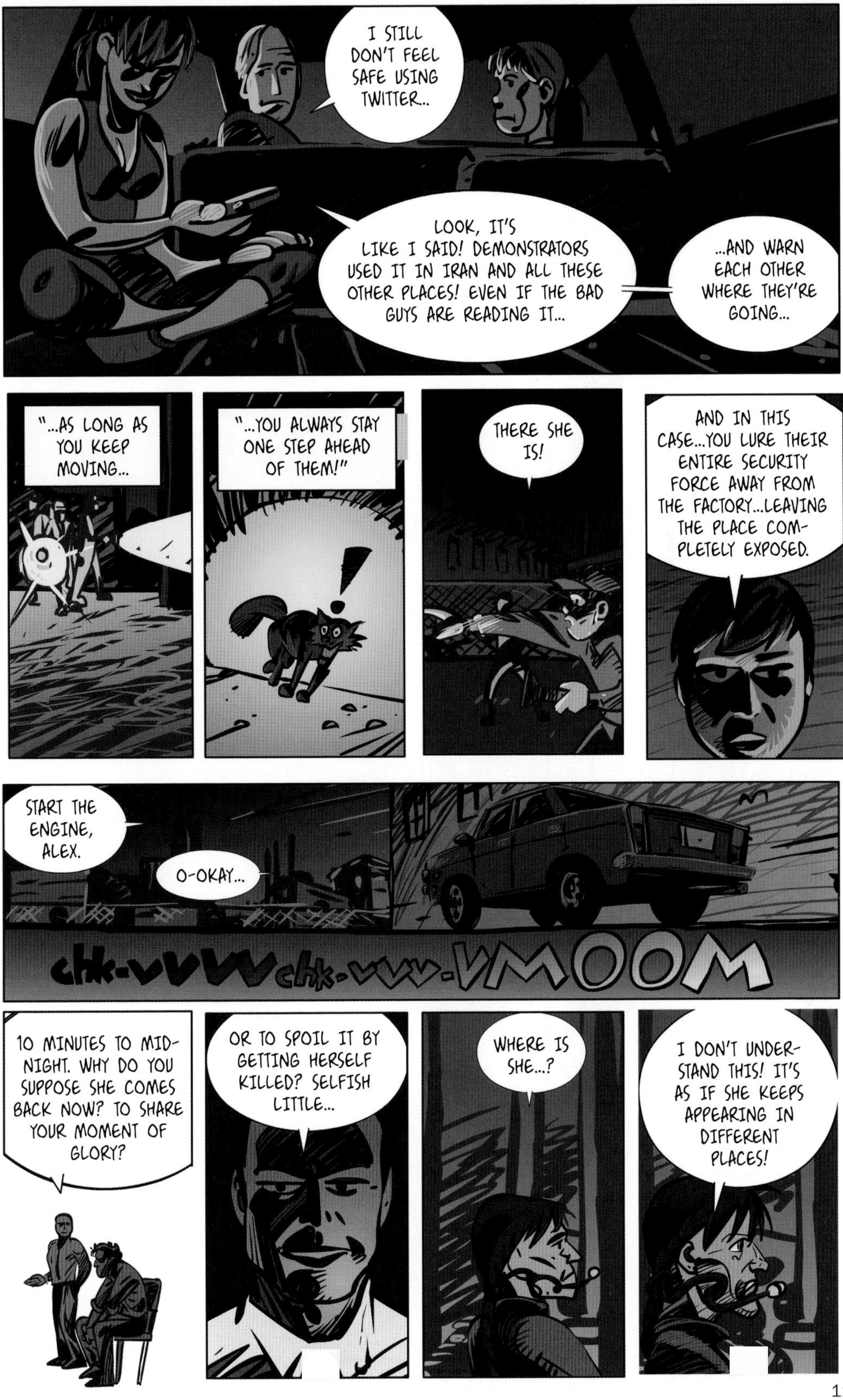
I STILL DON'T FEEL SAFE USING TWITTER...
LOOK, IT'S LIKE I SAID! DEMONSTRATORS USED IT IN IRAN AND ALL THESE OTHER PLACES! EVEN IF THE BAD GUYS ARE READING IT...
...AND WARN EACH OTHER WHERE THEY'RE GOING...
"...AS LONG AS YOU KEEP MOVING...
"...YOU ALWAYS STAY ONE STEP AHEAD OF THEM!"
THERE SHE IS!
AND IN THIS CASE...YOU LURE THEIR ENTIRE SECURITY FORCE AWAY FROM THE FACTORY...LEAVING THE PLACE COMPLETELY EXPOSED.
START THE ENGINE, ALEX.
O-OKAY...
chk-vvvv chk-vvv-VMOOM
10 MINUTES TO MIDNIGHT. WHY DO YOU SUPPOSE SHE COMES BACK NOW? TO SHARE YOUR MOMENT OF GLORY?
OR TO SPOIL IT BY GETTING HERSELF KILLED? SELFISH LITTLE...
WHERE IS SHE...?
I DON'T UNDERSTAND THIS! IT'S AS IF SHE KEEPS APPEARING IN DIFFERENT PLACES!

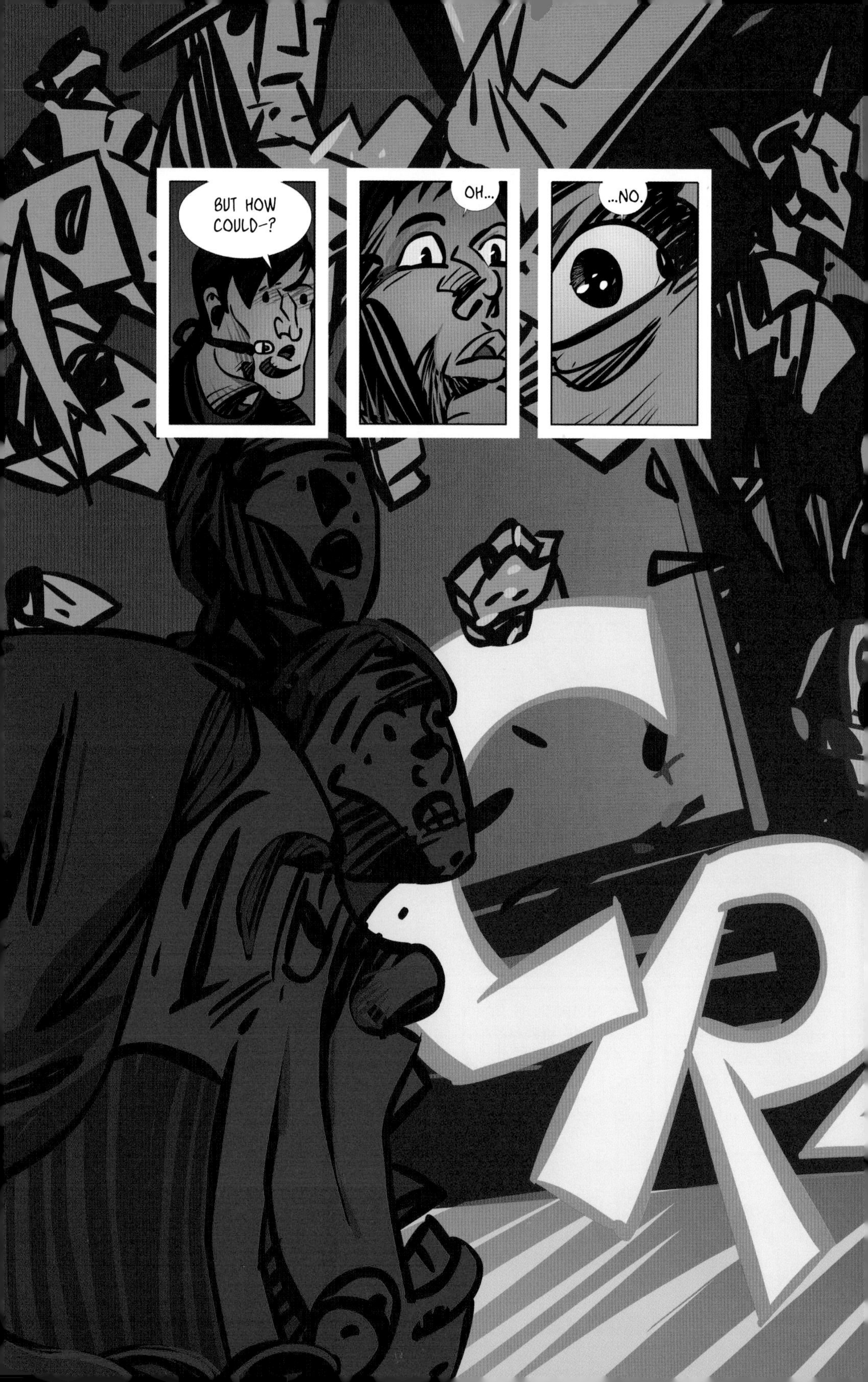
BUT HOW COULD-?
OH...
...NO.

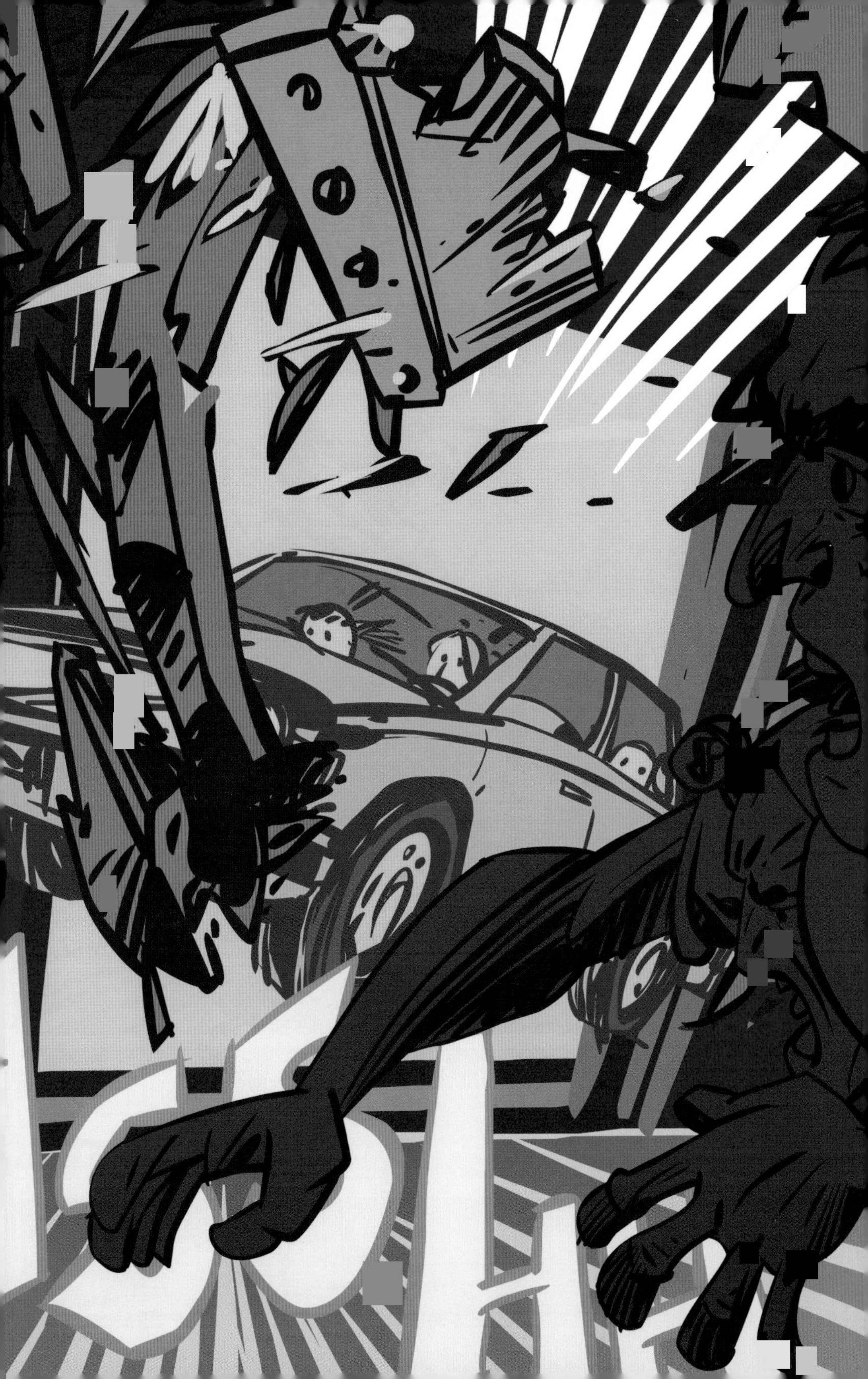

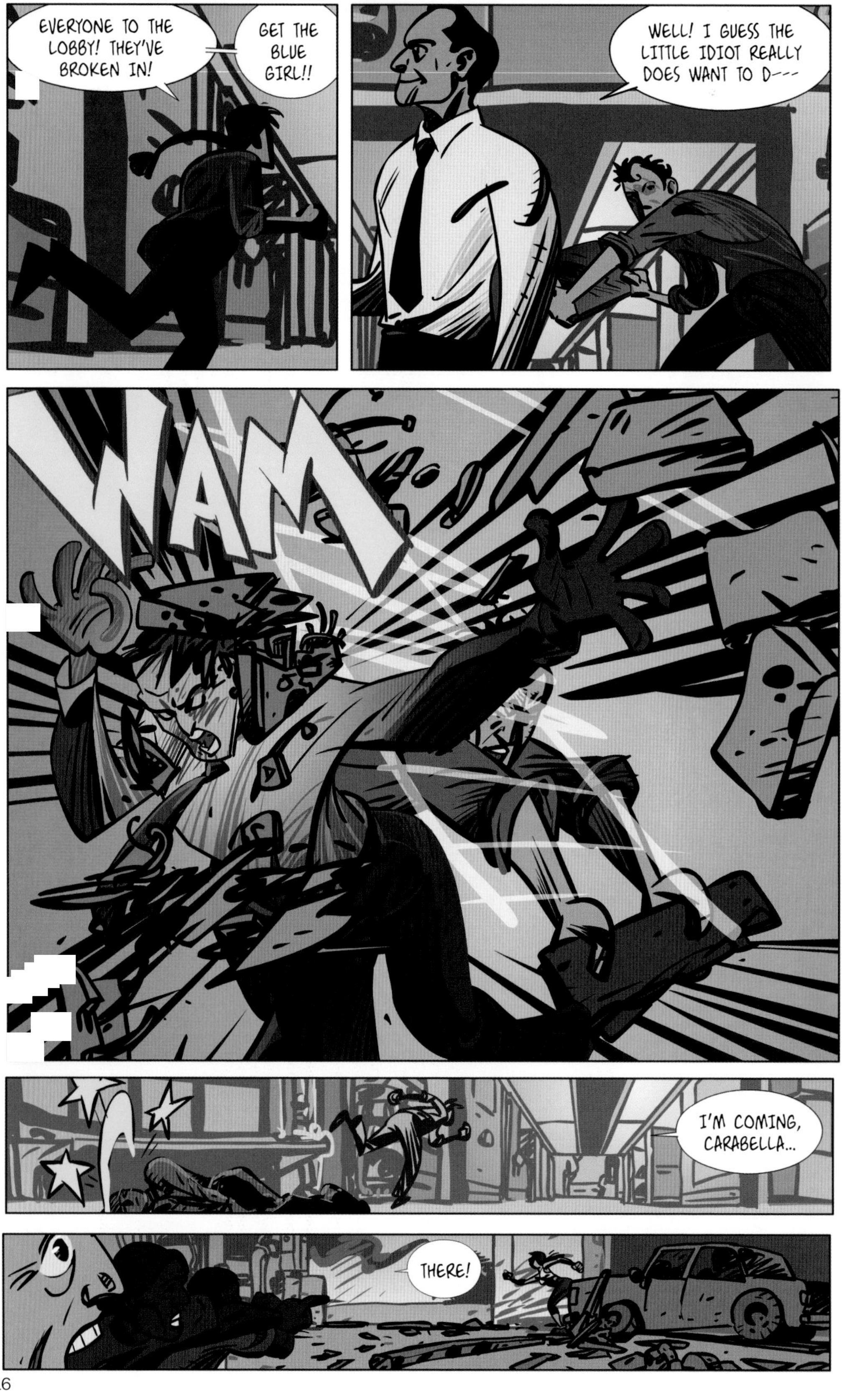
EVERYONE TO THE LOBBY! THEY'VE BROKEN IN!
GET THE BLUE GIRL!!
WELL! I GUESS THE LITTLE IDIOT REALLY DOES WANT TO D---
WAM
I'M COMING, CARABELLA...
THERE!

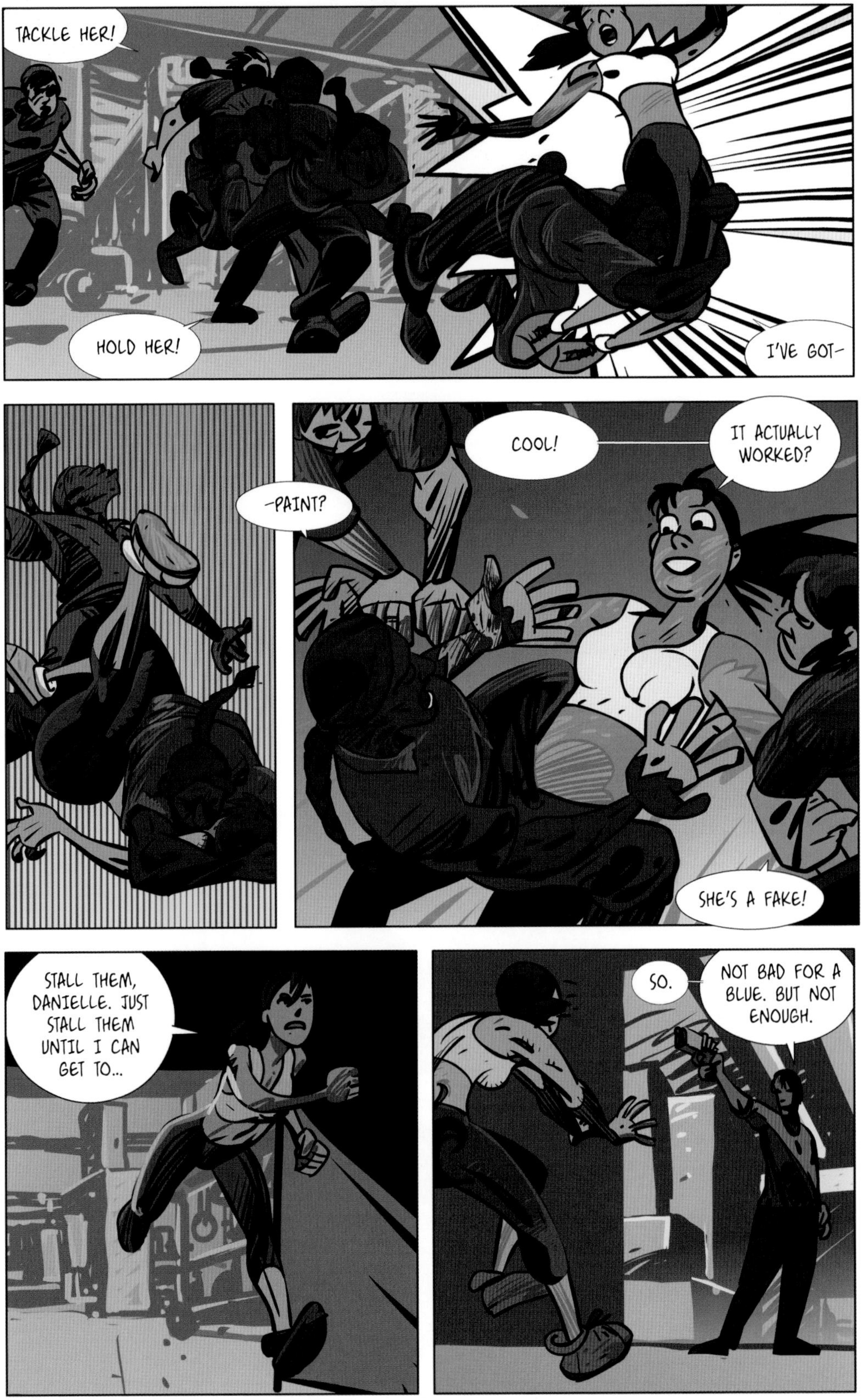
TACKLE HER!
HOLD HER!
I'VE GOT-
-PAINT?
COOL!
IT ACTUALLY WORKED?
SHE'S A FAKE!
STALL THEM, DANIELLE. JUST STALL THEM UNTIL I CAN GET TO...
SO.
NOT BAD FOR A BLUE. BUT NOT ENOUGH.

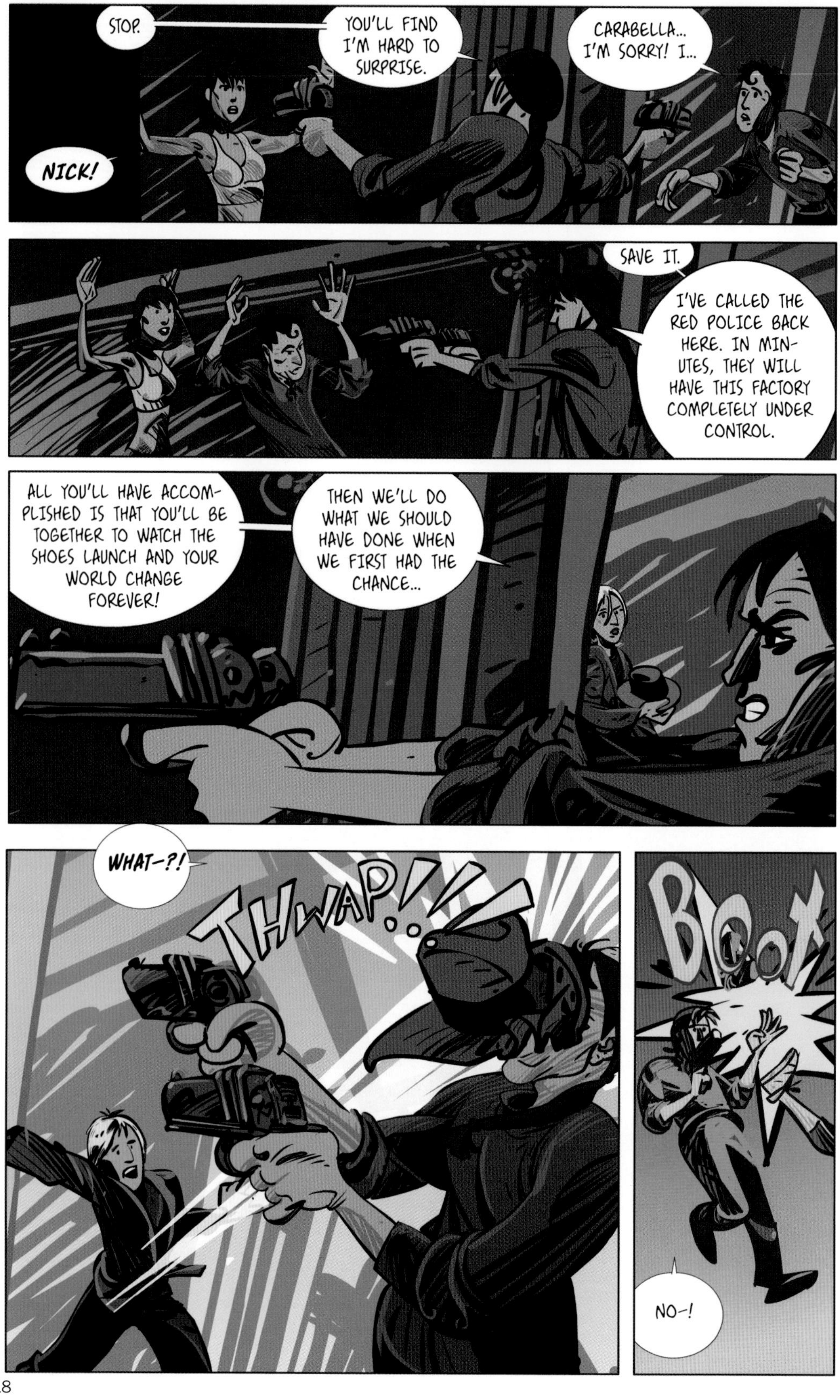
STOP.
YOU'LL FIND I'M HARD TO SURPRISE.
CARABELLA... I'M SORRY! I...
NICK!
SAVE IT.
I'VE CALLED THE RED POLICE BACK HERE. IN MINUTES, THEY WILL HAVE THIS FACTORY COMPLETELY UNDER CONTROL.
ALL YOU'LL HAVE ACCOMPLISHED IS THAT YOU'LL BE TOGETHER TO WATCH THE SHOES LAUNCH AND YOUR WORLD CHANGE FOREVER!
THEN WE'LL DO WHAT WE SHOULD HAVE DONE WHEN WE FIRST HAD THE CHANCE...
WHAT-?!
THWAP!!!
BOOOM
NO-!

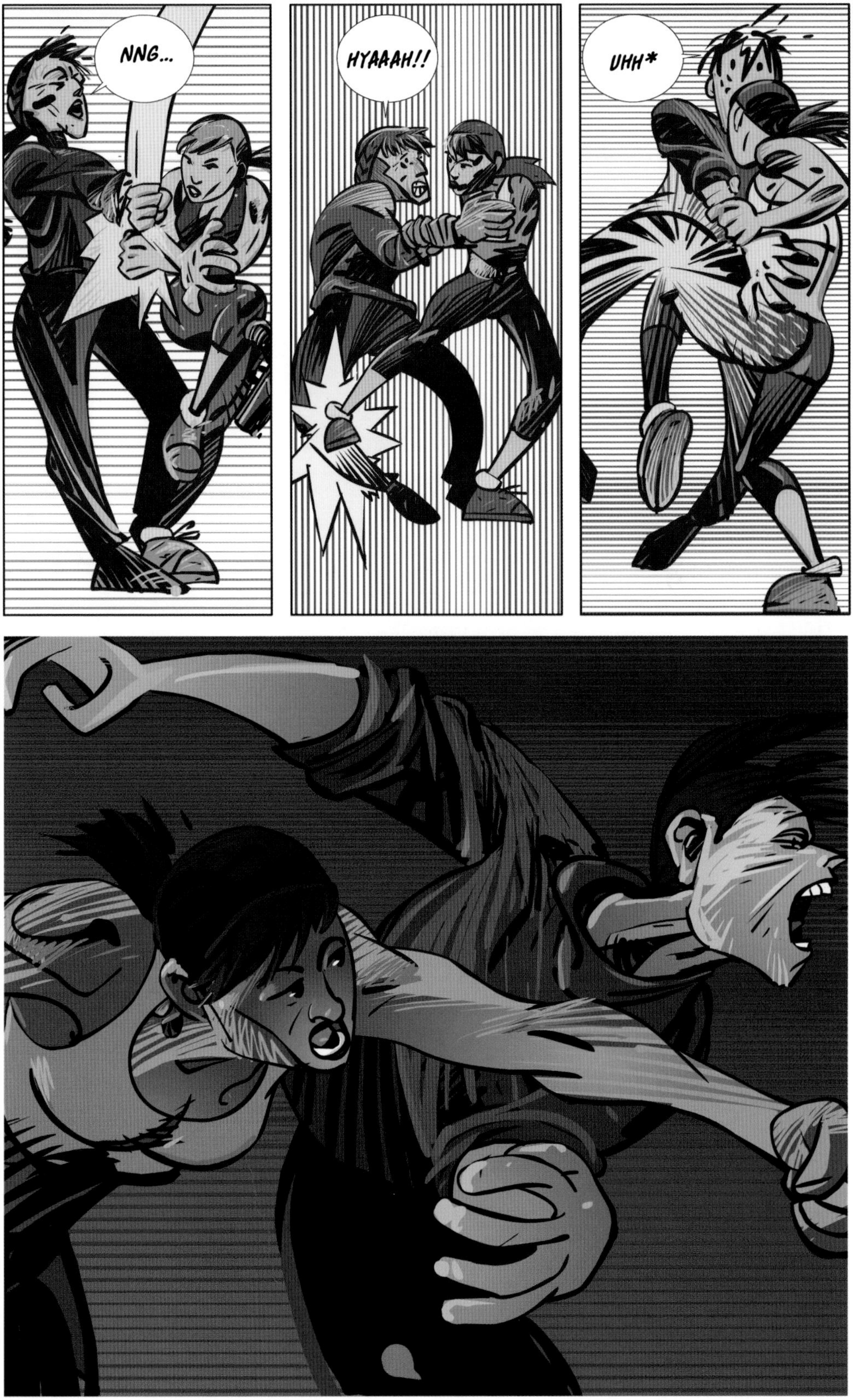
NNG...
HYAAAH!!
UHH*

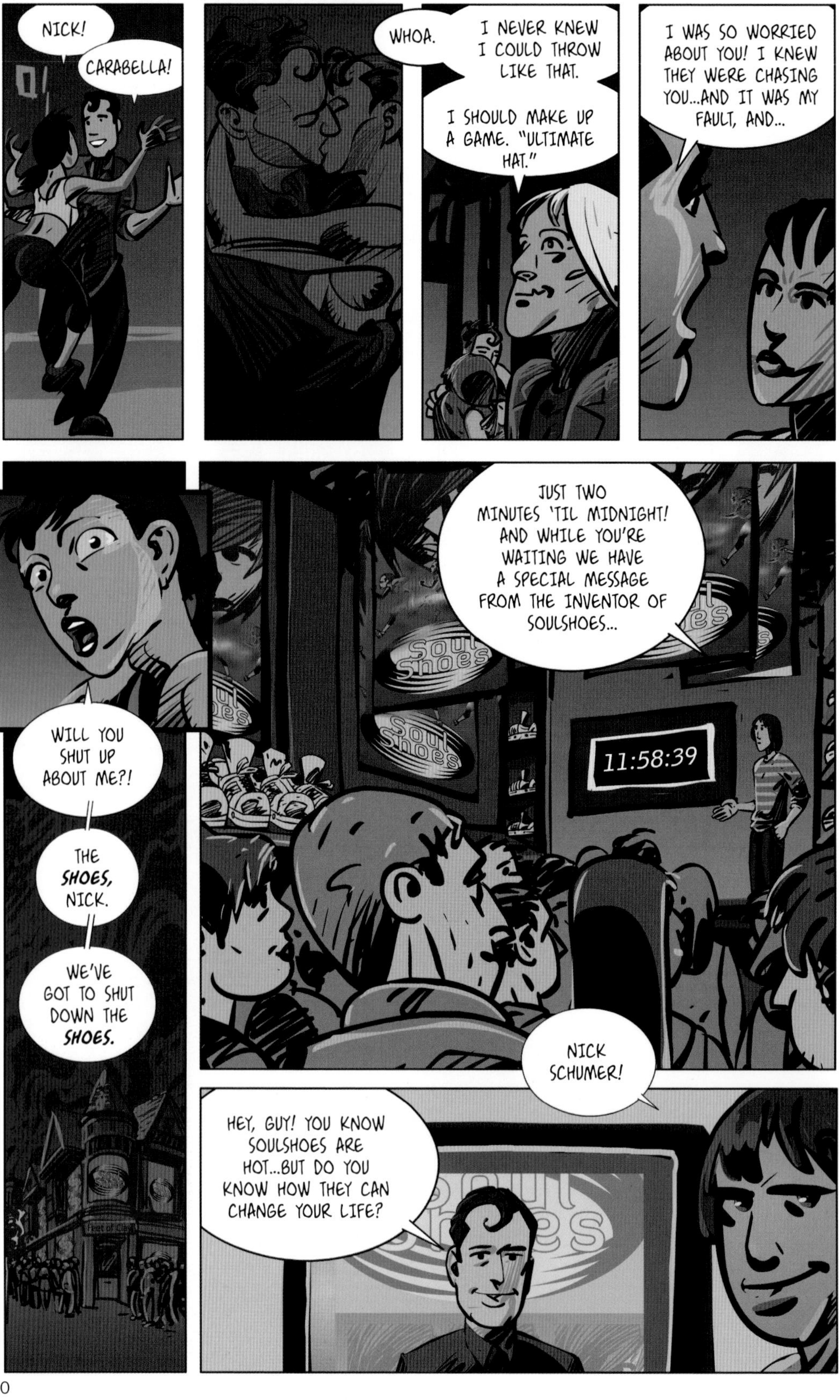
NICK!
CARABELLA!
WHOA.
I NEVER KNEW I COULD THROW LIKE THAT.
I SHOULD MAKE UP A GAME. "ULTIMATE HAT."
I WAS SO WORRIED ABOUT YOU! I KNEW THEY WERE CHASING YOU...AND IT WAS MY FAULT, AND...
WILL YOU SHUT UP ABOUT ME?!
THE *SHOES,* NICK.
WE'VE GOT TO SHUT DOWN THE *SHOES.*
JUST TWO MINUTES 'TIL MIDNIGHT! AND WHILE YOU'RE WAITING WE HAVE A SPECIAL MESSAGE FROM THE INVENTOR OF SOULSHOES...
Soul Shoes
11:58:39
NICK SCHUMER!
HEY, GUY! YOU KNOW SOULSHOES ARE HOT...BUT DO YOU KNOW HOW THEY CAN CHANGE YOUR LIFE?

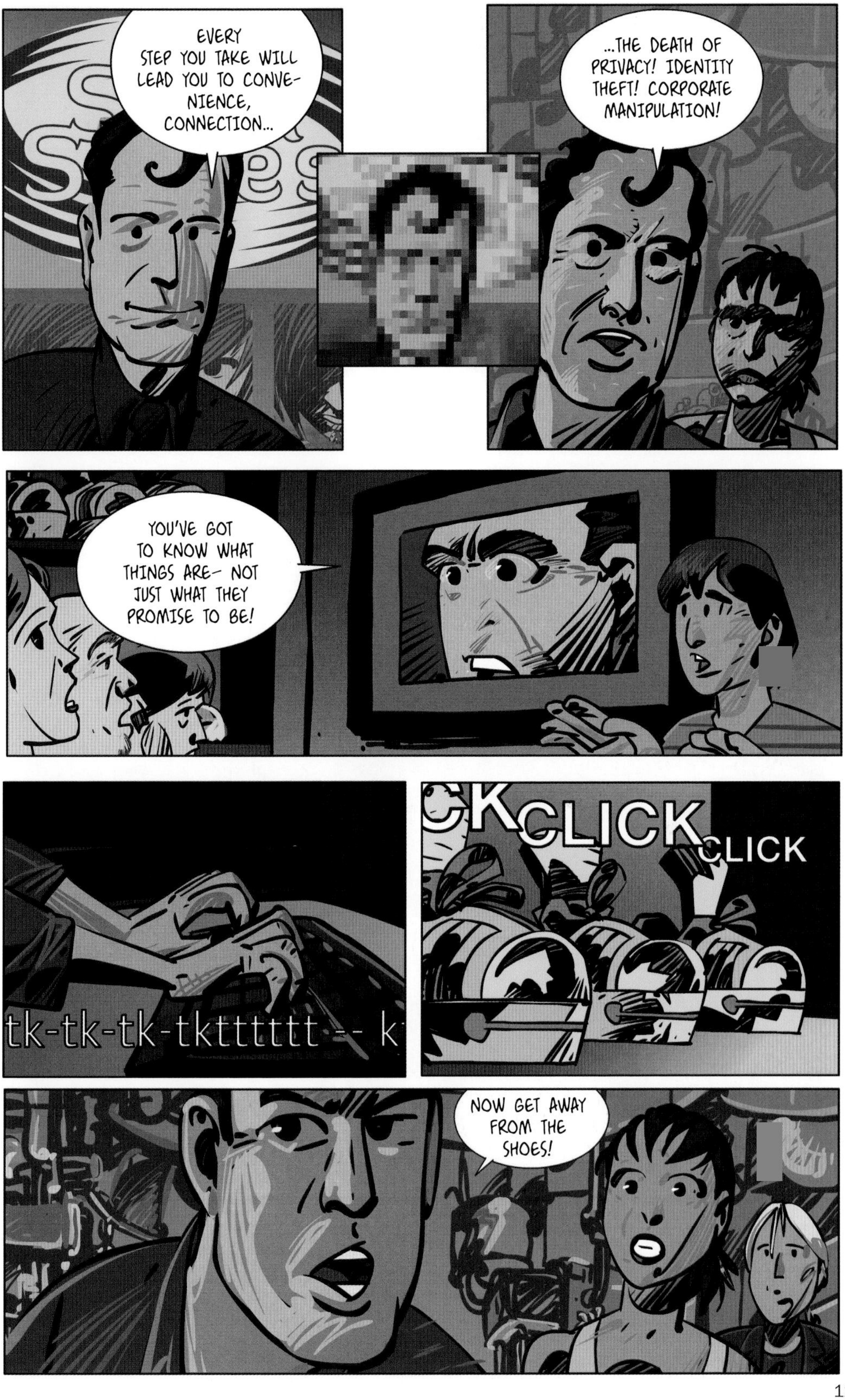
EVERY STEP YOU TAKE WILL LEAD YOU TO CONVE-NIENCE, CONNECTION...
...THE DEATH OF PRIVACY! IDENTITY THEFT! CORPORATE MANIPULATION!
YOU'VE GOT TO KNOW WHAT THINGS ARE- NOT JUST WHAT THEY PROMISE TO BE!
tk-tk-tk-tkttttt -- k
CK CLICK CLICK
NOW GET AWAY FROM THE SHOES!

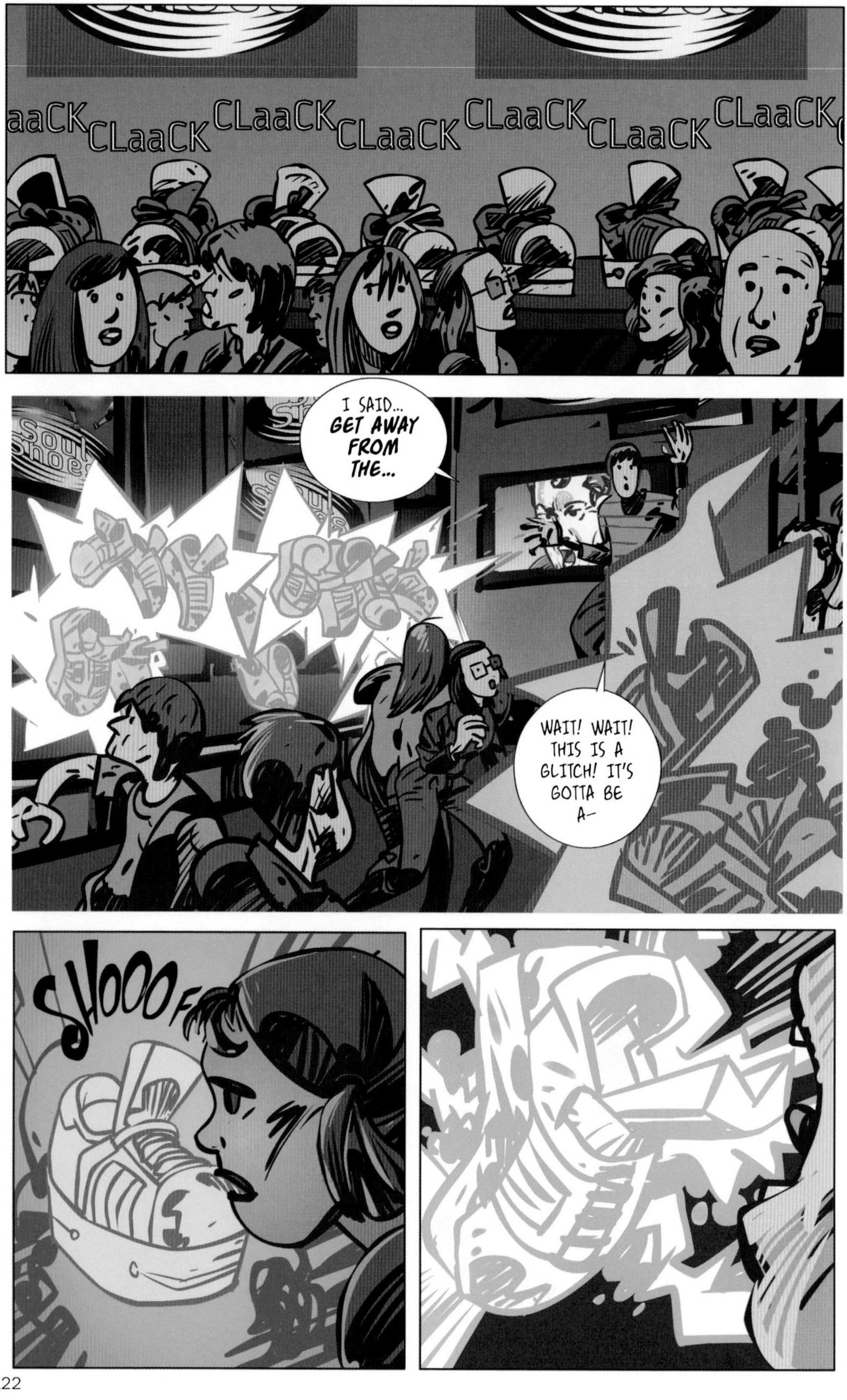
aaCK CLaaCK CLaaCK CLaaCK CLaaCK CLaaCK CLaaCK
I SAID... GET AWAY FROM THE...
WAIT! WAIT! THIS IS A GLITCH! IT'S GOTTA BE A-
SHOOOF

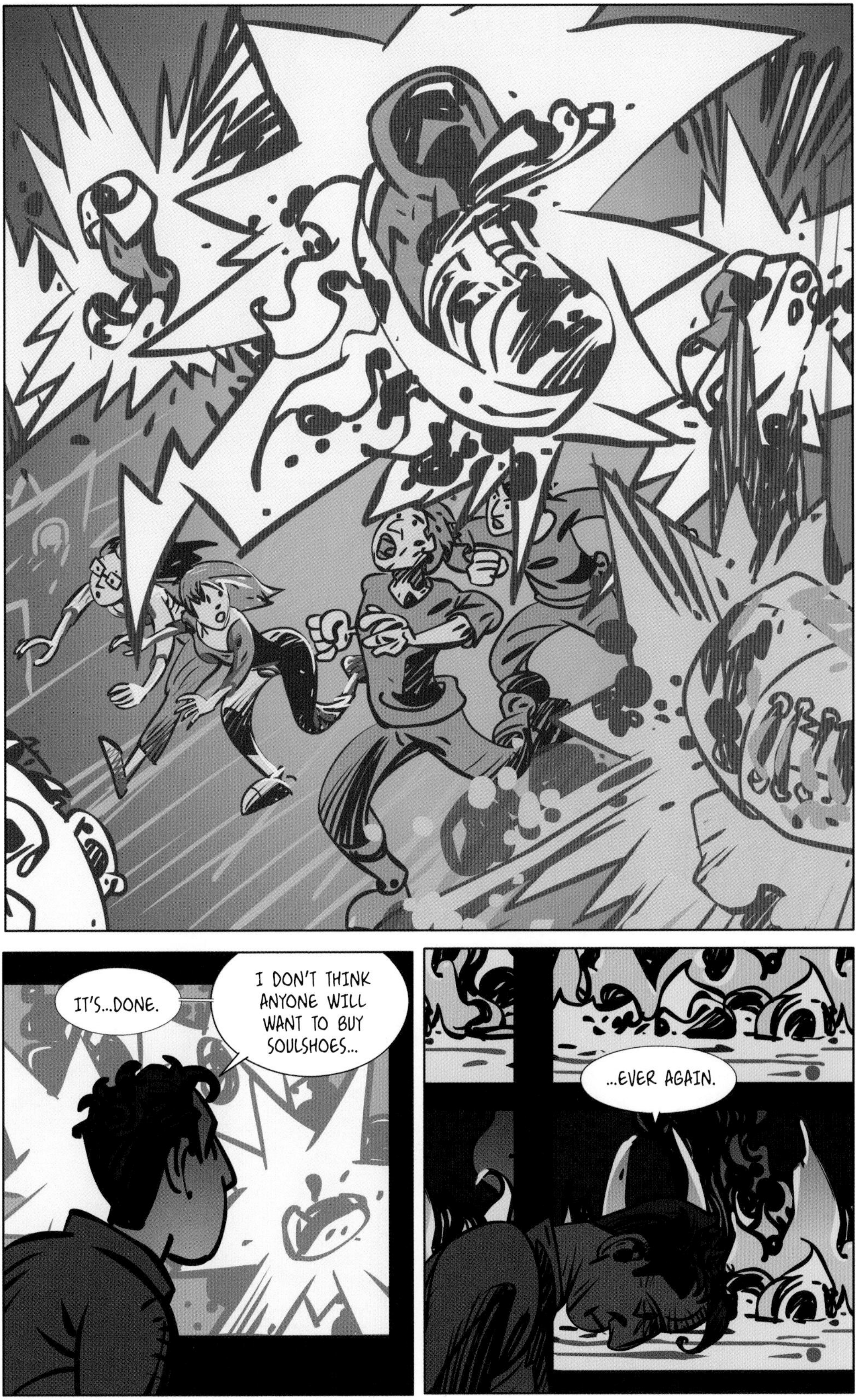
IT'S...DONE.
I DON'T THINK ANYONE WILL WANT TO BUY SOULSHOES...
...EVER AGAIN.

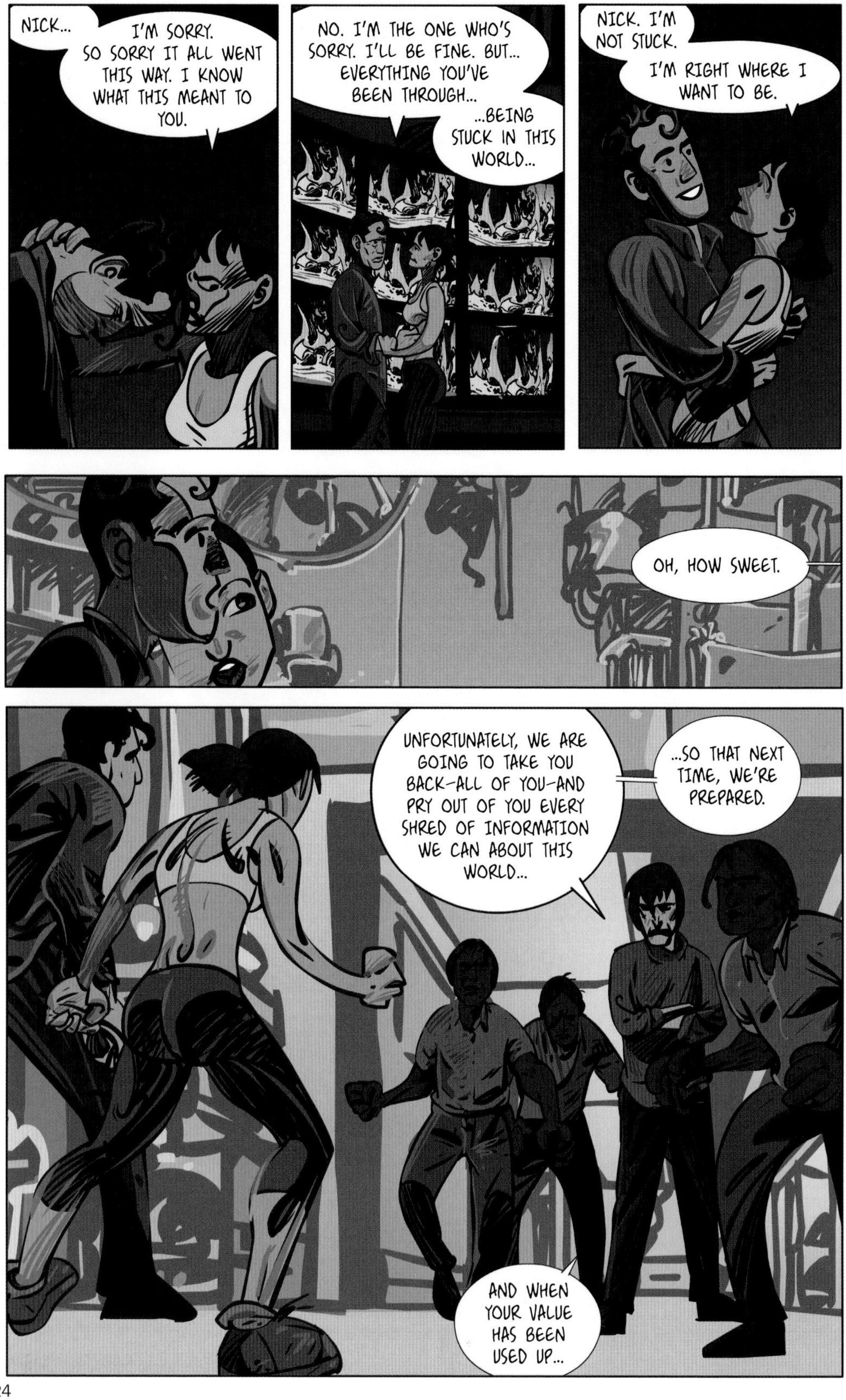
NICK...
I'M SORRY. SO SORRY IT ALL WENT THIS WAY. I KNOW WHAT THIS MEANT TO YOU.
NO. I'M THE ONE WHO'S SORRY. I'LL BE FINE. BUT... EVERYTHING YOU'VE BEEN THROUGH...
...BEING STUCK IN THIS WORLD...
NICK. I'M NOT STUCK.
I'M RIGHT WHERE I WANT TO BE.
OH, HOW SWEET.
UNFORTUNATELY, WE ARE GOING TO TAKE YOU BACK—ALL OF YOU—AND PRY OUT OF YOU EVERY SHRED OF INFORMATION WE CAN ABOUT THIS WORLD...
...SO THAT NEXT TIME, WE'RE PREPARED.
AND WHEN YOUR VALUE HAS BEEN USED UP...

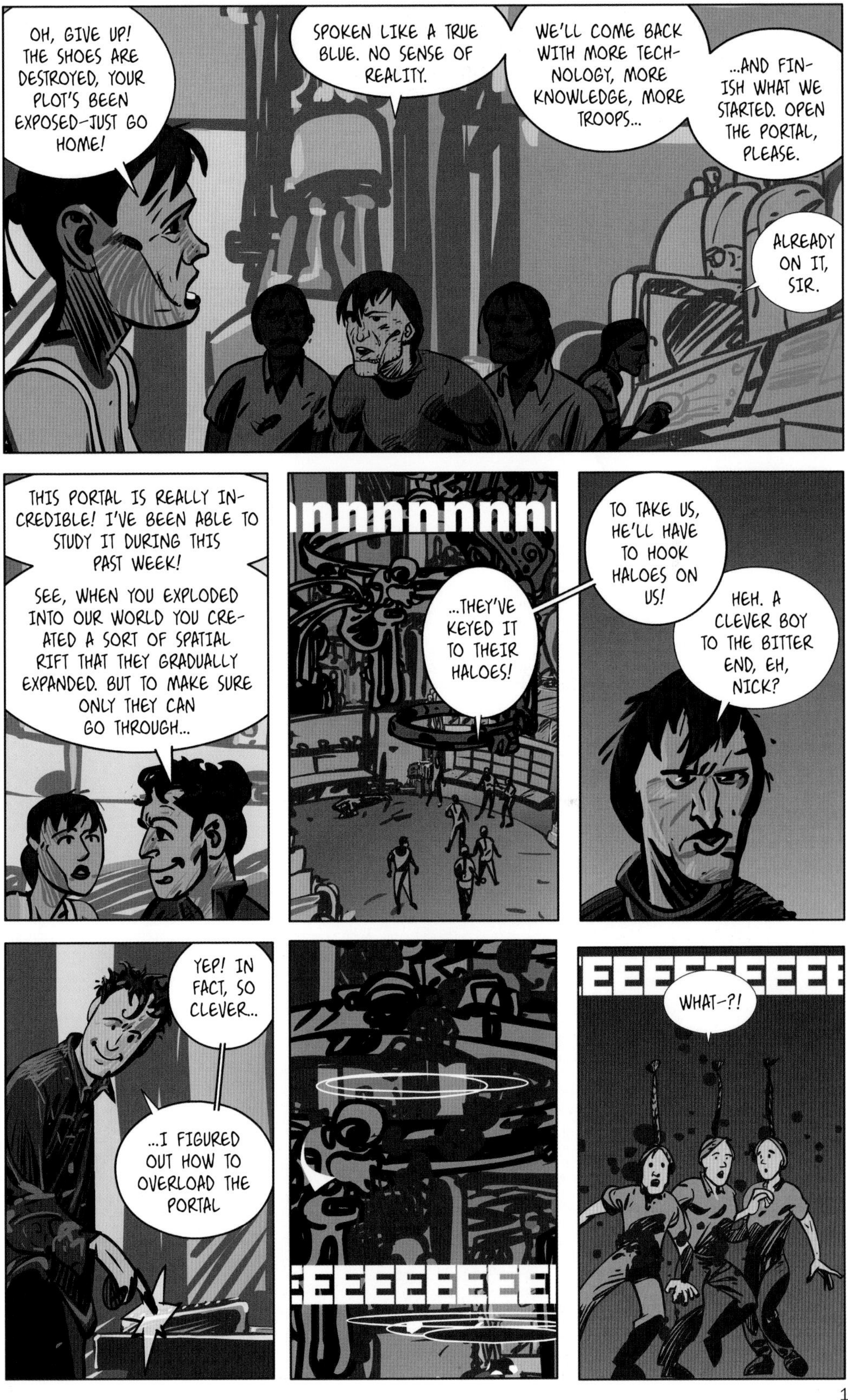
OH, GIVE UP! THE SHOES ARE DESTROYED, YOUR PLOT'S BEEN EXPOSED—JUST GO HOME!
SPOKEN LIKE A TRUE BLUE. NO SENSE OF REALITY.
WE'LL COME BACK WITH MORE TECH-NOLOGY, MORE KNOWLEDGE, MORE TROOPS...
...AND FIN-ISH WHAT WE STARTED. OPEN THE PORTAL, PLEASE.
ALREADY ON IT, SIR.
THIS PORTAL IS REALLY IN-CREDIBLE! I'VE BEEN ABLE TO STUDY IT DURING THIS PAST WEEK!
SEE, WHEN YOU EXPLODED INTO OUR WORLD YOU CRE-ATED A SORT OF SPATIAL RIFT THAT THEY GRADUALLY EXPANDED. BUT TO MAKE SURE ONLY THEY CAN GO THROUGH...
nnnnnnnnn
...THEY'VE KEYED IT TO THEIR HALOES!
TO TAKE US, HE'LL HAVE TO HOOK HALOES ON US!
HEH. A CLEVER BOY TO THE BITTER END, EH, NICK?
YEP! IN FACT, SO CLEVER...
...I FIGURED OUT HOW TO OVERLOAD THE PORTAL
EEEEEEEEE
EEEEEEEEE
WHAT-?!

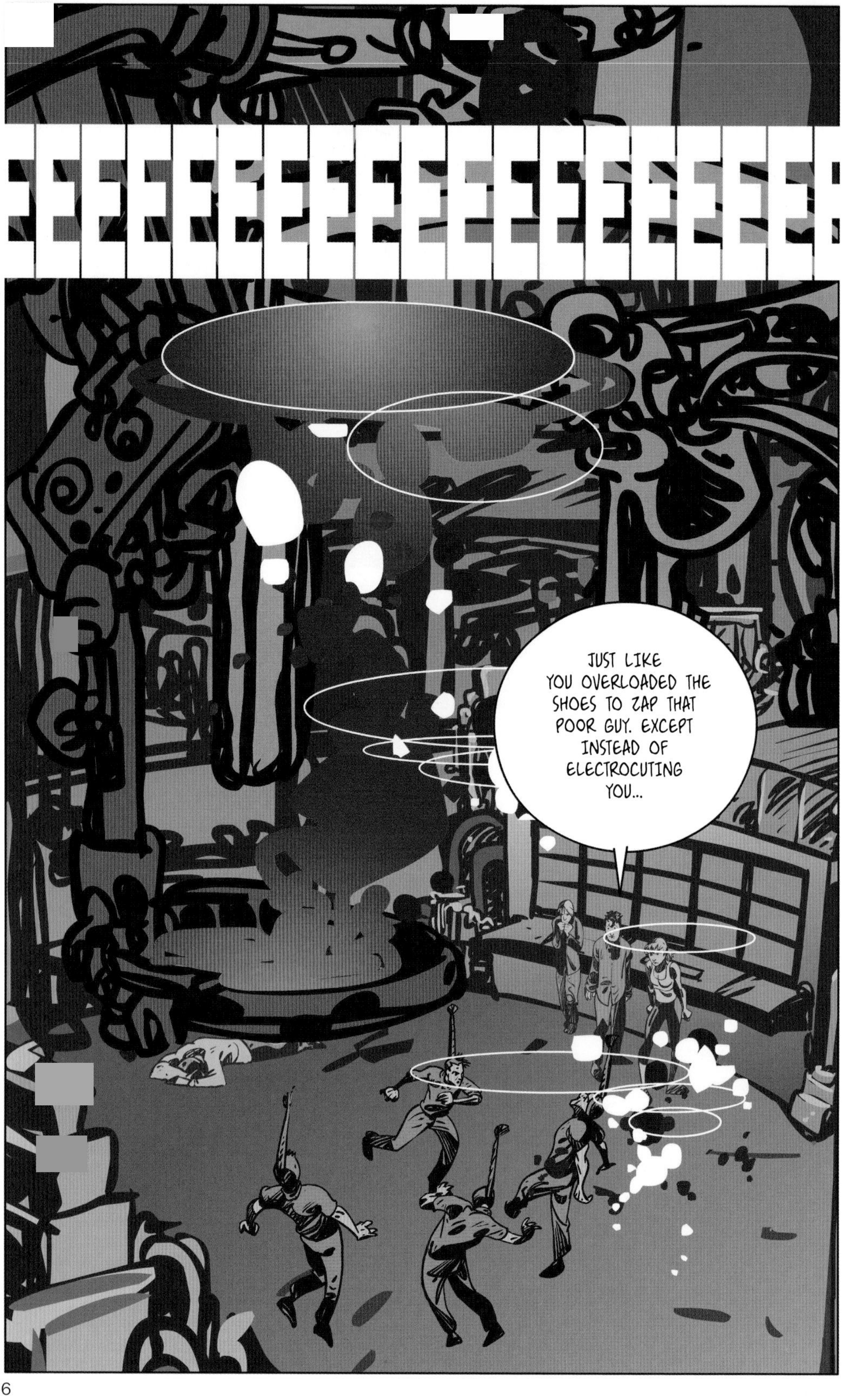
EEEEEEEEEEEEEEEEEE
JUST LIKE YOU OVERLOADED THE SHOES TO ZAP THAT POOR GUY. EXCEPT INSTEAD OF ELECTROCUTING YOU...

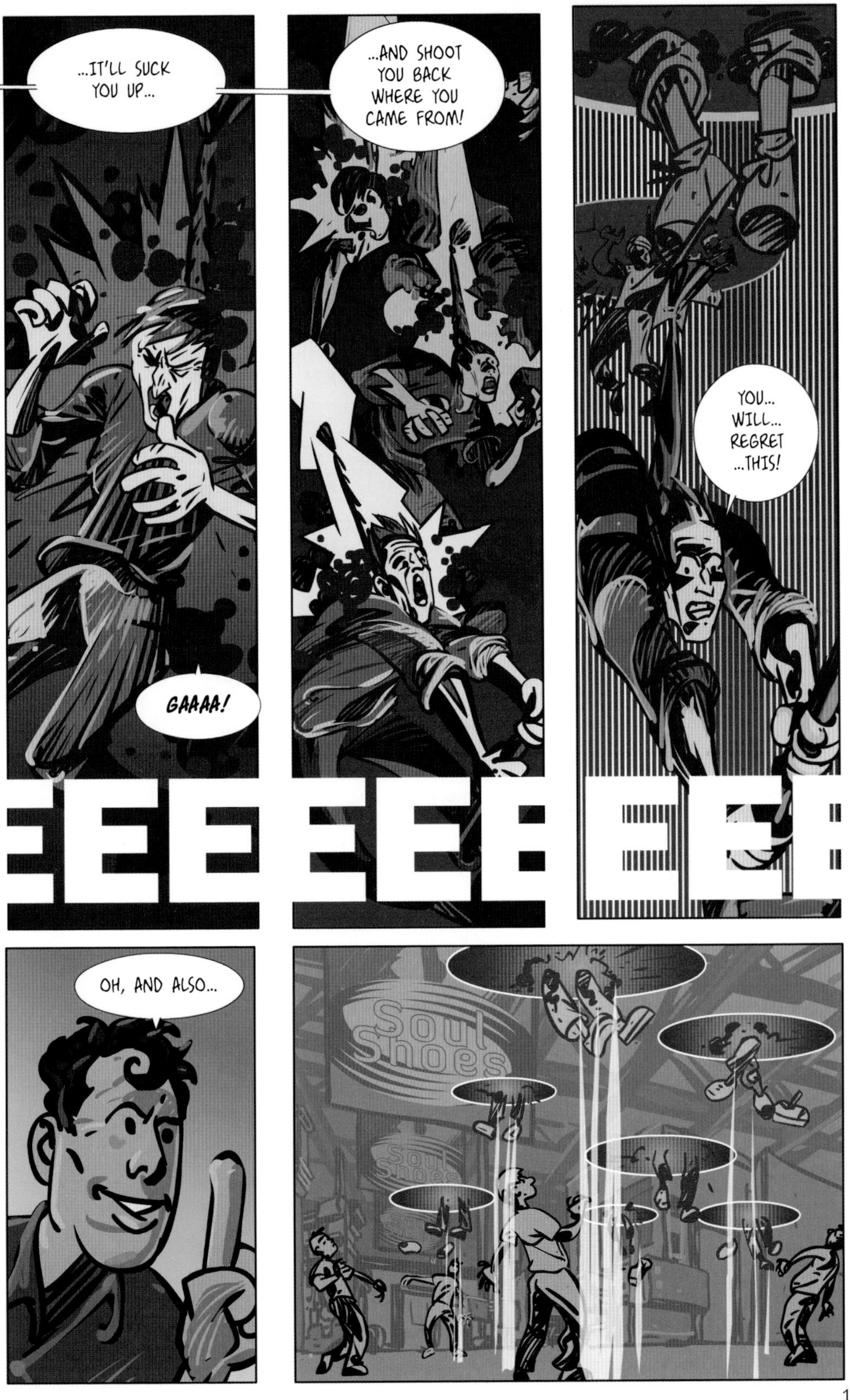
...IT'LL SUCK YOU UP...
...AND SHOOT YOU BACK WHERE YOU CAME FROM!
GAAAA!
YOU... WILL... REGRET ...THIS!
EEEEEE
OH, AND ALSO...
Soul Shoes
Soul Shoes

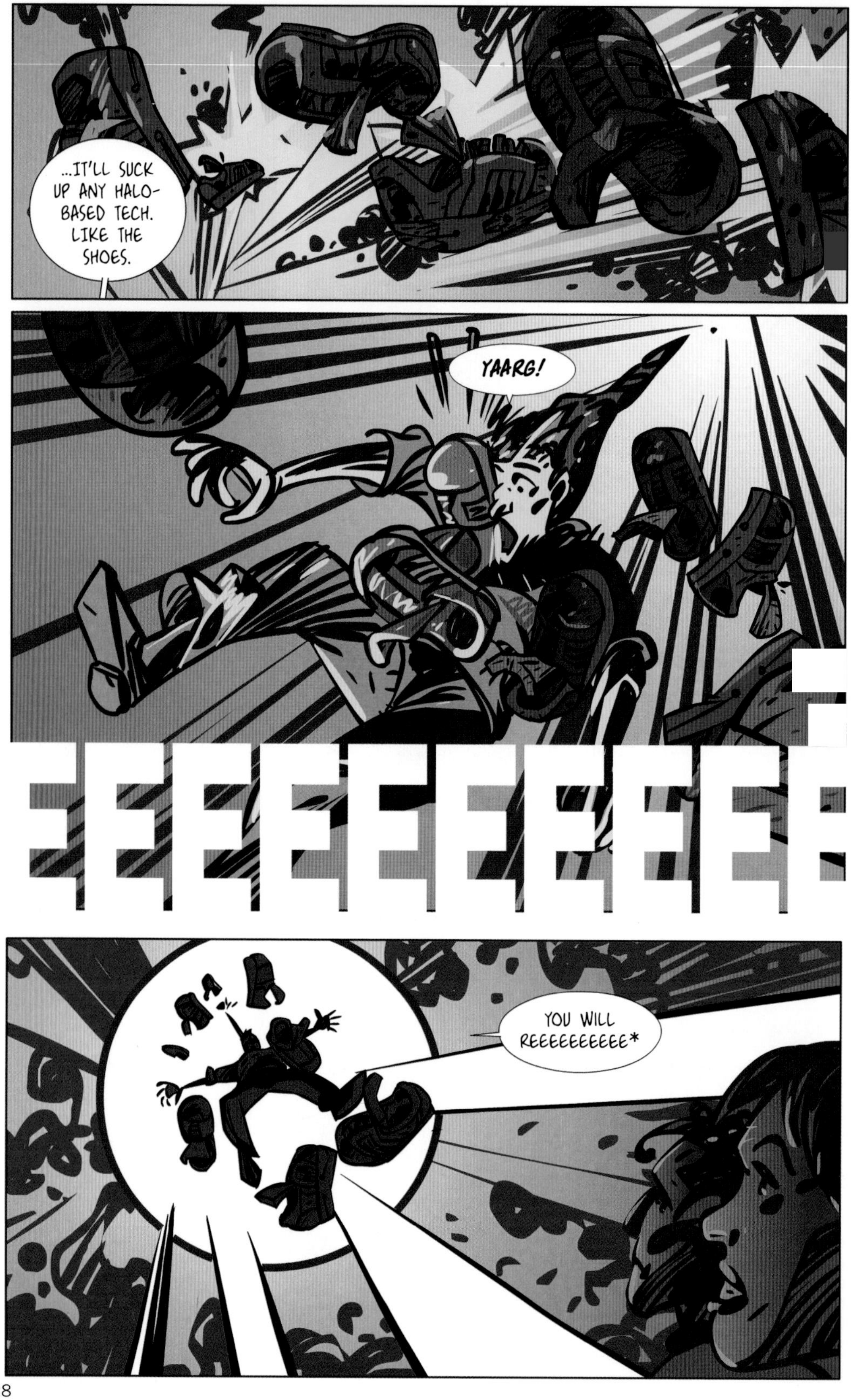
...IT'LL SUCK UP ANY HALO-BASED TECH. LIKE THE SHOES.
YAARG!
EEEEEEEEEE
YOU WILL REEEEEEEEEE*

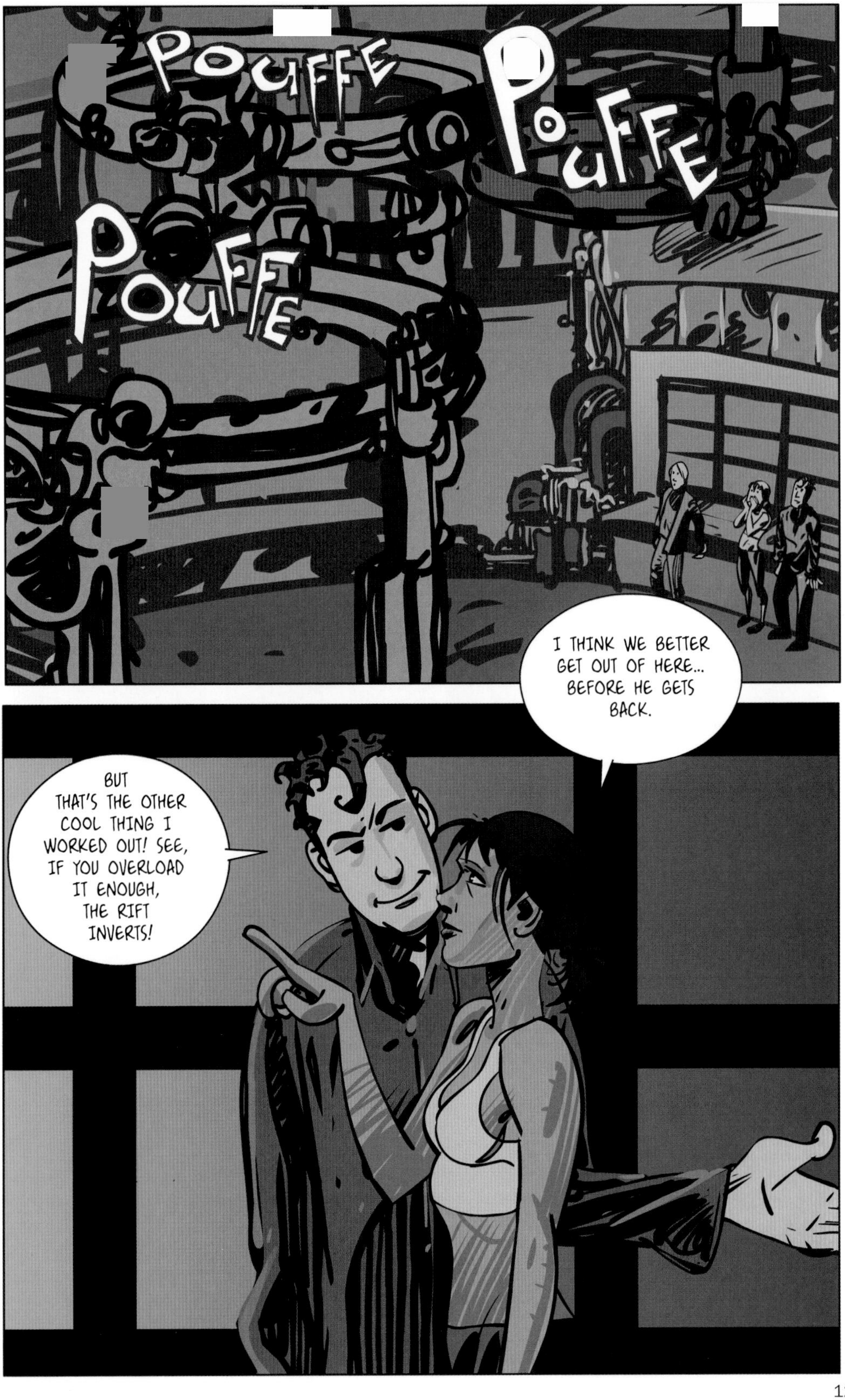
POUFFE
POUFFE
POUFFE
I THINK WE BETTER GET OUT OF HERE... BEFORE HE GETS BACK.
BUT THAT'S THE OTHER COOL THING I WORKED OUT! SEE, IF YOU OVERLOAD IT ENOUGH, THE RIFT INVERTS!

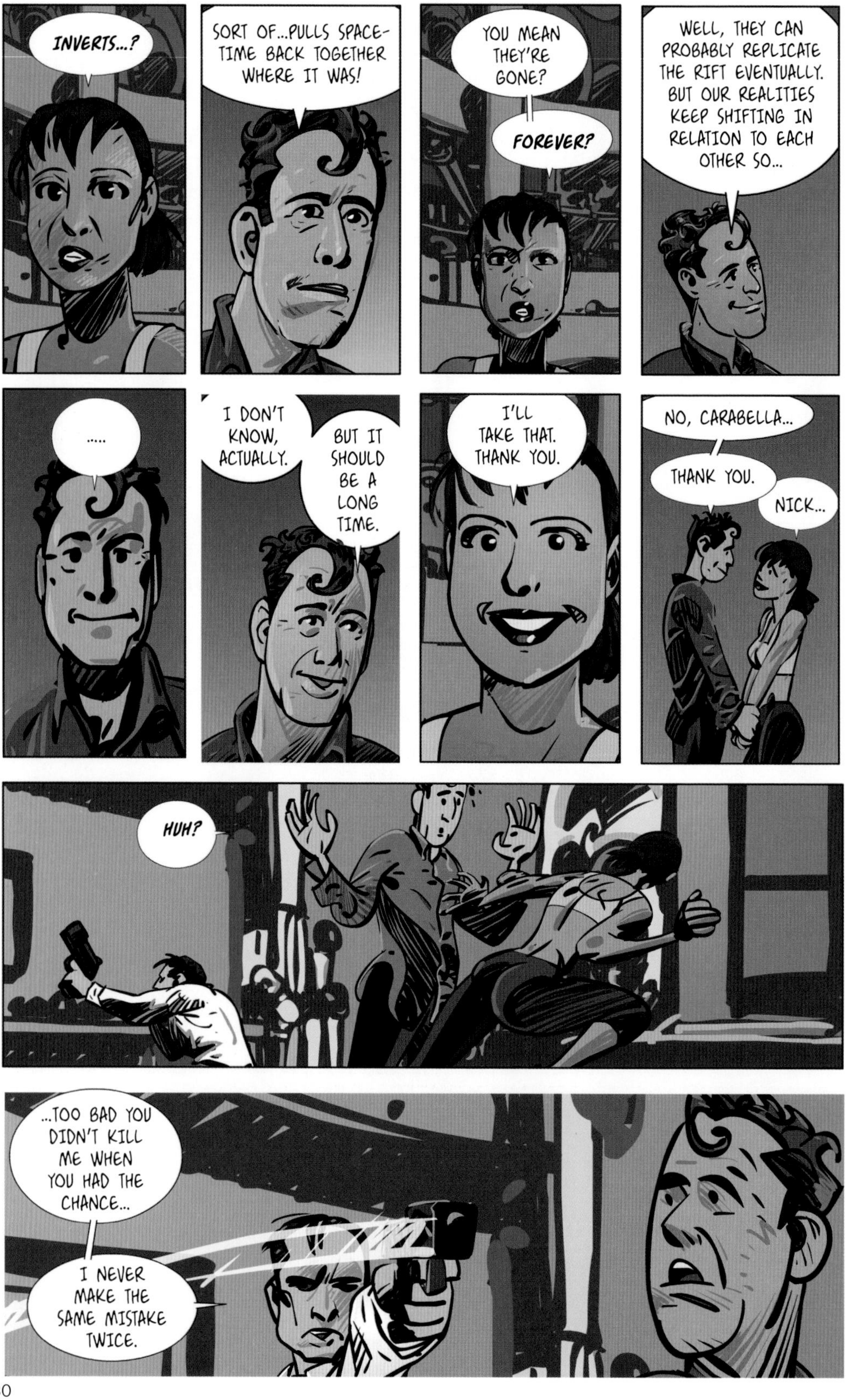
INVERTS...?
SORT OF...PULLS SPACE-TIME BACK TOGETHER WHERE IT WAS!
YOU MEAN THEY'RE GONE?
FOREVER?
WELL, THEY CAN PROBABLY REPLICATE THE RIFT EVENTUALLY. BUT OUR REALITIES KEEP SHIFTING IN RELATION TO EACH OTHER SO...
.....
I DON'T KNOW, ACTUALLY.
BUT IT SHOULD BE A LONG TIME.
I'LL TAKE THAT. THANK YOU.
NO, CARABELLA...
THANK YOU.
NICK...
HUH?
...TOO BAD YOU DIDN'T KILL ME WHEN YOU HAD THE CHANCE...
I NEVER MAKE THE SAME MISTAKE TWICE.

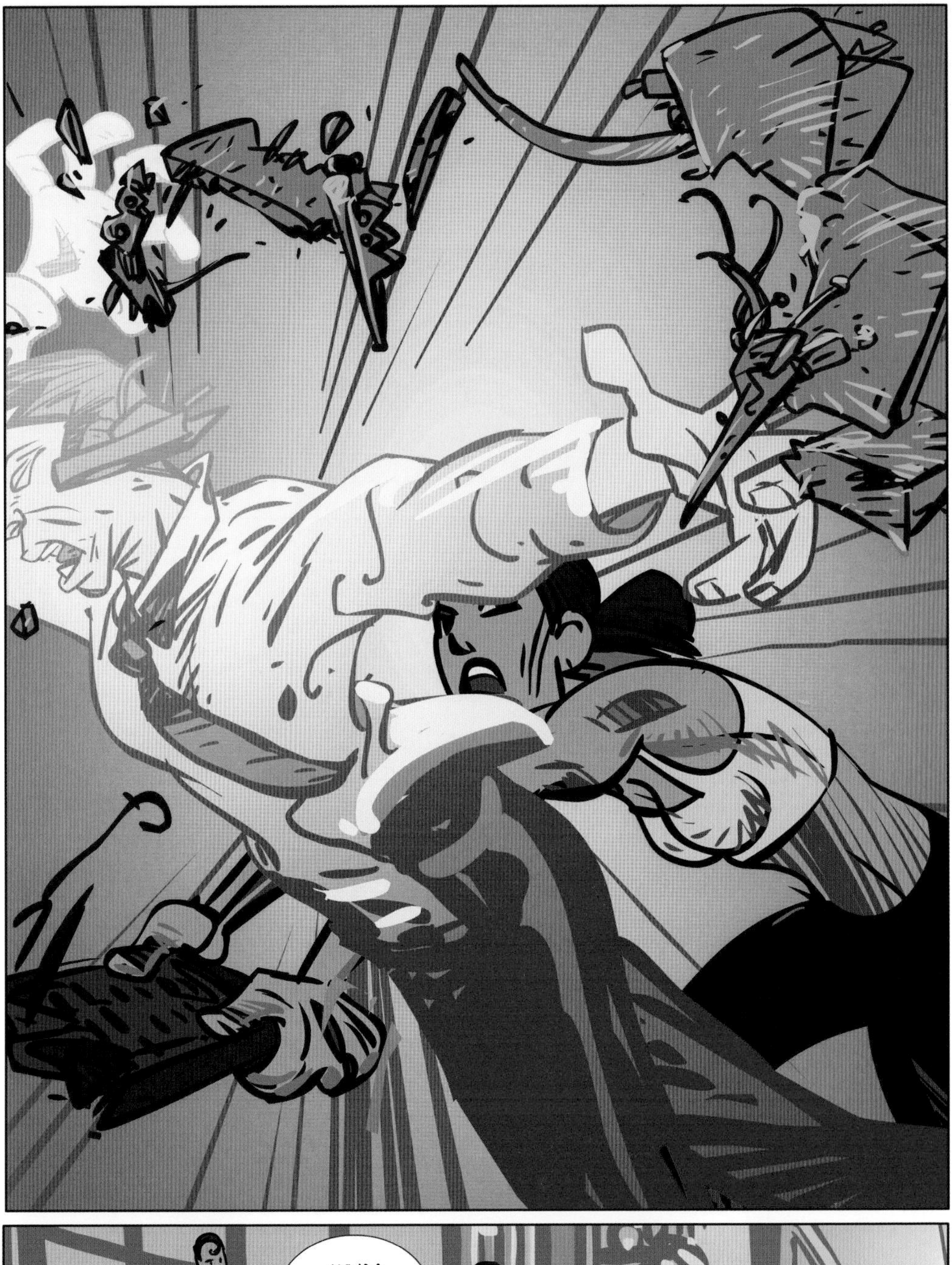

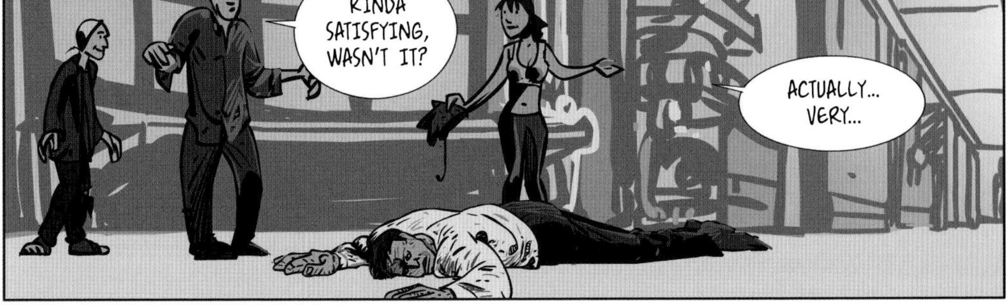
KINDA SATISFYING, WASN'T IT?
ACTUALLY... VERY...

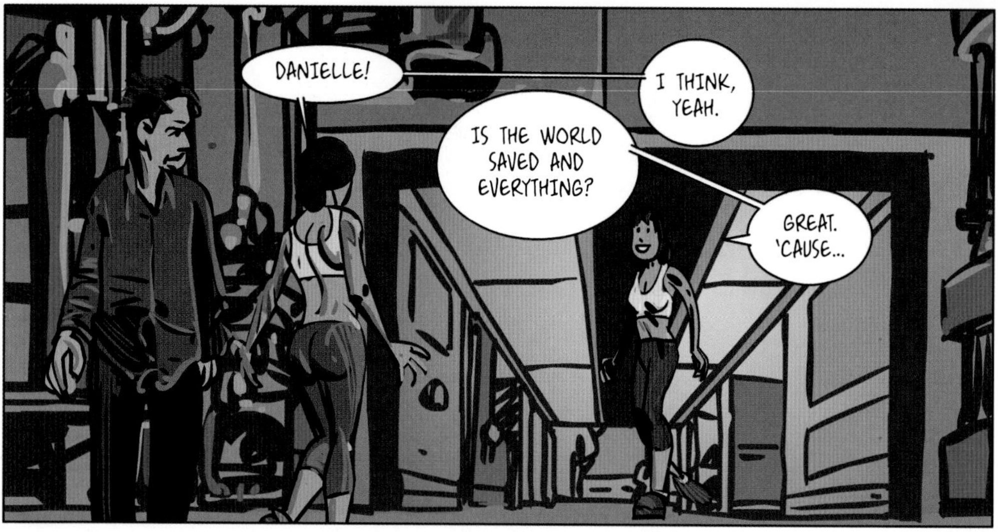
DANIELLE!
I THINK, YEAH.
IS THE WORLD SAVED AND EVERYTHING?
GREAT. 'CAUSE...

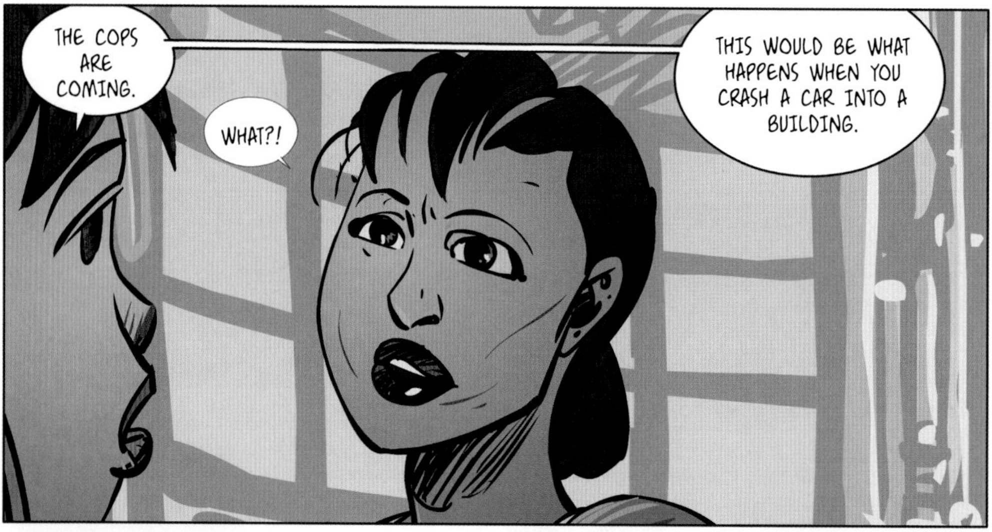
THE COPS ARE COMING.
WHAT?!
THIS WOULD BE WHAT HAPPENS WHEN YOU CRASH A CAR INTO A BUILDING.

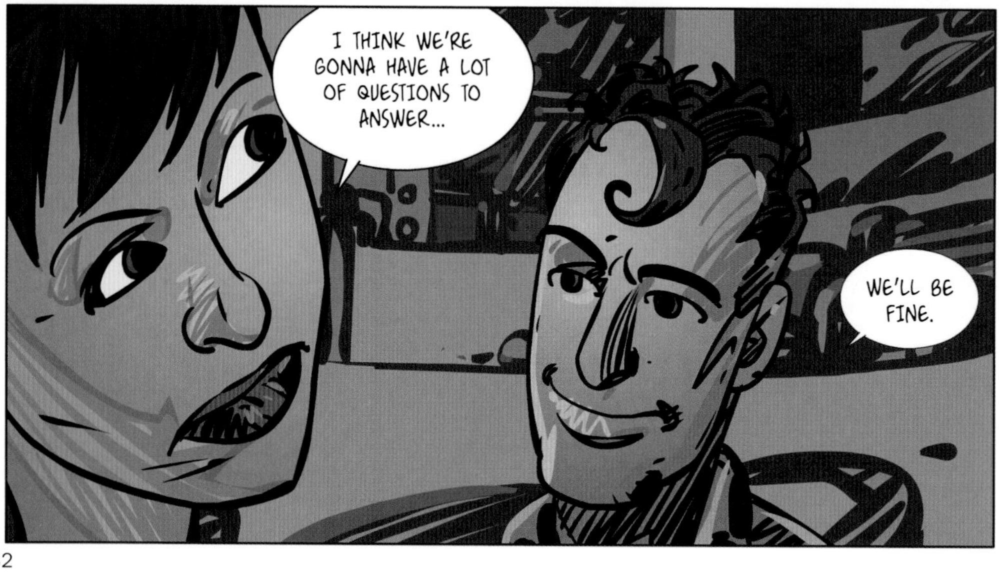
I THINK WE'RE GONNA HAVE A LOT OF QUESTIONS TO ANSWER...
WE'LL BE FINE.

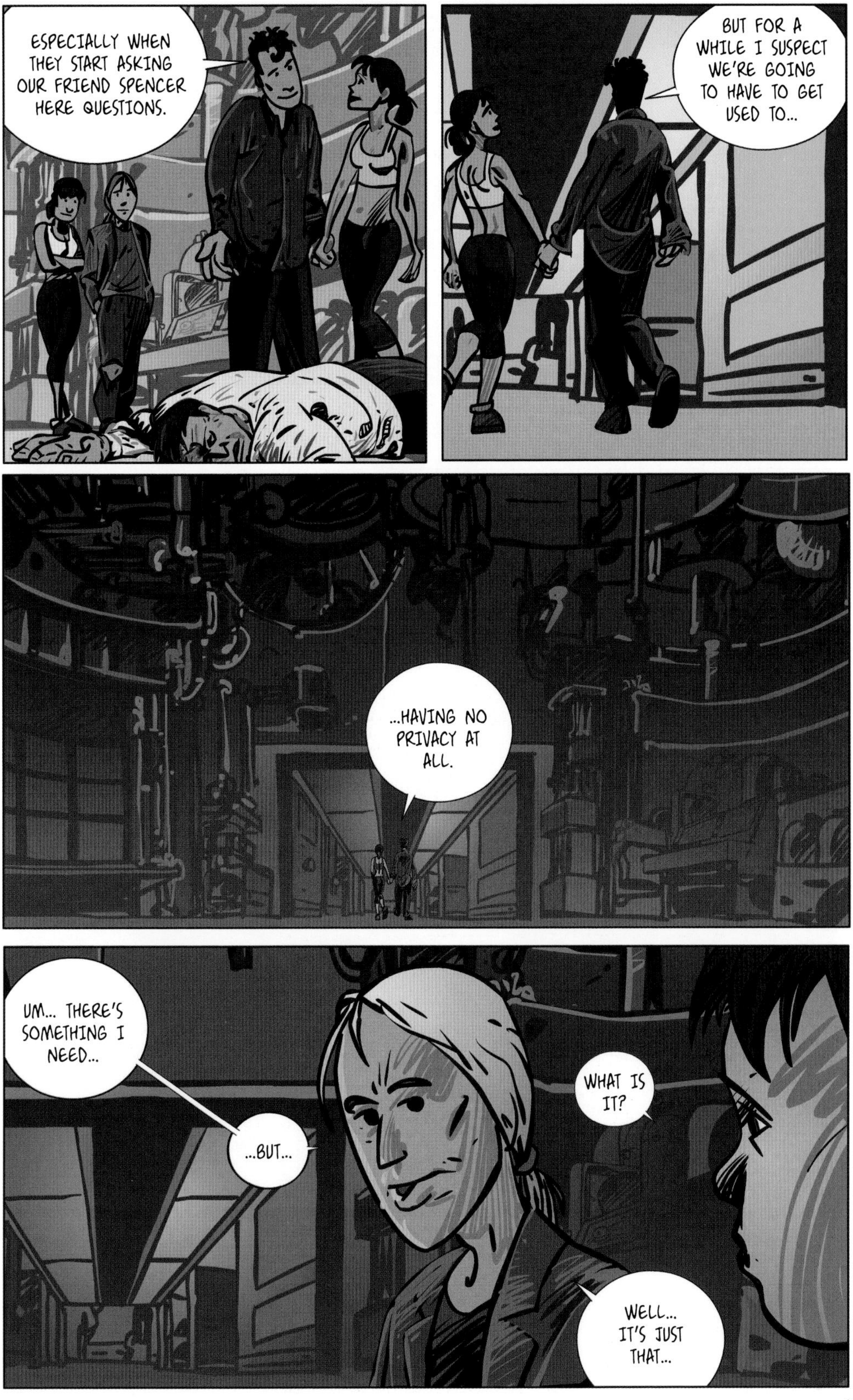
ESPECIALLY WHEN THEY START ASKING OUR FRIEND SPENCER HERE QUESTIONS.
BUT FOR A WHILE I SUSPECT WE'RE GOING TO HAVE TO GET USED TO...
...HAVING NO PRIVACY AT ALL.
UM... THERE'S SOMETHING I NEED...
...BUT...
WHAT IS IT?
WELL... IT'S JUST THAT...

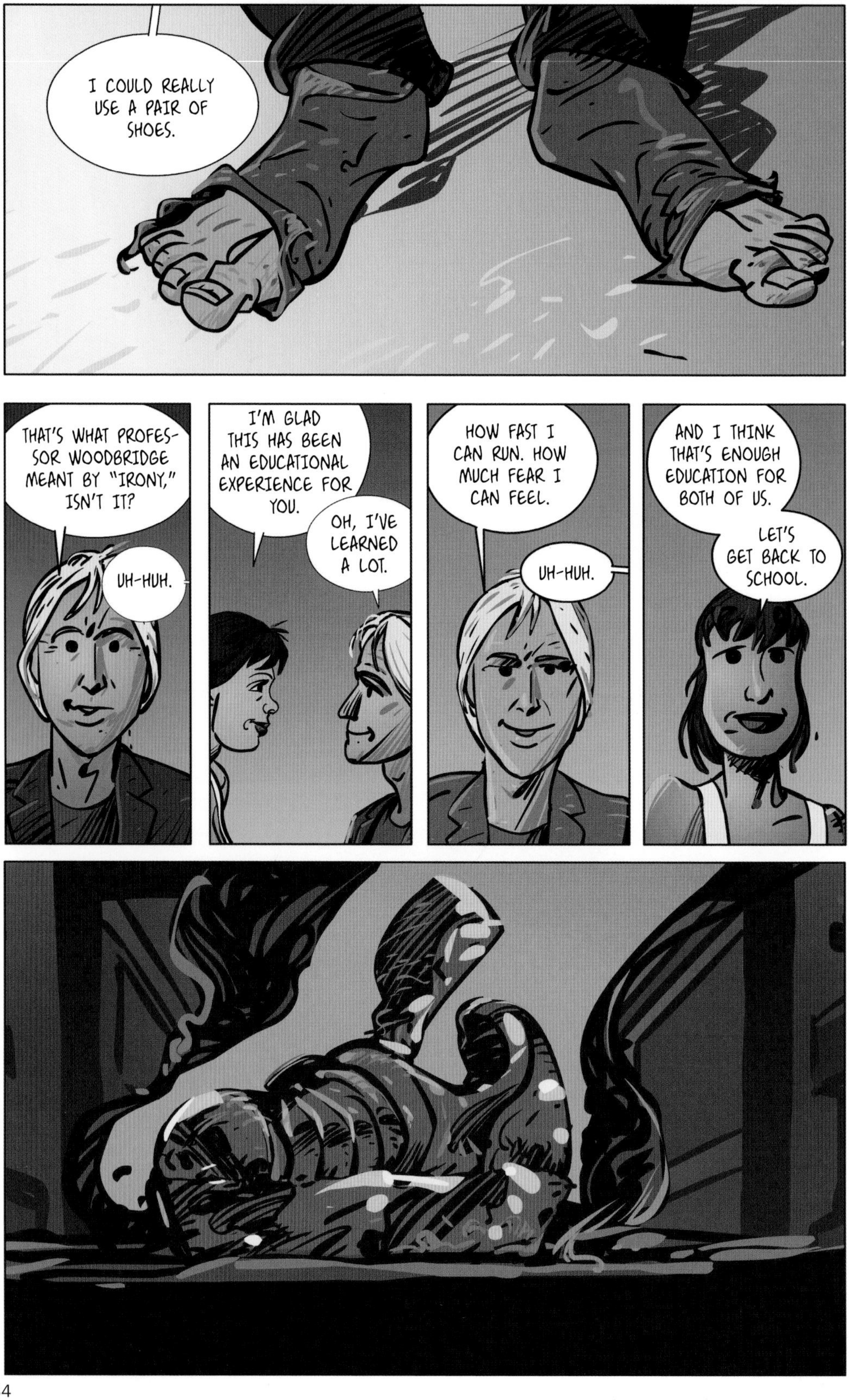
I COULD REALLY USE A PAIR OF SHOES.
THAT'S WHAT PROFES-SOR WOODBRIDGE MEANT BY "IRONY," ISN'T IT?
UH-HUH.
I'M GLAD THIS HAS BEEN AN EDUCATIONAL EXPERIENCE FOR YOU.
OH, I'VE LEARNED A LOT.
HOW FAST I CAN RUN. HOW MUCH FEAR I CAN FEEL.
UH-HUH.
AND I THINK THAT'S ENOUGH EDUCATION FOR BOTH OF US.
LET'S GET BACK TO SCHOOL.